FINDING MARISA

FINDING MARISA

A MOTHER'S STORY

A Guide to Raising a Child with Autism

SHERRY A. RUBIN

FINDING MARISA
A MOTHER'S STORY

iUniverse books may be ordered through booksellers or by contacting:

iUniverse
1663 Liberty Drive
Bloomington, IN 47403
www.iuniverse.com
844-349-9409

ISBN: 978-0-5954-2179-4 (sc)
ISBN: 978-0-5956-7980-5 (hc)
ISBN: 978-0-5958-6517-8 (e)

Print information available on the last page.

iUniverse rev. date: 08/13/2020

For Marisa,
my inspiration,
my husband, Dan,
who encouraged and supported my effort,
and my daughters,
Shoshana and Deborah,
who both contributed a great deal of time
seeking creative ways to help Marisa grow
intellectually, emotionally, and socially.

Contents

Preface

Nearly sixteen years ago, I gave birth to my fourth daughter, Marisa. At the time, I had no idea she was autistic, because she looked as normal as any newborn. However, by the time she was fifteen months old, my husband, Dan, and I started to realize that something about her was different. We took our beautiful little girl to a pediatric neurologist, who felt it was best to wait another six months before reaching a conclusion. She later confirmed our worst fears. We did not waste any time, obtaining the help of our school district Committee on Special Education to find an appropriate early intervention program for our two-year-old. This is where my story begins.

When Marisa started school, I started a journal marking her progress. I was determined to do everything I could to ensure a good outcome for our little girl. I was a teacher with a master's degree in early childhood, and I used my eight years of classroom experience to devise practical and fun ways to teach Marisa. I recorded my thoughts and Marisa's progress in my journal. As I watched Marisa grow, I realized that my efforts might be helpful to others going through the same struggle we were going through.

Two years ago, I started to review the twenty-three journals I had kept over the years. The result is a biography of Marisa's life growing up as a child with autism, struggling to fit in to a world of neurotypical people. This book documents not just her struggle, but our struggle as a family, and all the joys and sorrows that went along with it.

In my story I have stressed the things that I feel are most helpful in raising a child with autism. Developing rapport through activities that interest the child, monitoring and redirecting behaviors by charting goals that are age appropriate, and choosing rewards that are meaningful to the child are just some of the things covered in the book.

I am optimistic that this story will help others raising a child with autism, or with any other disability, have a more positive attitude as they face the future. This is not a story of miraculous recovery but rather a story that is meant to give hope to parents and provide them with the tools that will help children with special needs to not only reach their potential, but to achieve happiness and fulfillment along the way.

Introduction

This story is written from my journal entries over a thirteen-year period. Although the story does not go beyond the fifteenth year of Marisa's life, this does not mean that the story ends. Readers should understand that children with special needs sometimes have different educational goals than the so called "normal" or neurotypical children. At age fourteen, special needs children enter what is called a transition planning period. This transition period is the time when parents and school district personnel start planning for the future of the child once he or she graduates from the educational system at age twenty-one. This planning takes into account whether the child will be entering a day treatment program, a vocational training program, a community college, or a full college program before he or she is, hopefully, ready to enter the working world.

I could have waited till Marisa graduated from the educational system at age 21. However, I felt it was more important to cover the early growing years of Marisa's life. This is the time when a child's behaviors are molded and habits are formed, which will determine whether it is possible for an individual with autism to succeed in the adult world. Because autism is a disorder impairing social skills and language processing, these are the areas I have focused my attention on. The thirteen years I have spent helping Marisa control her impulsive behaviors, learning to process language, and improving social skills necessary to live in our world have poised her to enter adult life. Although autism is a lifelong condition, I believe it is possible for people with autism, like Marisa, to have fulfilling and happy lives if they are given the support and encouragement they need.

Chapter One

IN THE BEGINNING

It was a perfect day. The sky was blue, and the sun was shining brightly as I walked outside with Marisa to wait for her bus. It was September 15, 1992, her very first day of school, but Marisa was not going to a regular school for typical toddlers; she was starting a half day of school at a special preschool for speech-impaired children. I felt sure that after this day, somebody would recognize that our little girl was special, not in the way that one speaks of special needs children, but special because she had an eagerness for learning that I knew showed promise. To me she was special in the way that all parents think of their own children. How special it is to see one's little girl or boy do something new for the very first time. There were so many things about Marisa that seemed special to me: the way she smiled, the way she watched what was happening around her, the way she played with her toys in the natural, inquisitive way that fresh minds explore. Yet having had three older children before Marisa, I was nagged by the feeling that there was something different about her.

Marisa was just two years and two months old, a beautiful little girl with inquisitive brown eyes and curly, golden hair that framed her face with little ringlets, but she was not a typical toddler. In spite of her ability to do puzzles at the age of twelve months and her early walking skills at ten months, she was beginning to display more and more autistic-like behaviors. Her lack of speech and disinterest in relating to people around her gave us reason for concern. The decision to place her in a special school was a difficult one, but I was certain that this would turn out to be a short-term commitment—or maybe I was just in a state of denial. Marisa was a smart little girl, and I was under the misconception that autistic people were severely mentally impaired.

When Marisa was about thirteen months old, Dan, Marisa's dad, noticed that Marisa did not listen when she was spoken to. As a neurologist, Dan was concerned by her disinterest in responding. I, on the other hand, being an early childhood teacher, considered these first incidents to be signs of early "terrible twos" behavior, when toddlers gaining many new skills are typically trying to assert themselves.

To reassure myself, I started to observe Marisa's behaviors more and noticed that at times, while in the playpen, she would just sit still and stare into space, filling her time and thoughts with what seemed like nothing. I knew that this was not normal behavior for a toddler.

We decided to have Marisa evaluated for hearing loss, and when the evaluator found no abnormalities, we felt it was time to schedule an appointment with a pediatric neurologist. On October 31, I scheduled an appointment for the following month. That Halloween night, as I went out pushing a stroller and watching Deborah, my seven-year-old, go door to door trick-or-treating, I had to wonder if the little person I was pushing in the stroller would some day dress up and join the neighborhood kids to collect Halloween candy. I was overcome with a sense of loss and sadness at the prospect of trouble ahead.

The pediatric neurologist told us that, although at sixteen months it was too early to diagnose her as autistic, her aloofness, lack of speech, and disinterest in making eye contact made autism a very real consideration. We scheduled a BAER (brainstem auditory evoked response) test to be done under sedation at the neurologist's office so that we could more accurately rule out hearing loss. The test showed that she was able to hear but was apparently not able to process what she was hearing. The inability to process language is a common characteristic of autism. The doctor advised us to wait until she was a little older to bring her for a follow-up re-evaluation; she was not eager to diagnose a child under the age of eighteen months, because babies vary widely in their development of speech. Nevertheless, we braced ourselves for the worst, since Marisa, though inquisitive in her play, remained disinterested in relating to those around her and did not communicate, even through simple gestures. Upon visiting the pediatric neurologist again, Marisa was given a diagnosis of PDD. After doing some research, I realized that PDD, standing for pervasive developmental disorder, was a gentle way of labeling autism.

We went home hoping that things would improve, making all our concerns unfounded. We felt it just wouldn't be right if it were to turn out any other way.

Marisa was the fourth daughter to enter our family, and her oldest sister had been born with severe brain damage due to a chromosomal aberration; it would hardly seem fair for us to have to deal with another serious neurological problem. Our oldest daughter, Rebecca, was at age twelve nonverbal and unable to initiate her own need to use the toilet. She also had severe cognitive and fine motor impairments. Because she required constant care, it became impossible for us to care for her at home. When Rebecca was seven and a half, we made the very difficult decision to place her in a residential school. We did this because we had exhausted the possibility for improvement at home and because we knew that the time needed to care for Rebecca would cause serious consequences for our other children, Shoshana, then only six, and Deborah, just one.

So, on that sunny morning in September of 1992, as I sent Marisa off on her very first bus ride to school, I felt that things could not be as dismal as I feared. Here was this bright, energetic little girl! How could she be labeled autistic? I sent along a journal to correspond with the team of teachers with the idea that together we would be able to figure out what was going on in that beautiful little head, all the while hoping that she was not autistic. Little did I know at the time that my journal would be a source of strength to support me in my efforts to reach Marisa.

Marisa willingly got on the bus the first day, holding her school bag proudly and repeating, "Bus, bus, bus," which made me very happy to hear, since at this point Marisa had a very limited vocabulary. On the second day of school she seemed frightened and confused to be leaving home without me, so I decided to follow the bus to the school. Upon disembarking from the bus, Marisa was excited to see me, and we walked into the classroom together. I could see how happy she was to be there and was pleased that I could share that moment with her. I was anxious to hear positive feedback from the teachers at school and was disappointed though understanding when they told me that they didn't yet know Marisa well enough to answer my questions.

The entries from Marisa's first teacher were very routine, referring to Marisa's enjoyment of sensory activities like bubbles, shaving cream, painting, sand, water play, and Play-Doh. I was anxious for encouraging comments, and so I continued to write notes to the teacher about how happy Marisa seemed when she came home from school. More importantly, I decided to work with Marisa at home using my teaching skills, rather than waiting to see what would evolve.

I gave Marisa lots of drawing paper and encouraged her to explore with paint, pencils, and markers. This she did with great pleasure and enthusiasm, which made me happy. As this was going on, I hoped to read encouraging news from school, but as the days passed, all I received were notes that Marisa was having lots of fun and adjusting well to the school environment.

Within a couple of months, however, I started to notice small, positive changes in Marisa's behavior. She seemed to be showing more signs of awareness. One day when I asked my children, "Who wants Doritos?" Marisa surprised us all when she raised her hand and looked around to see who else was raising a hand, too. Then she kept her hand up till she got her plate of Doritos. Another day when she got on the bus, she blew a kiss to me with her hand. I found this amazing, because she didn't know how to kiss with her lips, but every night she saw me blow kisses to her from the bedroom doorway; she must have realized that she could do the same. Still another special moment occurred when Marisa repeated "sit down" after Deborah, my eight-year-old, told her to sit down to hold our kittens. Deborah then placed a kitten on her lap, and Marisa's delight showed all over her face! Yet another time, in the car on the way to the orthodontist, she suddenly started yelling, "Help! Help! Help!" in a loud voice. She had dropped her bottle. Shoshana turned around to get it for her, and Marisa happily started drinking. When Shoshana and I told her, "Say 'thank you' when someone helps you," she stopped drinking and said, "Thank you!" It was encouraging to see that she had actually listened, understood, and responded. Moments like these made me feel hopeful about the future.

Although I saw occasional encouraging moments, there were other causes for concern. Marisa was becoming a lot more capable in her large motor skills, such as running and climbing, which created new problems at home. She could easily climb over gates that my husband and I had deliberately placed to block off some sections of the house. She engaged in similar climbing activities at school, where the teacher had to work on teaching Marisa the meaning of the word "No." The teacher also informed me that she was working on teaching Marisa the phrase "Help me!" as something to say when she needed assistance, which we hoped would replace the tantrums and screaming behaviors that Marisa typically used because of her inability to communicate her needs. It was also important to teach Marisa to respond to her name, which she was unable to do at the time. At home I was eager to work on these very basic goals the teacher had set for Marisa, but I was also looking for new ways to stimulate her senses.

One night I prepared a bubble bath for Deborah in my bathtub. When Marisa saw this, she eagerly pointed to the bath and bubbles, so I decided to let both girls enjoy the bath. Marisa and Deborah got in the tub, and I turned on the whirlpool. The bubbles multiplied up to Marisa's neck. How delighted we were to see the look of joy and excitement on her face! It was also quite a funny scene: two cute faces peeking out above a mountain of bubbles. What a fabulous learning experience it was for Marisa, who had let me know what she wanted and was then rewarded with her request.

As time went on, I became eager to visit Marisa's class to see what the school day was like and to have a better sense of what Marisa was learning away from home. I was hoping to incorporate some of the school activities into my home schedule. I arranged to visit with my daughter Deborah, who was also interested in helping Marisa improve her speech and communication skills.

On November 20, Deborah and I visited Marisa's class, and we were surprised to find that the instructors were teaching Marisa sign language as a visual aide to use along with the words she was able to vocalize. Once I saw what Marisa was doing at school, I realized that she had been using sign language at home recently. However, because nobody had informed me that signing was being used at school, I had no idea what her hand movements meant. If I hadn't visited the classroom, I might never have known this. I asked the teacher to send home a list of all the signs for words that Marisa was using at school. I also noticed that items in the classroom were labeled so that the children could simultaneously learn the names of things and see the written words for those things. In my own early childhood classrooms I had used this same technique for building a sight vocabulary and teaching functional reading. I decided that I would start labeling things at home for Marisa, too.

During the visit, I also learned that the class regularly engaged in a nice selection of songs and finger plays, and I told the teacher that I would send in a blank tape for them to record the songs for us to have at home. I felt this would be a nice way for Marisa to reinforce the songs she was learning at school and give her extra practice time.

The teacher told me that one afternoon Marisa sang the class "good-bye song" at 2:30. Although it was somewhat early for the daily song to be sung, the teacher felt that Marisa was using the song to communicate that she knew it would soon be time to go home.

Later, Marisa enjoyed hearing the school songs on tape, and I noticed that she also liked studying the written word cards that I had made for her. This gave me the idea of introducing Marisa to some new word cards with pictures. I made my own shape and color cards and picture cards of family members that included our two cats, Shoshana and Deborah (Marisa's older sisters), and Marisa herself. Over time the cards became a source of entertainment for Marisa each day. At around the same time, Marisa began to show an interest in a map puzzle of the United States, and together we sat on the floor and worked on the puzzle over and over again. From the study of the map puzzle, new word cards evolved for states and cities on the map.

Marisa also enjoyed using a toy bus and ferry and some toy animals to role-play in a more or less appropriate way, as she lined up the animals and assembled them for a ferry or bus ride. The play activity seemed quite normal, except that Marisa usually played this game for a longer time than would be normal for most children her age, up to an hour at a stretch. She would line up the animals, taking them for a ride and then removing them from the ferry or bus after the ride, only to start all over again. I know that this repetitive behavior was typical of children with autism. Though I worried about the repetitive behaviors, I was encouraged when I realized that in some situations this trait would help Marisa master skills. For instance, the teacher told me that Marisa had mastered a ring-stacking toy by persisting in doing it over and over until she was easily able to complete the exercise correctly.

By December, Marisa had acquired many new skills. She was keeping busy at home with puzzles, word cards, books, and shape cards, and she was also starting to sing along with the nursery rhymes she had been listening to. She was watching fewer videotapes, and her play seemed more organized, more attentive to her toys, and she had stopped climbing and getting into things that were not for her. She seemed particularly interested in the basic shape cards, trying to say the names of each. Because of this new interest in shapes and because I knew Marisa enjoyed craft activities, I set up a collage project using different colored paper shapes. She was excited by this activity and seemed to enjoy it immensely, all the while reinforcing her knowledge of shapes.

During the Christmas vacation I kept Marisa as productively engaged as I could, jotting down the things we did each day, so I could feel a sense of accomplishment. Marisa also was delighted to receive a bubble blaster gun, a *Sesame Street* calender, a battery operated word game and some clothing for Chanukah. It was a difficult time, because my oldest daughter, Rebecca, was home from her residential school, and both she and Marisa required my close attention. I worried that the extra time I spent caring for Rebecca would affect Marisa's behavior. I hoped that some of the new toys would help keep Marisa occupied.

Things appeared to be going well the first few days of the vacation, until an unexpected and dangerous incident occurred one evening. My husband and I were in the kitchen discussing the prospect of moving our coffee table from the den to the basement, where it would be out of the way. Earlier I had noticed that Marisa was trying to move the very large, three-quarter inch glass top off the coffee table base. Though I was concerned, I felt the weight of the glass made it impossible for Marisa to move it a great distance. I did however feel it would be best to remove it as a precaution. As I was talking with Dan, we suddenly heard a loud and frightening crash. We rushed from the kitchen to the den, where, to our horror, Marisa was standing in front of a huge amount of shattered glass. She was unharmed, but she had both hands on her head in utter shock. We had to take her and Rebecca, who was sitting nearby, to their bedrooms in order to clean up the terrible mess.

An hour later I went to Marisa's room only to discovery another mess; having been temporarily locked in her room away from the danger of the shattered glass, she had taken it upon herself to strew her toys and clothing all over her room. Later that night I thought about what she had done to the coffee table and realized that she must have thought she had a good reason for moving the glass. I think she wanted to make a big slide, and knowing how smooth glass is, she expected this to be a really good idea. However, she had no concept that glass was breakable and could be dangerous. I realized just how unaware of danger Marisa really was.

During the next few days I kept Marisa busy reviewing her shapes as she watched me draw them for her. She also studied the magnetic alphabet letters I had placed on the refrigerator, even arranging some into familiar little words. She played with Mr. Potato Head, sang along with her nursery rhyme tapes, and practiced using a pencil to draw straight lines and circles. She spent time playing with her electronic word game, sang the alphabet, and perfected her counting of numbers one to twenty. I was pleased to see how occupied she was. Indeed she was a busy little girl, and I was happy and satisfied to see the results of my efforts.

My eight-year-old daughter, Deborah, decided to make a shape chart for Marisa. When the chart was done, we hung it on the refrigerator. Marisa traced the shapes with her fingers and practiced saying each one: "star, circle, square, triangle, rectangle, oval, and diamond." Seeing such great success, we proceeded to make a color chart.

All was going well for Marisa, but I had to carefully monitor her activities around Rebecca. In the last six months, Rebecca had become increasingly difficult at the residential school, taking out her frustrations and inability to communicate by grabbing hold of people's hair. In October, she had grabbed my thirteen-year-old daughter Shoshana by her hair, and I knew from the experience that it was extremely difficult to release her angry grip. One night at home, a particularly disturbing and dangerous incident occurred. It all happened very quickly and proved impossible to stop. Marisa and Rebecca were both listening to a *Kidsongs* video in the den. As Marisa danced around to the music, Rebecca sat quietly, watching the video and enjoying the rhythm of the song. As I helped Rebecca out of her seat to take a walk to the bathroom, I could see that she was visibly angry at the idea of leaving the room in the middle of the video. Marisa, in the meantime, was dancing down the hall. As I glanced at Rebecca again, I knew that her anger had mounted, and anyone in her path was likely to be a target. I backed away from Rebecca as I saw Marisa coming straight toward us. "Go back, Marisa! Go back!" I yelled, worried that she would not understand the urgency of my plea because of her inability to process language; she could also not comprehend the seriousness of the situation. As Marisa happily did a running dance, Rebecca became increasingly agitated. Then, as Marisa danced by, in an instant, Rebecca grabbed hold of Marisa's hair, so tightly that Marisa's screams were deafening. Not only did it require both Dan and me to release Rebecca's tight grip, finger by finger, but we also had to place ourselves between the two girls in order to prevent Rebecca from head-butting Marisa, who continued to scream and cry while waiting to be released. Fortunately, we separated the girls, and no serious harm was done. We then looked at each other in utter disbelief at how close we had come to a nearly tragic outcome.

In spite of the scary incident that day, I had much to be happy about. Although Marisa didn't show much interest in the color chart that Deborah had made, she did enjoy outlining the six circle shapes on the chart. She then went to the shape chart to make her first attempt at outlining the shapes with a black marker as she said the name of each one. Shoshana then decided to make twenty colorful number cards for Marisa, since she knew that Marisa enjoyed recognizing and saying those numbers. These numbers were brilliantly colored designs; each number itself was a genuine work of art. Marisa was very attracted to the numbers and gladly accepted the cards and enjoyed mixing them up and reading each one off proudly.

The day after the hair-grabbing incident, Marisa seemed to be more cautious around Rebecca, which I was glad about. To help ease the tension, I took out a hair-braiding book to look at with Marisa. Together we selected a hairstyle, and I braided her hair to make it more difficult for her sister to grab.

Throughout the day, Marisa continued her usual routine of coloring, looking at her alphabet book and word cards, and playing with small figurines of people and her bus. I noticed that she was starting to differentiate between boys and girls, probably because she had boy and girl word cards. She separated all the boy people from the girl people, then placed the girl people in seats on the bus and lined up the boys in the aisle. She also explored an alphabet writing chart I created for her; she enjoyed outlining the letters with her fingers.

That afternoon something happened that helped explain the scary hair-grabbing incident. Rebecca lost a tooth, probably alleviating pain in her mouth, and her behavior suddenly took a very noticeable turn for the better. Marisa noticed, too, and decided to get friendly and forgive her sister by going over to touch and smile at her. I was quite moved by this, since it showed a sense of compassion that I hadn't witnessed in Marisa, though in all honesty, mistrust and caution would have been a more appropriate response to Rebecca after the previous day's experience.

That evening Marisa continued to busy herself with many activities. She spent a good deal of time coloring a *Sesame Street* coloring book. I used this as an opportunity to name colors. She later pulled out the word *yellow* saying "Yellow! Yellow!" while looking for a yellow crayon to color Big Bird. Later that night she pulled out the word game Upwords, studying the tile letters, and she also enjoyed looking at the letters in the word game Boggle. She spent a good amount of time on these before going to bed.

Toward the end of the Christmas vacation, I noticed that Marisa was spending more time on puzzles and practicing writing her letters in the air. This was something she had learned from watching *Sesame Street*. But by the afternoons she would become restless at home, and she started climbing around the house. At times she needed to go to her room briefly to calm down.

The next morning she eagerly went to work on alphabet writing sheets. She pulled out the alphabet practice sheets I had made for her and insisted that Deborah and I write rows and rows of letters and numbers for her to practice. I was pleased by this self-initiated activity. Later in the afternoon, she played with a Barbie doll bathtub, washing a mermaid doll.

Rebecca and I went for a ride to return her to her residential school at 2:30, and when I returned at 5:30, Marisa was busy playing with her boat and animals. According to Shoshana, Marisa had kept busy with the giant United States map part of the time I was gone. Then in the evening, Marisa played with the Junior Monopoly game, matching the tile letters to the letters in the words on the board.

All in all, it was a busy and productive vacation at home; we filled the days and evenings with lots of fun learning experiences. Then on the afternoon of December 31, while watching *Sesame Street*, Marisa suddenly started screaming. I rushed in to the den and asked Deborah what happened. Apparently nothing had happened. I went over to Marisa, who was crying and screaming nonstop, to try to find out what was wrong. I asked her what had happened, and she just continued to cry and scream. Because she was holding her favorite stuffed Gund dog, named Mutsy, I jokingly asked her, "Did Mutsy bite your finger?" She suddenly jumped up to show me her finger, which was stuck in Mutsy's nose. The stuffed dog's nose had loosened, and Marisa's finger was tangled in some threads. I managed to untangle Marisa's finger, and then I told her that I would take her dog to "operate," remove the nose, and give him a new button nose. After I did so, she wasn't happy with the new Mutsy look, totally rejecting him and pushing him away throughout the rest of the evening. Though she usually slept with Mutsy, that night she chose Big Bird instead.

As the new year began, I reflected back over the past four months, and I felt a renewed enthusiasm. I realized that Marisa seemed to be making some genuine progress. I attributed this to a combination of the new experiences at school and my guided play at home. I felt that following Marisa's lead in choosing activities and developing the skills that she was interested in was crucial to learning. Marisa was a very visual learner, judging by her ability to do puzzles and her interest in shapes, letters, and numbers. I felt we were off to a good start, and this vacation made me feel so much more optimistic.

Although as a teacher I had always felt strongly about following a child's lead, it wasn't until five years later that I would realize the methods I believed in were practiced by Dr. Stanley I. Greenspan well known for his work with infants, young children, and their families. Stanley Greenspan and his colleague, Dr. Serena Wieder, used their research and experience to create a guide for raising a child with special needs by using the individual child's strengths, interests, and difficulties, and then applying Greenspan's "floor-time" approach. When I read *The Child With Special Needs*, co-authored by Drs. Greenspan and Wieder, I realized that what he called "The Floor-Time Approach," in which one connects with a child by engaging in activities with the child that are related to the child's interests, was very much like what I had been doing all along.

Marisa started off the new year in a restless mood. On New Year's Day, she was unable to sit still for any activity all morning. I spent some time making her boxes for storing number cards, shape cards, and extra word cards. I wondered if she was just fed up with me and my enthusiasm, so I decided to leave her alone and observe her for most of the day. I watched as she sang songs; played with her puzzles, animals, and garage toy; and spent much time running around to get rid of excess energy.

Later she seemed to settle down to quiet activities, and her interest turned toward looking through her books. Once again I was encouraged. I took out an additional twenty to thirty books that were appropriate for her age—pop-up books, word books, nursery rhyme books, simple picture books, etc. She was very excited with them.

That evening she took out the game Perfection. She removed all twenty-five completely different puzzle shapes and then proceeded to replace them all in the correct location. There were funny shaped stars, parallelograms, triangles, squiggly shapes, and the usual circle, square, rectangle, and various triangles, too. She needed a little help at first, but the second time around she was able to complete the task all by herself.

The next day Marisa enjoyed looking through some of the books I had given her the day before. One book I read aloud seemed to fascinate her, so I read it a second time, pleased that she was paying attention. It was a Golden Book called *My First Book*, about a little boy's things around the house. The book starts out asking the question, "Where is Timmy?" Then the story proceeds to show all his things around the house, but no Timmy. Finally, at the end of the story, Timmy is found waiting in his bed.

Over the vacation I realized that Marisa was spending a great deal of time studying the alphabet, reading letters everywhere, and trying to write them. Marisa was also enjoying studying the word cards I had made for her. I felt that this would help her develop a sight vocabulary that would make beginning reading more fun and less frustrating later on. She also was extremely interested in magnet letters. Marisa would spend time matching the magnet letters to the words that were on the cards. She also was using a shape chart and playing with the felt shapes that I made for her.

On the last day of the Christmas vacation, Marisa spent the morning perfecting her skill at Perfection and looking at me with a proud smile each time she placed the twenty-five shapes correctly. She also spent a good amount of time drawing carefully with her magic markers. Another activity that Marisa regularly performed was running up and back in the living room for about half an hour each day. Since the living room was free of furniture, this was actually a good place for her to release some of her energy. I noticed she had made time for this each day during the vacation; we weren't able to spend time outside since Marisa and Rebecca both had colds. In the evening an overtired, overenthusiastic Marisa pulled out a bunch of toys. Together we worked on Perfection, a giant peg board, giant Loc Blocs, soft shape puzzles, the ring toss, alphabet letters, and word cards. Finally it was time for bed, something that Marisa was ready for by 11 PM. I was not one to stick to a strict bedtime since many children with autism have difficulties going to sleep and staying asleep through the night. I was happy to have Marisa tire herself enough to sleep through the night even if her bedtime was late. The good news to start off the new year was that Marisa accepted back her Mutsy dog, nose job and all, and happily took him back to bed with her.

It seemed to me that over the Christmas break, Marisa had started to blossom in ways that made me feel very positive. She became interested in colors from a rainbow her sister Deborah drew and placed on the refrigerator. I put the rainbow to a song, and Marisa quickly learned the colors using the song. She would practice little phrases like "hello" and "bye-bye" using little people figures on her ferryboat toy. At around this time Marisa started to use single words and also started to identify the parts of the face and body. She had an alphabet desk with word cards that she started to read. She learned to say "Thank you" when someone turned on her tape recorder so she could listen to music, but nothing before had given me a thrill like the day Marisa looked in the mirror and drew her first human face—and brought tears of joy to mine! Though I didn't realize it then, this was significant of the uneven splintering of skills among some people with autism.

Chapter Two

FORGING AHEAD

By February of that first school year, there was a sudden explosion of activity and excitement in the air. Now Marisa seemed to be putting so many things together. She could draw a face, and I would label the parts for her. Then I added a story to the picture so she could associate the picture with the words and learn to read. She also practiced puzzles out of the puzzle frame, putting them together on the table and then moving them back to the frame. She used her stencil letters to chalk in the letters on her chalkboard rather than using the magnets. Then she would try writing the letters without the stencils. I could see that she had her own wonderful way of learning, and all she needed were the tools and encouragement to continue.

I madly ran around labeling objects in the rooms of the house, figuring that this would be a way of helping Marisa gain a functional vocabulary. She seemed interested and did pick up on many of the words.

To encourage her interest in writing letters and words, I gave her a tracing chart to practice, and she spent a good deal of time perfecting her penmanship. She showed such a strong interest in shapes that I pulled out the Mr. Mighty Mind game of thirty wooden shapes and pictures to build objects using the shape pieces. Marisa worked on these twenty-four progressively more difficult pictures. This all by the age of two and a half.

I was greatly encouraged, and the staff at Marisa's school started to recognize that indeed Marisa did have a good deal of potential. It was an exciting time for me, because I felt that I had my goals laid out. Even though Marisa had autism, her abilities gave me hope regarding her future. I wanted to maximize her potential in any way I could. I saw so much growth through her eagerness to learn! Marisa had been in school for just five months, and already she was tracing and eagerly saying numbers up to thirty and asking for things in our supply closet by name, such as *brush* and *paint*. She was singing along with videos and at school was interacting nicely with another student while singing along with Hap Palmer songs. Marisa also started to sing the rainbow song I had taught her in order to learn her colors.

Not only was I pleased with her cognitive development, but I started to see in her a glimmer of understanding others' feelings as well. One evening during the family dinner, Marisa was pestering me to get a game from the upstairs closet. I explained that the family was eating, and I would help her after dinner. She kept pestering me, and finally I lost my temper and yelled at her, "You're inconsiderate, not nice. Can't you see we're eating dinner?" A moment passed, and then Marisa took my hand and said, "I love you!" She pulled me down to kiss my face and said, "I give kiss." Then she went around the table to her dad and gave him a kiss and said again, "I give kiss." It was the first time she ever did that, and it brought our dinner to a complete halt, just to take in the beauty of that moment. I realized that, in her own way, she was apologizing and letting us know she was sorry.

During the February recess from school, Marisa was busy with singing and dancing to videos and practicing shapes and alphabet letter writing, when she suddenly came down with a fever and vomiting. In spite of her illness, she was determined to stay busy with the business of learning. One morning while Marisa was resting on the couch watching *Sesame Street*, I left the room to put away some laundry. When I came back, I was surprised to find Marisa sitting in the kitchen practicing her writing and saying letters, even though she was still ill. She practiced drawing the shapes for circle, square, rectangle, and oval but could not yet master the diamond or triangle. She wanted to learn to draw a star, and so I showed her.

Marisa was also showing a strong interest in drawing people and used the shapes she knew to create faces, but I wanted to help Marisa acquire more language using her strong visual ability. I decided to introduce a new toy called the Headsmart Talking Typewriter that vocalized words and how to spell them. The child is supposed to type along with the voiced letters and make up words. Although Marisa had a strong interest in letters and new words, she found it too frustrating to have to find the letters on the keyboard, so for the time being I took the toy away. I gave her a Magna Doodle toy instead, so she could write what she wanted and then erase it and start again.

Marisa also seemed interested in people's social interaction. She would frequently use objects as make-believe people that she would pair up and pretend they were saying "Hello" and "Good-bye." She used stacking cups in this way after becoming bored with the idea of stacking them. I thought this was a very creative idea.

One afternoon I walked in to the kitchen to find Marisa sitting close to the cat while he was eating. Her head was down low watching his mouth, and she was petting him while he ate. I sensed a wonderful connection and interest in the family pet and thought perhaps our gentle pet could help Marisa to develop into a caring, gentle person. Up till this point we had only observed Marisa picking up the cat by the neck as she would pick up her stuffed toy. We had been concerned that if she was not closely watched she would choke him without realizing it. It was refreshing to see Marisa looking at the animal as a living thing rather than as an object to play with.

By the end of the February recess, Marisa had mastered her rainbow colors with ease and learned to trace letters well using stencils and draw all her shapes. She also enjoyed reading some sixty-five word cards and even managed to type beginning sounds of words on the talking typewriter that she had initially found so frustrating.

Back at school, Marisa seemed very comfortable with her accomplishments and was using more words to express herself. After playing with bubbles at school, she would say "All done!" when the container was empty.

I decided that it was time to work on simple commands at home in order to get Marisa used to following directions. I tried this with things that she liked to do, using commands like: "Bath time!"; "Sit down to eat!"; "Bedtime!"; "Get your coat and hat!"; etc. I noticed too, that when Marisa played with little toy people, she would start to add her own commands and new phrases.

I continued to be amazed by Marisa's own unique learning style. One evening Marisa pulled out Mr. Mighty Mind, the game with different colored shapes and picture cards. She enthusiastically worked through the picture cards, placing the shapes on the grey forms to complete the pictures. She was excited as she pointed out to me that two half-circles together would equal one whole circle and that two squares together would equal a rectangle. As I shared her excitement, I was fascinated by the way she was learning. It was so rewarding to watch her new skills evolve with a minimum of guidance from me.

I enjoyed watching the conversations she created, too, using the toy people.

Writing letters was another skill that she learned in her own unique way. The letter *N* became an important letter, because it went with the word "No" that she heard so much when she got into things that weren't for her. The letter *A*, I realized, as I watched Marisa write, was first written as a triangle, and then the upper bar was added.

She also mastered writing her name and the cat's names, traced words successfully, and said "Thank you" when she received help. Not only was I pleased to see her growth in language and visual skills, but also around this time I noticed Marisa was trying to connect with other people. One night Marisa snuck into bed with her sister Deborah and decided to get cozy with her for the night. Upon checking the situation in her own bedroom, I found that she had tangled her bed sheets and could not manage to straighten them out so that she could comfortably go to sleep. It seemed to me that because she didn't have the words to ask for help, she chose to join her sister in her bed. Although it was so cute to see her in her sister's room, I realized that it was important to teach her how to ask for help with a few simple words like "Come" and "Help."

It is amazing how much we can learn from our own children if only we stop long enough to pay attention to the way their minds work, rather than imposing on them our own ideas and ways of doing things. One afternoon Marisa was working on a difficult picture in her Mr. Mighty Mind. After she completed the picture, she would say "Betcha" and then take the next card to work on. I didn't understand what she was trying to say. I thought she meant to say "Next," as in "next picture." Later that day we were watching *Lamb Chop's Play-Along* with Shari Lewis. One segment on the show was called Betcha, which stood for "bet you can do anything." As I watched the segment, it dawned on me that Marisa was playing the Betcha game from Shari Lewis's show. I realized that she was betting me that she could do the next card in the Mr. Mighty Mind game. How amazed and delighted I was!

I began to pay much closer attention to the little clues that helped our little girl learn. One day I was drawing a picture of a boy and a girl for Marisa, and I drew a dress on the girl. Marisa immediately went to look at herself in the glass of the oven, which she frequently used as a mirror. She removed her pants and pointed to the picture of the girl in the dress. Understanding her desire to look like the girl in the picture, I went to get a dress for her to wear. She was so delighted by the dress that she spent the rest of the afternoon dancing around and then pulling her sister Deborah to dance with her.

Soon after this, a problem developed; Marisa was suddenly afraid to go to school. Once again I felt it was important to pay close attention to the clues Marisa was giving me. She had seemed to love going to school up to this point, and it seemed odd that suddenly she didn't want to go anymore. After speaking with the teacher, who said that things at school were just fine, I decided to send her favorite toy dog, Mutsy, on the bus ride. When this did not help the situation, I decided to go on the bus with Marisa to see what was happening. Judging by Marisa's nervousness and frightened reaction when the new matron on the bus approached her, it became apparent that there was something about the woman that made Marisa uncomfortable. Although Marisa could not tell me why the matron was upsetting her, her body language said it all. I spoke with the director of the bus company who agreed to change the matron on Marisa's bus to see if it improved the situation. After that was done, the problem was resolved; Marisa was happy to go off to school once again.

Around the middle of March I received a call from Rebecca's residential school that she had come down with chicken pox and needed to come home to recover. I then made the mistake of mentioning this to the psychologist at Marisa's school. The next thing I knew, the nurse at the school informed me that since Marisa was being exposed to chicken pox, she should stay home from school during the incubation period so as not to expose anyone at her school. I felt this was ridiculous and unfair but was given no choice in the matter.

Marisa and Rebecca were both to be home for at least ten days. During that time, Marisa seemed to be competing for attention as she realized that her big sister was actually very much like a dependent baby. Marisa took every opportunity to get in trouble. During her bath, she poured water out of the bathtub, creating floods; she used her booster seat as a springboard for jumping off; and she colored her face black with Magic Markers (I assumed to see what she would look like if she had dark skin like some of her classmates). She used the couch as a trampoline and a somersault platform and the arms of the couch as a balance beam. I realized it was time to bring out some active toys for our very overactive Marisa. After all, Marisa wasn't sick! As dumb as it seemed, we had just been waiting for her to get sick. So out came the rocking horse.

I've always been interested in observing the way children study new things, and children with autism are no exception. Marisa pointed at the horse and said "horse," looking at me for approval, and she then proceeded to study the horse from every angle. She walked around it and examined its face, saddle, feet, tail, and spring action. Then she climbed on to try it out. She climbed on and off constantly that first morning. She moved the horse around the room to various positions and then would try it to experience the new vantage point. All day she practiced getting on and off the horse and trying different riding techniques. She took breaks that day to work on stencils or coloring but kept returning to the horse. Later that evening she practiced mounting and dismounting with great speed, sang to the horse while riding, talked to the horse and petted it, and even dramatized her approach to the horse by mounting as if she were a cowgirl. The horse was a wonderful outlet for all the energy Marisa had to release while spending her days at home waiting to get chicken pox.

In spite of having the horse for those times when she needed to release some of what seemed like endless energy, Marisa still managed to get into a lot of mischief. Her curiosity was boundless. I considered it to be a good thing, as most two and three year olds have a healthy sense of curiosity that helps them learn, but to be on the safe side, I decided to purchase some cabinet safely locks.

At the store Marisa spotted a Lamb Chop puppet, and it seemed like a wonderful toy for her. A puppet would be a good partner for make-believe conversation. I decided to buy the Lamb Chop puppet and some new Magic Markers for her. Marisa held the puppet all the way home, and it was plain to see that Lamb Chop had become her new best friend. She immediately put the markers to good use once we reached home; she tested the colors by creating a display of happy heart faces on a piece of drawing paper.

During the days at home, Marisa also seemed to be developing an interest in the toilet. This was quite normal for someone approaching a third birthday. However, unraveling a whole roll of toilet paper was not my idea of the best way to learn to use the toilet. Not wanting to discourage her interest in acquiring toileting skills, I decided to make sure that her bathroom visits would be supervised. I placed safety doorknob grips on the bathroom doors and instructed Marisa to ask for help in trying the toilet.

During another shopping trip, I purchased some videos for Marisa. *Barney at School* and Big Bird's "Read Along" video *I Want to Go Home* seemed like excellent choices. Barney taught Marisa how to mix colors and the days of the week. I noticed that the videos captivated her attention, and since she seemed so receptive to the Barney video, I felt she would be able to learn a great deal by watching the character's regular TV show. She seemed to focus well on this children's show, and since she liked it so much, it became an extra tool for learning.

New experiences and anything outside her regular routine were difficult for Marisa, and I hadn't come up with a plan for dealing with them. Since Marisa did not understand many things that were spoken to her, any deviation from her familiar routine left her feeling lost and confused and often would result in mischievous behavior. This is typical for children with autism. During the stay at home, we took a trip to the beauty parlor so Deborah could get a haircut. This was an all-new experience for Marisa, which meant that a total exploration of the beauty parlor equipment was in order. She tried out every hair-cutting seat and checked out the hair driers and the tanning room before she wandered out the door to a car parked on the street. It took a lot of convincing to get Marisa into a stroller to go for a walk while Deborah got her hair cut.

To pass the time, we went down the street to the shoe store and purchased her a pair of sneakers from a choice of three. Marisa definitely had her preferences and, even at this early age, was showing a flair for fashion. Her decision was quick and decisive. Later that evening, it was pretty clear that she had had a very satisfying day as she carried her new sneakers around the house. When she came into the den and said, "Good night" later that evening, I walked her to her room, where she snuggled in tight with Mutsy, Big Bird, and Lamb Chop.

The last week of March Marisa was still home waiting for chicken pox to arrive, so it seemed like a good time to go through the children's spring clothing. Deborah gave many of her things to Marisa, who was excited to receive them. She held up every item to herself, spinning around and smiling delightedly. It was a joy to see!

Later in the day my parents came to visit. When it was time for them to go, Marisa said "Bye-bye!" Then she decided to stop them from going by pushing her grandpa back from the door, all the way through the kitchen, and into the den. It was nice to see that she was actually disappointed that they were about to leave and was clearly expressing her feelings through her actions.

But in spite of the occasionally appropriate social interactions, sometimes Marisa would engage in repetitive behaviors that were dangerous. Once she busied herself by removing bottles from a wine rack to line them up. For Marisa this was a self-initiated lesson in taking the wine bottles out to form lines and then putting them back again. For children with autism, engaging in repetitive behaviors is a form of self-stimulation.

To help prevent dangerous situations I started to videotape the *Barney* show, which was on every morning before Marisa got up. It seemed like a good idea, since being home for so long was making Marisa a bit more restless than usual. I felt that organizing a clear routine for Marisa during her extended time at home would help prevent some of the inappropriate behaviors. In making *Barney* and *Sesame Street* available for a morning activity, I was hoping to eliminate some of the self-stimulating behavior such as lining up little people or coloring the same words over and over again. Marisa tended to busy herself with such behaviors if left to her own devices.

The videotaping did help to bring order and routine to the long days at home. She was able to start her day with *Barney, Sesame Street,* and breakfast and then take a short trip out to the supermarket. She spent the afternoons with drawing, practicing word cards, and using the horse and indoor slide. One day she traced her Lamb Chop puppet onto a piece of paper, which she had seen done on *Lamb Chop's Play-Along* show. She then would cooperate at cleaning up when I asked her to. It seemed to me that the morning shows were teaching Marisa some very useful skills that she could practice on her own. I was pleased when, at dinnertime one evening, I called her for pizza, and she responded by dropping her toys and running to the kitchen, saying, "Pizza, pizza pizza!" She took her place at the table, ready and waiting. It was a rare pleasure for me to have Marisa join us for dinner because she did not like too many foods. Her diet consisting of cereals, cheese, crackers, macaroni and cheese, pizza, chicken nuggets and French fries, was usually eaten before the family dinner hour. Pizza night was always a pleasure because I didn't have to prepare a separate meal for Marisa.

March 31 was Marisa's last day at home; she never did get chicken pox. I had learned a few things about Marisa during her time at home. Videos had become a very useful teaching tool, and I was going to continue to use them to help Marisa organize her time. But this particular morning was beautiful with temperatures in the sixties, and spring fever was in the air. Marisa was itching to get out of the house by 11:30; she had clearly had enough of her morning *Barney* and *Sesame Street* shows. She went to her room, grabbed a jacket from her newly arranged spring wardrobe, and came running back to the kitchen, saying, "Jacket, jacket, jacket" while struggling to get it on. She then took my hand and pulled me all the way to the front door. We went out immediately and spent more than an hour swinging, playing in sand, and running around the yard.

Then Marisa started to get out of hand. She wanted to climb the fence to the neighbor's yard and had one leg over before I managed to pull her back. Next, she wanted to explore the backyard of the house across the street. At this point, it seemed to me a better idea to bring the play indoors, since she had become a bit overactive. Marisa was disappointed to have to go inside and kept letting me know that she wanted to be outside again by getting her jacket and repeating "Jacket, jacket" while trying to get it on.

Since it was almost time to pick up Deborah from school, I decided that a ride to the school would be a good compromise. When we arrived at the school, Marisa was happy to get into the stroller while we waited for Deborah to come out. When the buses pulled up and she saw the kindergarten children coming out of the building and getting on the bus, she started to scream and struggle to get out of the stroller. She wanted to go to the buses, too, and I understood that she was missing her own school bus, but there was no way of making her understand that she could not go on those buses. Fortunately, Deborah arrived, and we hurried back to the car and home.

Once at home, Marisa collapsed from fatigue but woke up an hour later to fill her time with jumping off her booster seat, riding a bike, and playing with water at the sink. Later, when she decided it was time to go to bed, she picked up her quilt and her three animals, came to the kitchen, and said, "Good night!" Then we went down the hall to her bedroom together.

The day Marisa was to return to her regular afternoon session of school, she spent her morning watching *Sesame Street, Mr. Rogers, Lamb Chop*, and *Barney*. She worked on a twenty-four piece puzzle with assistance and did some number writing and animal play. Then Marisa's first session back at school went well. I was happy to read the teacher's note, when she arrived home from school later that day.

> *She seemed happy to be back. I was amazed at how well she participated in the group today, including circle time. She did quite a bit of talking and spontaneous singing.*

This was just the kind of reassuring note I had been waiting for all year. It was nice to hear some good news.

Unfortunately, the return to school activities was short lived, because the spring recess was approaching, and Marisa was to spend more time at home. Rebecca was to come home for vacation, too, and Shoshana and Deborah had left on vacation with my parents. Marisa was confused and disappointed by the changes and started to cry at the kitchen table. She seemed so sad, and all I could do was explain to her that her sisters were away on a trip with grandma and grandpa and would be back in a week. I told her that when she grew up, she would get to go on trips, too. I didn't think she could understand my explanation, but the crying did stop. I knew that though she may not have understood everything, there was a good chance that she was understanding enough to calm down and it was certainly worth a try. It always was particularly difficult to make Marisa's time at home pleasant when Rebecca was home also. However, Rebecca's love for musical videos became a common interest for the two girls. In the evening Marisa stayed up watching the movie *Annie*. She loved the movie so much that she wouldn't be interrupted to take her bath. I was glad to see that she was happily occupied and decided to allow her to watch the movie to the end.

The week turned out to be extremely difficult, because my other children were not around to help out. I had to juggle caring for Rebecca's needs, which involved toileting and feeding supervision, while at the same time ensuring that Marisa didn't get into any major trouble. This was becoming increasingly difficult as Marisa's curiosity and skill increased. Even though it was hard for me not having Shoshana and Deborah around to help, I was glad that they could have the opportunity to go away on a trip with their grandparents since it was too difficult for us to take family trips while Rebecca was home for vacations.

One afternoon while I was cleaning up after Rebecca's lunch, Marisa went upstairs to the game room for longer than usual. She would usually go upstairs and return with a game from the closet, but this particular day, she did not come down. When I went upstairs to check, I found her digging her hands into the large plant that was up there. There was potting soil all over the room—on the window ledges, the blinds, the couch, the desk, the floor, and everywhere! There was no way to remain calm, especially since this was something Marisa had done once before. I gave her a spanking, something I had never done before, and took her directly to her room, where I instructed her to stay till I came for her.

For the next forty-five minutes I was busy cleaning up the room. I never did figure out why Marisa did this. I wonder now if she got some sort of tactile stimulation from this experience. At the time, all I could think was that what she did was just crazy, and my anger made me react in an inappropriate way, because I didn't know what else to do. However, all these years later, after reading and understanding autism more clearly, I'm sure there was some very logical reason why she chose to dig in that plant.

Later that day, we spent time outside, and Marisa did seem more cooperative about not climbing the fence and going in the road. I had noticed that lately Marisa seemed to have become more interested in physical activities rather than the reading and writing activities she engaged in all winter. Perhaps it was related to the change in season. I had her climb the hill on the front lawn and wait for me to call the command of "Get ready, set, go!" before she would run down the hill and then climb back up again.

In spite of the outdoor activities, by the end of the week, Marisa was pulling me to the basement door for something new to try; she knew that all the extra toys were stored in the basement. We went down to the basement to retrieve the teeter tot toy. I brought it up as Marisa eagerly followed me. She could barely wait while I cleaned it off and removed the handle bar to make it easier for her to get in and out. The teeter tot became the toy of the day! Marisa invented different ways to climb in and out—from the front, from the side, from behind. She tried standing on the seat and balancing and jumping on the seat as if she were on a diving board.

She spent the evenings watching the movie *Annie*, and by the end of the week, Marisa knew all the songs and even enjoyed acting out the scenes with the girls in the movie.

One very rainy day toward the end of the vacation was difficult for Marisa. We couldn't even go out in the yard, so she was very frustrated and upset. In spite of her frustration, she did finally manage to entertain herself well for part of the day. She spent time reviewing many of her word cards and playing with puzzles. She also learned to say "Bless you!" to my great surprise, after she herself sneezed. This day I refused to allow her upstairs, because of the incident with the plant the day before.

Two days later it was time to return Rebecca to her school, and Marisa was only too happy to get in the car for the hour-long ride to Port Jefferson, Long Island. Through my rearview mirror, I could see Marisa sitting contentedly in her car seat smiling to herself.

Later that day Marisa managed to get into enough trouble to need her shirt changed multiple times. She poured her own drink very enthusiastically, but overflowed the cup when she couldn't stop pouring in time. She soaked herself playing with water at the sink, and then managed to dirty herself when she put her hand down her very messy diaper to check it out. All this happened before my very eyes in a thirty-minute period, but no matter how difficult things were to that point, one simple incident that followed ended up lightening the day. That evening Marisa climbed onto a chair to open an egg carton and appropriately said, "No eggs!" It was a moment like this that made me feel all my efforts were well worth it.

Back at school, Marisa fell into a familiar routine, and she was also happy when her sisters returned home. By that weekend we needed to take a trip to the toy store for a birthday present for an upcoming party. While in the store, Deborah showed Marisa the Barney stuffed animal, which she immediately became attached to. This seemed unfortunate, because there was no way I would be able to take her favorite TV character from her arms. Her inability to comprehend the reason why I would take it away would most likely have caused a major tantrum, so I paid for Barney, and Marisa had another new best friend. On the way home Marisa surprised us when she sang the "I love you!" Barney song. She did not let go of that stuffed doll for the rest of the day—or the next day, for that matter.

At school, Marisa's speech teacher decided to make a picture word board for Marisa, which would help her communicate some basic needs she could not yet express. This seemed like a good idea. At home, I experimented with a talking doll to see if Marisa would interact with it in some way. She seemed to enjoy listening to and playing with the doll, which she had sit with her during *Sesame Street* time.

By the end of April, the teacher and psychologist asked to hold a meeting soon to discuss the following school year. I had some concerns, because they had hinted about not accepting overactive children into the three-year-old program, since the main focus of the school was on speech problems only. I began to suspect that Marisa was going to be bumped from the program.

At the end of April, Marisa attended her very first birthday party. This occasion provided a perfect example of behaviors manifested by autism. Children with autism have difficulty understanding the social skills that would help them get along with their peers. From their perspective, what matters is more likely to be the things rather than the people around them. The party was in a small party place with very structured activities in which the birthday girl was the main focus at all times. This was an extremely difficult situation for us, because Marisa could not understand why the birthday girl got all the attention, while everyone else had to just watch. From a teacher's standpoint, I knew this was not an ideal atmosphere for any normal two- or three-year-old. Though other kids may have been disappointed by the overabundance of attention given to the birthday girl, they were more able to control their feelings and understand why the birthday girl was the center of attention. Even at such a young age, neurotypical children are able to understand the basic social skills that are such a puzzle for children with autism.

Marisa, on the other hand, was continually getting into a power struggle with the birthday girl, who was supposed to be the center of attention. After struggling to keep her out of the way for the first forty-five minutes, I realized that I had no choice but to pick her up and leave the party. We went out to the car, where I just sat and cried, thinking what a disaster this experience had turned out to be. Though I explained to Marisa how wrong her behavior was, I didn't know how much she could understand, and I had no way to justify the insensitivity of the staff in charge of the party. They continually reprimanded Marisa for trying to gain attention, not realizing that she was a child with special needs. Even though I knew this was not a well-planned party, I still felt vulnerable being the one with the "flaw." I drove home angry with Marisa and angry with the people running the party.

I later discussed the party problem with Marisa's teacher and psychologist at school. Both felt that Marisa needed to stay away from over-stimulating environments at this time. They again hinted about not accepting Marisa into the school program for the following year.

In spite of these difficulties, I continued to receive encouraging notes from the school in regard to Marisa using many new words correctly to ask for help. The teacher also informed me about how appropriately she was using the dress-up center in the classroom. In addition, she was paying close attention to the circle-time activities and was singing and doing the hand and body motions that went along with the songs. Marisa's teacher wrote:

> *Marisa entertained us all at snack time by singing "Head, Shoulders, Knees and Toes." When we all joined in, she was so pleased. I think she felt like the star of the show.*

As I mentioned earlier, Marisa seemed to like the idea of developing her own bedtime routine. It was so nice to see that when she was ready for bed, she would pick up her little quilt, Mutsy, Big Bird, Lamb Chop, and Barney, and come to get me, saying "Good night!" We would go to her room, where she would make all the preparations for bed by herself. She would raise the window shades (I discovered that she liked to sleep with the moonlight shining in). Then she would fold down her bed covers. We enjoyed some intimate time together as I sang the "I love you!" song from Barney. I was pleasantly surprised when Marisa sang the Spanish version back to me which she had learned from watching the show.

Structure and routine were becoming increasingly important to Marisa. One day, Marisa arrived at her afternoon school session asleep and was carried into the classroom sleeping so as not to awaken her. Unfortunately, when she woke up, she was miserable and crying. I could not explain this to the teacher, since Marisa had been happy and active all morning, so I suggested that perhaps she was disappointed that she had slept through the first activities of the school day. Marisa needed the security and order of the familiar routine, and that had been broken. I suggested to the teacher that if Marisa came to school asleep again, she should be awakened so that she would not miss any of the regular activities.

Along with the need for routine, Marisa showed signs of improved eye contact and more functional speech. Marisa actually sat for dinner with guests we had over one weekend, and started to use the phrase, "I ready." She would select her own clothing, and after she was dressed she would say, "I ready." When her grandmother would suggest some playtime with blocks, Marisa would go to the blocks, sit down, and say, "I ready." She also started to say, "I take a bath," with good eye contact, when she knew it was time for a bath.

At school, her speech teacher started to use the computer to do a song activity called "This is the way we ..." She placed pictured objects next to different phrases, such as "comb our hair, brush our teeth, eat our food." Marisa would have to select from the objects that corresponded to the words for the objects. Marisa would appropriately choose the correct object when each verse was sung.

At around this same time, I decided to set up a home center in Marisa's room as a way to encourage some make-believe play. While Marisa was at school one day, I rearranged her room to create a house center with dishes, pots and pans, and a sink and stove. This was a pleasant surprise for Marisa when she came home. She and her sister Deborah used the house center many times during the weekend.

I hoped that Marisa would be moving in a new direction, spending more time in the make-believe play activities that I knew were normal for her age group. I felt that Marisa was showing more of an interest in dramatic play, and I was happy to encourage it. I thought it appeared that she was much less interested in letters, writing, and drawing at this time, and I hoped this was a good sign because I had read that children with autism often are fascinated with letters, numbers and words and I wanted to see a better balance of activities. She was doing a lot of very nice singing and acting out to TV videos, too.

But I thought too soon that Marisa's play activities were shifting in a more normal direction, so to speak. Marisa quickly reverted back to playing with magnet letters, creating the words she learned, and practicing saying them. In spite of my concerns about her fascination with letters, I felt the arrangement of letters into words was still a productive and meaningful activity.

In the meantime, the school advised me to check out two options for Marisa for the following year. I went to see Variety Preschooler's Workshop and a BOCES (Board of Cooperative Educational Services) program in Nassau County, Long Island. Both schools were for special needs children with varying disabilities and both were conveniently located near my home. I was very impressed with the well-stocked, large rooms at the BOCES classes but was concerned with the slightly larger class sizes of nine children to one teacher and one assistant. I was worried that the environment might be too over-stimulating for Marisa who was currently in a class of six children with one teacher and two assistants. I next went to see Variety Preschooler's Workshop, where the class sizes were smaller (no more than six children, with one teacher and two assistants) and the rooms were smaller. I felt that this less stimulating environment was probably a better choice for Marisa's needs, enabling her to more easily focus on her tasks.

My husband and I decided that Marisa would attend Variety Preschooler's Workshop, which in later years changed its name to Variety Child Learning Center. She would be turning three in June, and the school's staff suggested that it would be best to transition to the new program during the summer.

Over the course of the next few weeks, I realized that Marisa had made many gains during this year. At the end of May, Marisa's sister Deborah celebrated her ninth birthday by having a crafts party at our home. Marisa was very excited to participate at the party with Deborah's friends. She greeted everyone as they arrived, ate pizza with the other children, and sat and painted a doorknob sign along with the group. She was delighted to be included in the fun, and I was happy to see her participating with the group.

I could see that being around other children was a wonderful thing for Marisa, who was becoming quite sociable and was eager to have her own friends over. We arranged a play date with a little boy her age from her class. They played with a school bus with toy people and, with guidance, nicely took turns at a game. When the boy left with his mom, Marisa sang a Barney good-bye song.

I also noticed, to my surprise, while Marisa was playing with her toy typewriter by herself, that she had learned the letter placement on the keyboard. She was learning as she enjoyed typing words that she knew. This was an indication to me that she was once again using the tools provided to learn at her own pace. It was so nice to see! I was also somewhat relieved because I knew that a higher cognitive ability, though it would not mean Marisa would ever be neurotypical, would more than likely mean a better prognosis for someone on the autism spectrum.

On Memorial Day weekend we went to a barbeque at the magnificent, large home of some friends. Marisa could not make herself stay outside where the party was; she only wanted to explore the house with all its amazingly beautiful rooms, each with large picture windows overlooking outdoor gardens. What normal person would not want to see such a beautiful home, but what normal person would have the nerve to go through someone else's house without being invited to do so? There I was following Marisa around this magnificent home and feeling just awful doing it. I wanted to be outside with everyone else but I did not want to make a scene. Marisa, of course, had none of the inhibitions of the the rest of the guests, and after exploring the entire house, she settled in the playroom upstairs. When I wanted her to go downstairs, to eat or have dessert, I reminded her of the beautiful fish tank in the kitchen. She ran down yelling "Fish, fish, see fish!"

When it was time to go home after a tiring, six-hour visit, I held Marisa as she repeated over and over to the group of remaining people, "Good-bye, good-bye!"

At home Marisa was making swift progress with her alphabet desk toy, which had six modes. By pushing the buttons, one would hear the names of the letters, shapes, and numbers. Marisa could successfully complete this first mode. The second mode asked *Where* questions, for example, *Where is the letter B?* The child must then push the correct letter. Marisa was also able to do this mode. The third mode recited the letter and named an object beginning with the letter, for example, *S is for sun.* Marisa could complete this mode and enjoyed and studied it frequently. The fourth mode asked, *What letter comes before C?* or *What letter comes after C?* Marisa could not do this, because she hadn't yet learned the concept of *before* and *after*. The fifth mode asked questions like *Where is the sun?* and then would spell *Sun.* She hadn't mastered this mode yet. Mode six asked what letter a certain word begins with. Marisa was able to do this mode. Marisa enjoyed my applause when she was able to correctly answer the *Where* (mode 2) and *What* (mode 6) questions. This was really a good listening exercise for her, and the toy helped me realize the things Marisa needed help with.

At around this time, Marisa was showing more interest in domestic activities like sorting laundry and helping out around the house. She also expressed increased displeasure at having a messy diaper. I felt these interests were quite normal for this age, and once again I was encouraged.

With Marisa's third birthday approaching, we decided to have a small party for just the family. Marisa's grandparents came over, and we all wore party hats while we sang happy birthday and gave the birthday girl a chance to blow out the candles on her cupcake. Then she opened her presents. Marisa especially enjoyed playing with a seven-room dollhouse with furniture she received, and a large pedal sports car. She also enjoyed playing in the big cardboard house that I made for her out of the box that the pedal car came in. We took lots of pictures, and it was a terrific day!

On June 14, 1993, two weeks before school ended, Marisa's school held an outdoor graduation for the two-year-olds, something that the children had been rehearsing for some time. Marisa sat in a row of graduates, beaming with pride, and sang the graduation songs. When a little boy next to her was called to receive his diploma and hesitated to get up, those around me, myself included, were touched to see Marisa reach out to him and offer a helping hand, gesturing to him that he should go up. Then the teacher called Marisa's name, and she stood up to receive her diploma.

After the ceremony, Marisa was very excited to play with some colorful balloons that decorated the field for the graduation ceremony. When her teacher said she could take them home, she was just thrilled, and she spent the rest of the afternoon running and playing with the balloons and saying, "Balloons, balloons!" Later Marisa lined up her rubber toy animals and played graduation with them, having them each walk forward to accept a diploma.

That afternoon Marisa also went into our swimming pool for the first time of the season. She wore a bathing suit with built-in floats to help her while she was learning. She had no trouble remembering, from the summer before, how to kick and use her arms for swimming. She swam to the ladder in the deep end, climbed out, and jumped in about five times, holding my hand, before she decided to push me away and swim to the center of the pool on her own.

Over the next few days, Marisa was eager to jump off the diving board but was afraid. All winter she had practiced jumping off her booster seat, but now she could only jump up and down on the diving board. This was a nice start. She was able to jump in the pool from the side, and she didn't seem to mind when her face went under water. Marisa also spent lots of time watching her sisters in the pool and trying to copy the swimming strokes. She seemed to do well with floating and the breaststroke.

On the weekend, Marisa was lucky enough to have two older sisters to entertain her. Shoshana, thirteen, enjoyed drawing pictures for Marisa to color, and Deborah, nine, did a lot of imitative activities that Marisa liked to follow along with. These included hopping, clapping, funny arm movements, dancing, and talking.

In the morning when Marisa sat down to eat Cheerios for breakfast, she delighted us all by saying, "I eat Cheerios!"

Back at school, I received a note from the teacher.

> *Today I came in with a new haircut, and you should have seen Marisa inspecting it. She was so funny! She looked at me from all sides, touching, etc., and when I said, "Yes Marisa, I got my hair cut," she was satisfied. She doesn't miss a trick!! My husband probably won't even notice! HA!*

It was nice to know that Marisa was more in tune to things around her than we thought. When Rebecca was home from her residential school this week, I noticed Marisa taking a very active interest in all the things I had to do for Rebecca, things like bathing, dressing, and eating. Watching these things made Marisa curious about why her sister couldn't do these things for herself. It seemed as though she was beginning to realize, even at the age of three, that Rebecca is very different and very disabled.

June 30 was the last day of school, and I wrote a sentimental note to the teacher in the notebook we used to correspond.

The final day has come. It's a happy and sad day. Marisa had a great year! I hope she will hold onto some of the memories and remember all of you too. I've told her it is the last day. It's time to say good-bye, but a happy good-bye. She's moving on to new adventures now. I know this will be a positive experience for Marisa. We will visit Variety Preschool's playground after Rebecca returns to her school, so Marisa can have a chance to see what it is like. We have talked about the new school with Marisa and tried to compare it to other new things like new shoes or a new dress. Perhaps we will visit at some point in the future.

Though one door was closing, another was opening to a new and exciting beginning. I knew Marisa had autism, but I was feeling optimistic.

Chapter Three

A New Beginning

On Marisa's first half-day of the summer program at Variety Preschooler's Workshop, I wrote a note to the teacher.

> *I will use this notebook for corresponding. At this point, the only thing I'm going to tell you about Marisa is that if there is a way for her to escape to bigger and better things, she will do it ... slip out the door or climb out the window ... these are very definite possibilities for Marisa. P.S. Mutsy (favorite dog) is coming along to school.*

The teacher returned a note that said, "Marisa had a successful first day and didn't escape once." I was happy to know that the new teacher actually had a sense of humor. I felt as if she appreciated Marisa's feisty and curious nature.

Over the next few days, it became clear that Marisa was adjusting nicely and loved her new school environment. Each day she was eager and ready to go, with her lunchbox in hand. She was enjoying sensory activities like water play, sand art, shaving cream art, Play-Doh, and running through the sprinkler on hot days. Over the course of the next six weeks of the summer program, Marisa participated in music sing-alongs, and was actively engaged in gym time that required interaction with others. There were also sensory art projects related to a special theme for the summer. The theme that summer was the study of animal life, so many projects focused on different animals, and when possible, the teacher brought in live animals.

The teacher also was working on the group's eating habits at lunchtime. Lunchtime had been a problem for Marisa, because she had no patience to sit down and eat. Marisa was not yet able to eat at the dinner table at home because of her limited diet. This same problem became apparent at school, though I tried to send in foods Marisa would eat. Although eating remained a problem over the summer, seeing other children eat had some impact on her. Marisa sometimes expressed an interest in trying something she had seen. With the teacher's recommendations I would try sending in some of the new foods. Marisa remained finicky, but at least she was trying more new foods at school.

On a routine trip to the pediatric neurologist, I asked the doctor what educational approach would be best for Marisa. She suggested that Marisa have a total communication program, meaning that we should try anything and everything available, including speaking, sign language, computers, communication boards, and so on. Since all children learn differently, trying every way of reaching Marisa was important at this young age.

At home we were seeing some progress with speech and interaction. When Marisa's grandparents returned from a month-long trip to Alaska, they brought Marisa a train whistle. When Marisa blew into it, she said, "I do it!" Later, when they were leaving, Marisa surprised us all by saying, "Good-bye, Grandpa; good-bye, Grandma!" Then on another night when my older daughter poured soda for Marisa during dinner, Marisa surprised us again when she responded by saying, "Thank you for the soda!" Wow! That was actually a full sentence! And yet another time Marisa snuck into her sister's room, sat at the dressing table, and sang, "Put on a happy face …" as she brushed red blush all over her face. These exciting moments seemed like little miracles and brought such joy to us all.

As the summer drew to an end, I sensed that the teachers working with Marisa had grown very fond of our mischievous little daughter. "She is a joy!" was one comment I received from the teacher. "We like her, too!" I jokingly replied. "She manages to get away with a lot by being cute."

One afternoon, I laughed when I watched her get off the bus trailing sand from her sneakers as she walked. I could imagine the fun she had had playing in the sand that day. Later, Marisa tried to eat a whole peach. She stubbornly had refused to eat the one I had cut up for her, but I was delighted to see her eagerly trying to eat a whole one instead. She tackled it pretty well with her little, baby teeth, as she left a puddle of juice on the floor in front of her.

I had been using videos as reinforcement and to teach Marisa new skills. I purchased and played *Preschool Power*, a video that teaches a number of useful life skills, such as how to put on a jacket by placing it upside down on the floor and flipping it over one's head, zipping, and buttoning, as well as pouring liquids into a cup and preparing simple foods like a peanut butter sandwich. She seemed to study this video very carefully, taking it all in and learning each new skill. I was happy to see Marisa using her new skills to prepare a peanut butter sandwich, cut a banana, and proudly show how she could put on her own jacket by using the video technique.

The summer session at Variety Preschooler's Workshop ended on August 13. It had been a fun-filled and rewarding summer for Marisa. It had been easy for her to become accustomed to the new school because of the relaxed summer atmosphere. Marisa was to spend the next three weeks at home until school resumed in September. I was determined to keep structure and routine in place for the three long weeks, because I knew that Marisa would be happier if she had order in her day.

During this time I kept a journal of Marisa's activities and progress. She spent a great deal of time singing and painting, and she enjoyed placing the colors on the paper in different designs. She also was developing good organizational skills, cleaning up appropriately after painting. She would cover the paint jars and put them away in the proper storage area.

Marisa was also busy with many other activities at this time. She was spending less time studying words and letters and more time playing with other toys, trying to learn the names of real objects. The first Monday home during the break from school, we took a trip to the supermarket. Marisa enjoyed this a great deal. She willingly remained harnessed in the wagon while observing everything she saw … even naming some foods. Later, at home, she played with a Barbie doll that I bought her at the store for showing such good behavior.

By noontime she suddenly became very sad, and she started to cry as if she were mourning some great loss. I realized that this was the time that Marisa would usually leave for school, and I could think of no other reason for her to cry. Assuming that she was sad not to be in school, I told her in the simplest way possible about vacations and changes from the usual school routine. As she sat listening to what I had to say, she calmed down and climbed on to me for a hug. I sensed that she understood what I had said, because she was fine from that point on.

Later in the day, Marisa was upstairs with the cats, Pablo and Milo. I heard a crash and ran up. A record player speaker had been knocked onto the floor, and Milo raced past me. I walked in and said to Marisa, "What happened?" While standing on the couch, Marisa immediately replied, "He fell!" I looked at her in amazement as she casually shrugged her shoulders and stretched out her hands in reply.

What a miracle, I thought! She had listened, responded, and spoken to me appropriately, all in a split second. I paused to think and wonder about this. At times she could seem so normal. I wondered if she really knew everything that was happening around her but just couldn't always find the words to express her thoughts. That incident opened up a whole new way of thinking about Marisa. I began to feel that she really did understand a lot more than we thought, which was why it was so important to talk to her all the time; even though she didn't always respond, I had to assume that she was listening and understanding.

Early in September, before the new school year began, I reminisced and recorded Marisa's summer achievements. These journal notes helped me put Marisa's progress in perspective and appreciate the slow but steady improvements that were occurring.

Being home with older sisters during this time was a true blessing, too, because it gave Marisa an opportunity to practice her social skills. Marisa learned a lot from her sisters, who were always eager to draw her into activity. Deborah frequently would engage Marisa in dramatic play. One day she initiated a game of cowboy play: the girls would dress up in boots and hats and take toy guns to act out a cowboy scene. Deborah built a make-believe horse out of some furniture, so she could ride alongside Marisa on the rocking horse. She also played a game of school with Marisa, to which she was very receptive. Deborah would have Marisa sit at a desk and follow instructions, which was a playful way of developing her listening skills. She also would encourage Marisa to copy words off the blackboard, which gave her practice in visual discrimination and fine motor coordination. And on her own, Marisa also enjoyed following the words of songs in her sing-along book as she listened to the song tapes. I was happy to see the progress though I also knew that Marisa did not have a balance of skills throughout. She had amazing fine-motor coordination when it came to drawing and writing numbers and letters, but she had no ability to hold a conversation or even speak a simple sentence at this point. This imbalance of skills is often characteristic of people with higher functioning autism.

Getting ready to go back to school was exciting, too; Marisa practiced holding her new school bag and walking with it. She would, of course, stop to check herself out in the mirror as she walked. She was eager and ready to go! School resumed and seemed to be going smoothly, and Marisa liked her new teacher immensely. Once again, Marisa was to attend for a half-day program, which was standard for children before kindergarten.

By the end of September, I felt a need to review Marisa's progress in my journal. As I recorded my notes, I realized that Marisa was making good use of her time by playing appropriately with her toys and trying to develop her language skills. I had eased back on working with Marisa, allowing her space to explore her own world. What I observed was a little girl struggling to fit in to the world around her, though she seemed to have little need, understanding, or interest in the social skills that would make it easier to get along with others.

In spite of this I still remained optimistic and hopeful because she was making progress in some areas. She enjoyed setting the table for dinner on those nights when she would join us for pizza, engaged in some nice imaginative play with her toy people, and even showed an interest in talking on the phone though it was just to babble. Although she still had limited eye contact and an inability to engage in even the simplest of conversations, she seemed much more attentive to commands. However, she still remained unable to handle large social gatherings.

September 25 we celebrated Shoshana's fourteenth birthday. Our party was great fun! Marisa participated in the party lunch and craft activity and patiently waited as Shoshana blew out her birthday candles. She then sat down and ate her cake with the rest of the kids.

Back at school, Marisa was getting practice with using a toilet—a potty seat, actually—and at home she had graduated to a regular twin bed. She seemed very proud to be using a bed like her sisters and was also happy to be learning to use a toilet. These were encouraging signs to me.

Variety Preschooler's Workshop offered a Sunday program that was beneficial to both parents and children. It was an opportunity for parents to have some respite—a day to spend with the rest of the family without having to worry about the special needs child. It was also an opportunity for the child to socialize with his or her peers and not spend a whole weekend at home. Over the next few years I fully enjoyed those Sundays, and so did Marisa.

The first year at Variety Preschooler's Workshop was very special. Marisa's teacher seemed to be drawn to Marisa in an affectionate, maternal way. The relationship Marisa developed with her teacher, and the ongoing communication notebook I kept with the teacher, helped Marisa to make many positive gains. Marisa made new friends in her class with whom we were able to arrange play dates. She also mastered her toileting skills, at least the use of the toilet to urinate. She had many enjoyable learning experiences through the use of crafts, stories, music, cooking, gym equipment, community outings, and out-of-class speech lessons for 30 minutes a day for 5 days a week.

By the end of September, I had seen some amazing progress in Marisa's emotional development. One day she ran eagerly to the bus and, once she was seated, she waved and repeatedly threw kisses. Watching this affectionate gesture was a real joy to see!

That same afternoon, Marisa's bus was very late arriving home. When I called the bus company, I learned that a substitute bus driver had apparently gotten lost while bringing Marisa home. Marisa was on the bus till 5:30 PM. I kept imagining a crying, upset little girl, but when she arrived, I was surprised to see my child happily smiling and waving as she said good-bye to a very distressed bus driver and matron. They both looked as though they had just arrived back from a trip through the desert, but Marisa seemed not to have been affected by the long drive home as she happily ran down the driveway to the house.

Early in October, we were celebrating my parent's fiftieth wedding anniversary at the Crest Hollow Country Club. It was on a Sunday, and Marisa spent part of that time at her Sunday program in school. Later, I picked her up and brought her back for the last hour of the party. She seemed drawn to the band, and when the players left the room for a break, Marisa rushed to the drums and took a seat. She picked up the drummer's sticks and immediately started to play a pleasant, rhythmic beat. Unfortunately, the drummer came back and yelled at me for allowing Marisa to play his drums. I quickly removed her, but the sympathetic singer in the band offered to let Marisa sing into the microphone. Then Marisa sang along with the back-up music of the band. As the crowd watched in silence, Marisa beamed with pride at having been given this chance to sing. When she finished her little tune, she got a round of applause. It was Marisa's first opportunity to perform in front of an audience, which she thoroughly enjoyed! Watching this little girl at the microphone brought tears of joy to my eyes, not because she had a great voice, but because one very kind and ordinary person had recognized her desire to be in the entertainer's spotlight and had taken the time to make that moment happen.

During the next month we started to notice Marisa's more consistent use of language. She came up with more spontaneous phrases, like "Come down," "Go up," and "Let's go!" She even asked a worker in our house, "What's the matter?" when he smiled at her.

To help make it easier for the teacher to plan what to work on with Marisa, I felt it would be a good idea to send in a list of things Marisa had already learned. She also had a sight vocabulary of at least thirty words and enjoyed reading book titles. The teacher used this information to help decide what new games and equipment to order for the classroom.

Although Marisa seemed to have a fair amount of skills in the academic area, she remained socially and emotionally immature. On a trip to the orthodontist for Shoshana, Marisa was impatient. The secretaries felt it would help to let her into the examining area, where there were some toys to keep her busy. Against my better judgment, I let her go. Unfortunately, Marisa had other ideas than playing with the toys; she focused on the secretaries' computers and was also interested in playing orthodontist with some patients who were being examined.

No compromise was agreeable to her. I had to carry her out, kicking and screaming, to wait in the car. It was a very embarrassing afternoon. If I could find any positive from the trip to the orthodontist that day, it was when we had first arrived, and Marisa climbed the reception counter to say "Hi!" to the secretaries behind the counter. Unfortunately, though, that was the moment when she first saw the computers that attracted her and caused all the fuss that was to follow.

After this incident, the teacher recommended the use of visual aides such as pictures to show Marisa the appropriate things to do in different situations. They were using such materials at school, because Marisa's strong will sometimes would get in the way of her making the right choices. The pictures would hopefully serve as a reminder.

Along with being very strong willed, Marisa tended to be overactive. She had so much energy and not enough space to release it. One day she was playing on the couch and leaped down onto the rug in front of the fireplace. She seemed to like repeating this jumping routine, and it seemed harmless enough. Unfortunately, on one of her jumps she lost her footing and went too far forward, smashing her forehead into the stone platform of the fireplace. She had a bad cut in her hairline and cried, refusing to let me bandage the area.

When she stopped crying, I took her to show her the cut in the mirror, so she could understand why I needed to bandage it. She screamed in disbelief and cried just from the sight of it. After about fifteen minutes, she got up and went to style some curls over her cut, while looking in the glass of the stove, which she frequently used as a substitute mirror. I could see that her appearance was her first priority. I didn't realize it then, but so much attention to the minutest details of her appearance was to become an important part of Marisa's personality.

By November, Marisa seemed to be getting into a fairly consistent bedtime routine. She would say "Good night, good night!" and take my hand to go to her room. Over Thanksgiving, she used many more new phrases, such as, "What's wrong?"; "I know!"; and "I'll be right back!" She used these phrases appropriately in response to things that people said to her. She also was using the toilet more frequently during the day, but would only indicate the need to go by pulling her pants down in the middle of the room, rather than asking to go with words.

The next month, Marisa was showing real signs of developing her own sense of style. She started to spend time trying on clothes to wear for school and would go through a number of outfits before finally selecting something that met with her approval.

By mid-December, Marisa had gained a few new useful skills. She learned to accept her cup more readily, as I reduced the amount of liquid in her bottle, and was going to the bathroom regularly to urinate. I was even pleased to see that her behavior at the next visit to the orthodontist was greatly improved. I prepared her in advance regarding how to behave in the doctor's office, and we also took a book of baby pictures to keep her occupied while her sister met with the orthodontist. I could see her actively controlling her urge to go to the back rooms where the computers and examination rooms were. She did, at one point, stand on an end table briefly to see the computers behind the counter. I quietly encouraged her to sit down to continue browsing through her album of pictures, as I quided her back on to the couch.

The Christmas vacation was approaching, and I was not looking forward to the long days at home. Rebecca had to come home from her residential school for the week, and Marisa did not respond well to the inevitable loss of attention to her. I tried to organize Marisa's days so she would be busy and occupied enough to stay out of trouble, but I also worried about the huge responsibility of caring for Rebecca as she was getting older and harder to handle. Marisa, too, was getting older, and I worried about her increasing abilities to get into more trouble. For example, though Marisa hadn't walked out of the house yet, I knew it was just a matter of time before she would figure out how to move a chair to the door to reach the latch. Autism has no boundaries when it comes to good judgement and safety issues. The result was that vacations were always such difficult times for me. I wanted Rebecca to share our family time, but it was impossible to make it relaxed, free of stress, and enjoyable for everyone.

Once Rebecca returned to school, I took Marisa for a ride to the toy store; my parents had given me some money to use for a Chanukah gift. Upon arriving at the toy store, Marisa said, "What are we doing here?" I was so happy to hear that sweet voice and appropriate question. When I explained that we were there to buy something for her with her grandparents' gift money, she quickly said, "Let's go!" Such phrases never ceased to surprise me, especially when Marisa would say something entirely new and unexpected. Whenever that happened, it felt to me like another miracle. I could see that she was so much more aware of things than she appeared.

Marisa was not just aware; she had a unique and different way of seeing the world. She viewed the world from her perspective, that of a child with autism. She had her own way of handling situations, and the way she saw things might not make sense to us, but it made sense to her. For example, for days she walked around with a stomach ache, until it occurred to me that perhaps she was afraid to have a bowel movement (BM) in the toilet. She was wearing underpants all day, since she was now using the toilet to urinate, but she wouldn't go to the toilet to have a bowel movement. Instead, she would wait until I put a diaper on her at night. I had to wonder if she just didn't know how to express her fear of using the toilet for her BM, so she patiently waited for a diaper.

I decided to make sentence cards with pictures to help her communicate her needs, and I found that they worked well for Marisa. She would point to the words as she read them, adding to her list of sight vocabulary. At the same time, the cards were helping Marisa communicate some of her needs. When it came to using the toilet for her BMs, however, she decided that she would rather bring a diaper to me to put on her for that purpose. I guess this was her way of telling me that she just wasn't ready to use the toilet for her BMs yet.

In spite of her increased vocabulary and improved ability to communicate, Marisa still remained impulsive in new situations. When we picked up her sister Deborah from a friend's house, Marisa only wanted to explore, and I had to carry her tantruming from the house. These impulsive outbursts made me uneasy about taking Marisa anywhere. I started to reduce the number of situations that were likely to create her problem behavior until I could find a way to control her impulsiveness. I was angry and frustrated at not knowing what to do about the frequent outbursts in public.

By March, Marisa was officially toilet trained. When she was learning to occasionally use the toilet for her BMs, a thought had occurred to me: knowing that she was now fully capable, I thought that an incentive might do the trick. I told Marisa that if she could use the toilet for her BMs three days in a row, we would reward her with something that she wanted. She asked for Grow to Pro Basketball for kids, a freestanding basketball net. I made a chart showing the three days, and at the end of each day she would get a sticker for using the toilet for her BMs. To my amazement, the technique worked, and after three successful days, Marisa was thrilled to receive her basketball set.

Understanding the needs of a child who can't express her thoughts to you requires some detective work on a parent's part. A good example of this was when Marisa's teacher was absent for a few days. It became apparent that Marisa was missing her greatly; she walked around with a sad face and expressed the same feeling in her drawings. This all came to an end once the teacher returned.

On another occasion, I had signed Marisa up for an after-school gym program, but it was plain to see that she was not happy there. Although the program was in her school with the same special needs kids she went to school with, she would cry and cover her ears whenever she entered the gym. This was surprising, because Marisa usually liked gym activities. However, this program was noisy and overcrowded with many more students than she was used to. Marisa's classroom teacher felt that Marisa's sensitivity to the noise level made her uncomfortable, so we switched her to the after-school art program instead.

Incidents like these made me realize how important it was to pay attention to detail, and because Marisa was using more words, I continued to add important phrases and illustrations to a book that she could refer to for assistance. On one occasion at school, Marisa caught her hand in a toy. The teacher was happy when Marisa called out "Help me, help me!" This was one of the key phrases in her book at school and at home.

I was thinking ahead to Marisa's birthday, which was coming up on June 16th and decided to ask the teacher if she felt a birthday party with children from the class would be a good idea. Marisa seemed anxious to have friends over, and I felt that this would be a good opportunity to celebrate her fourth birthday and see her friends from school, too. Marisa's teacher felt the party would be fine, but she suggested that I not invite the whole class, because some of the children would have difficulty. Since all the children in Marisa's school had varying learning disabilities, some of the children might not be ready or able to comfortably participate at a party.

By April, the teacher had noticed Marisa engaging in some very nice pretend play with another little girl in the class, Brittany. Marisa took Brittany's hand, and they both went pretend shopping with pocketbooks. Then they went to the play kitchen, where Marisa said, "Eat," and they pretended to cook and then sit at the table to eat. They drew a little boy into the play, and Marisa used the pretend doctor's kit with him. It was nice to hear that Marisa was engaging in some healthy pretend play that was giving her practice in social interaction.

I decided it was time to arrange a real play date with Brittany, and I thought it would be a good idea to have a friend over before the birthday party, which was coming up in June. It would be good practice and preparation for a group of friends. I spoke to Brittany's mom to plan for a get-together scheduled for the end of May.

Not only was Marisa developing an interest in friends, but I also began to sense that she was capable of sharing emotions in a very healthy and normal way. This became most apparent when Dan and I took a trip for a few days and left Marisa in the care of her grandparents. When we returned, it was so nice to realize that she had missed us. We walked into the house, and she looked at me and didn't seem to know whether to laugh or cry. Then she just cried—it was the cry of relief! Though she couldn't verbally express her feelings she clearly was showing that she had them. It was a very touching moment for me.

According to my mom and Marisa's teacher, while we were gone, Marisa would go to school and ask for me. When she returned home, she would look through the house and climb into my bed. It was nice to know that I was more to Marisa than just a caretaker. She was showing real emotions and expressing them, which was an encouraging sign to me.

The after-school art program started out with some difficulties, but Marisa's regular classroom teacher was willing to spend time carefully evaluating what was going wrong. This proved to be a worthwhile effort on her part, and the program, which could have been a failure, turned out to be a successful and positive experience. Marisa wasn't interested in waiting for the instructor to tell the children what to do. Instead, she seemed drawn to other things in the room. Marisa's teacher and I talked about ways to make the program work, and we felt that perhaps if I arrived at the program ahead of Marisa, things would go better. Though my presence improved the situation a bit, Marisa continued to have little patience while waiting for the art teacher's instructions. To help overcome this problem, we decided that having the materials ready and waiting would help things go more smoothly for Marisa. This prevented her from being easily distracted by other things in the room and kept her focused on the project set before her. I was very grateful!

Though we did successfully complete the art program, Marisa's impulsiveness continued to be a problem in other areas. Deborah's birthday party was coming up on May 21st. Unfortunately Marisa's behavior at the party, once again, would remind me of just how much we still needed to work on her social skills. We felt the birthday party would be good practice for Marisa, since her own party was scheduled for just a few weeks after Deborah's. As it turned out, Marisa was unable to handle being at the party. She was confused, thinking the party was for her, and she kept wanting to open all of Deborah's gifts. She was so uncooperative that I had to lock her in her room halfway through the party. It was disappointing, but I knew that Marisa's impulsiveness and inability to fully understand the situation left me no other appropriate alternative. Likewise, in a similar situation at school, during a puppet show, Marisa wanted to touch the puppets, running up to them during the performance, and also had to be removed from the room, which once again left me feeling at a loss for what to do.

By the end of May, Marisa did have her first play date at Brittany's house. She was very excited to go to a friend's house and kept saying, "Brittany's house! Brittany's house!" She enjoyed meeting Brittany's dog, and the girls played side by side with toys in the bedroom, while Brittany's mom and I talked near by. This was the first of many terrific play dates that would follow, as we alternated between homes.

As Marisa's birthday approached, I had to think of what would be a good gift for such an overactive soon-to-be-four-year-old. I decided to purchase an indoor trampoline so that she could jump and release some of her endless energy. A few days before the birthday party, Marisa found her birthday gift hidden in a room upstairs. She was so excited! There was no keeping it from her at that point, so down it came into our then-empty living room, where she excitedly jumped for joy.

We also planned to set up the trampoline for her party on June 18. At the party there would be six children—four from the school class, Marisa, and one other little boy whose parents were friends of ours.

The night before Marisa's fourth birthday, she did something that was very precious to me. When I was putting her to bed, I handed her a milk bottle, and she said, "No!" Then I said, "Don't you want your bottle?" and she replied, "No, stupid baby bottle! Good night!" On her own, she had decided that it was time to give up the bottle. I was happy to see that she had reached this milestone independently. I was never one to push my children to do anything before they were ready, whether it was toilet training or giving up the bottle. To me it wasn't worth the anxiety it could cause both the parent and the child. But hearing Marisa express in her own words that she was ready to move on was a thrilling and rewarding moment.

Looking back over that past year, I thought that it really had been a terrific year at school. She loved her teacher and her speech therapist and had learned to enjoy her classmates. Marisa was turning four and was finally just beginning to show signs of real listening. She was beginning to pay attention to requests like, "Show me the baby in red" or "Show me the girl with the curly hair." She actually answered "OK!" when I told her she would swim after school one day. I could see that she was speaking more spontaneously, remarking on things and feelings. Things seemed to be looking up.

Marisa had a party at school to celebrate her birthday. I sent cupcakes, and the teacher told me that Marisa walked around singing happy birthday as she wore her birthday crown for the day. When she arrived home, she opened the Bing Bong Paddle Ball set the classroom staff had given her. Marisa enjoyed the paddle game and listening to the noises it made.

Marisa was very excited watching, as we prepared for her birthday party that Sunday. We had decorated the party rooms, our large atrium center hall and the connecting living room that still was free of furniture. The decorations and the party table made her realize her day had finally arrived. When the balloons were delivered, her excitement escalated.

The first party guest was a little boy named Ross. Marisa screamed and rushed to the door, a big smile planted on her face. She took his hand and led him around the two party rooms. Then she showed him the Styrofoam bath I had set up in a big, blow-up swimming pool. She jumped in and invited him to join her. Then her friends Tony, Thomas, and Brittany arrived, and everyone got busy with party activities. Aside from the Styrofoam bath, there was the trampoline, a balance beam, a seesaw, and a box cut to look like a TV screen so the children could imagine they were on TV. By the time Evan, the last guest, arrived, the party was in full swing, as the children engaged in the activities set to background music.

The free-play activities were followed by a pizza lunch, cup-decorating craft activity, and parachute games. I also handed out instruments and led the children in a marching band around the party rooms. Then the children all enjoyed an ice-cream birthday cake. When the party ended, Marisa was upset and cried. It was a sad and emotional moment for her, but a very important one for us; her tears made us realize just how important people were becoming to her.

Marisa then opened her gifts and enjoyed them all, from dolls to sand art. A week after the party, Marisa had completed all the sand art in the kit, played with finger puppets she created from a puppet-making kit, and enjoyed her Barbie dolls and a mermaid doll she had received as gifts. She spent the last few weeks of school playing with her dolls and dollhouse as she acted out dramatic play activities. She also enjoyed using sewing cards that she had received.

The school year ended on June 24 with a party at school. There was to be a break before the summer program would begin, then Marisa would return to the same class for the summer session so as not to break up the continuity of her progress.

The interim week at home was a difficult one. Marisa had become extremely demanding, and she always seemed to insist on getting her way. I decided that it was time for Marisa to learn that sometimes she just would have to wait. For example, if Marisa wanted ice-cream, but it was before dinner, she would have one of her screaming tantrums in order to try and get her way. Tantruming usually would escalate out of control. Once this happened, there was no way to stop it and no way to reason with her. Sending Marisa to her room, I hoped would help her learn that outbursts were not acceptable. She clearly needed to learn to pull herself together before coming out of her room. I hoped that this technique would help her learn to prevent some of the outbursts. It was worth a try.

The summer program started at the beginning of July. Once again, Marisa remained in the same class with mostly the same students. The children spent a lot of time engaging in various outdoor activities, including running through a sprinkler. I noticed that, although Marisa was enjoying the relaxed summer program, she seemed somewhat sad. I wondered if she was beginning to realize that she was different from other children. Though the children in Marisa's school had special needs also,they were not necessarily on the autism spectrum. I felt it was conceivable, too, that she was becoming more frustrated by not being able to express herself fully. I tried new things to see what would interest her. Of course she still enjoyed our pool, which had a very calming effect on her. The pool remained the most pleasurable activity of the summer. Marisa enjoyed swimming with her body float swimsuit, so she didn't have to constantly be held up or have me hovering over her in the water.

During that summer Marisa colored words in block letters, but I was not happy to see that she was becoming very particular in what she chose to color and how she colored it. She had been watching some *Kidsongs* videos when Rebecca was home and decided to create her own art out of the word "Kidsongs." She would make block letters and then color them in exactly like the word was written on the video box. She continued to do this, always coloring the word the same way from memory. I realized that she was developing a pattern of repetitive behavior so typical of autism.

What bothered me was her lack of interest in coloring other words, or other things for that matter. She was totally preoccupied with the sameness of the one word. Along with this preoccupation was the sadness that seemed to overcome her during that summer. Although she had made slow but steady gains in her speech and other skill development, she seemed bored with her own accomplishments and seemed to be unable to move forward. I started to wonder if I had been too relaxed that past year, relying too heavily on the teacher at school to help Marisa move ahead.

She had kicking and screaming tantrums that seemed to spring up out of nowhere as a result of her frustration and inability to express her needs and feelings. Marisa also had tantrums when she couldn't get her way. At times she had numerous tantrums in a single day, and sometimes it was hard to know what the tantrums were all about.

During that summer, Marisa spent a good deal of time locked in her bedroom because of the uncontrollable tantrums. She would have to stay in her room until her screaming would stop. I knew that the separation was a good way to allow her to regain her composure. Once she regained control, I knew I would have a better chance of making her understand the reasons for not getting what she wanted at that time. However, I began to think that she was enjoying the time she spent by herself. Although the periods of solitude had a calming effect on her, I was concerned that she liked the time alone too much. Children with autism often craved these times alone.

I tried to watch her closely in order to figure out what caused some of the tantrums. If I could pinpoint tantrums occurring out of frustration or an inability to express a need, then I would be able to prevent some of the occurrences and reduce the time she was spending in her room by herself.

In spite of my concerns about Marisa's tantrums, she did have some good moments in the summer of her fourth year. Marisa spent time with her sisters, engaging in some make-believe activities like shopping at the supermarket and doll play. These dramatic play periods were a good way for her to improve her social skills. One day Marisa surprised me by letting me know that she knew her last name. I was writing her name on a play purse for her to bring to school when she suddenly blurted out "Rubin!" after I wrote her first name. I was once again delighted by her awareness!

Marisa was developing a very particular taste in her choices of clothing. She showed great assertiveness in selecting certain flared dresses with matching socks. She also wanted to match her hair ribbons or clips and made sure to give her favorite stuffed animal, Mutsy, a matching ribbon too. One morning I walked into her room to help her get ready for school. Marisa had selected her clothes to wear and was sitting fully dressed when I entered the room. She said, "Hi!" as she sat perched on her bed, smiling, with her shoes in her hands. What a pleasant surprise this was for me!

Another day I was struck by Marisa's enthusiasm to put an outfit together. She decided to wear her Barney hat that day, and then she remembered that she had a Barney shirt to match. "Barney shirt, Barney shirt!" she said, and she rushed to look for the shirt. I was thrilled by her sudden enthusiasm, and I helped her find the shorts to match. She got dressed and then said, "Cookie Monster shoes!" She rushed to the closet to find the sneakers with the Cookie Monster laces. The entire day she wore her Barney cap, and when she temporarily misplaced it, she cried and ran to me saying, "Barney hat, Barney hat!" I was happy to see the excitement come back in her eyes.

Marisa also started to respond quickly to requests when she was reprimanded. When she turned the kitchen light out while I was working, she immediately turned it back on when I told her to. I tried giving her more commands as practice. I would ask her to bring the red cup or close the door, for example. This gave her practice in listening and following directions.

Because Marisa was good at decoding words phonetically, the teacher continued to use written phrases to help reduce Marisa's frustration level. Marisa's teacher labeled things around the classroom to increase the children's sight vocabulary, and she wrote out key phrases for Marisa to use when she wanted to ask for something. Phrases like "Give me ___" and "I want ___" gave her the tools she needed to ask for a particular item. I did the same at home.

In the meantime, Dan and I had decided it was time to consult with Isabelle Rapin, a pediatric neurologist with extensive experience in research about and treatment of autism. Consulting with this doctor was specifically for a second opinion as to what treatment would be best for Marisa. Because of Dr. Rapin's experience in treating autism, we greatly valued her opinion, and welcomed any advice she could give us. We traveled to meet Dr. Rapin on August 1, 1994, at her office at the Albert Einstein College of Medicine in Bronx, New York about an hour away from our home.

The visit was extremely difficult. Marisa was darting all over the place in the waiting room, climbing on furniture, and moving around the room nonstop. When we finally went in to see the doctor, it was difficult to contain Marisa for any kind of evaluation. Marisa ended up on the floor in a full-blown tantrum. After a good twenty to thirty minutes of observation, Dr. Rapin sat down with us and had just one thing to say: "Given the clear-cut autistic behavior, the best advice I can offer is to get the behaviors under control since this will be a decisive factor in terms of her future prognosis." That was the bottom line. It was the first time anyone had actually used the word "autistic" to diagnose Marisa's disability, and we were taking every word she said very seriously. Dr. Rapin gave us the name of a neuropsychologist on Long Island, near our home, who she felt might be able to help in creating a behavior management plan or recommending someone else who could. I went home and immediately gave Dr. Frances Taylor a call.

Although I didn't know it at the time, it was a turning point in the way I would work with Marisa.

Chapter Four

THE POWER OF
REWARDS

Meanwhile, a new school year began on September 12, and Marisa was to have a new teacher. To ease the transition, the previous teacher had given Marisa a picture of her new teacher. The note I sent the first day of school expressed some of my biggest concerns.

> *I'm sure Marisa will be thrilled to be back at school. There are two things I will warn you about for now:*
>
> 1. *Marisa sleeps, eats, and bathes in her necklace and bracelet. She won't take them off and generally doesn't lose them. If she does lose them, she will definitely become extremely upset.*
>
> 2. *She may decide to walk out or escape unnoticed. At home the doors are always locked. I won't overburden you with any other details at this time, so good luck!*

I had major anxieties about Marisa beginning the year with a new teacher, and the only way to ease the fear was to communicate my concerns. Parent input was actually the best way to help the teacher understand the idiosyncrasies of a child, and this school actually welcomed parent input, encouraging and applauding it as a collaborative team effort. I later sent a list of activities Marisa enjoyed at home, and I also informed the teacher that we had started to meet with Dr. Taylor, a psychologist who was helping us set up a behavior plan for Marisa.

One weekend in September our family went to look at new cars. Marisa was totally uncooperative in the public setting, unable to stay with the family and unable to control her tantrums. We had to cut the outing short. Such difficulties as this became examples of the problems I faced on a daily basis, and I used these outings as examples for Dr. Taylor.

When we first met with Dr. Taylor, we talked about Marisa's impulsive behaviors and tantrums while she sat on the floor playing with Marisa. It was a very relaxing meeting and Marisa seemed to enjoy it a great deal. Dr. Taylor then suggested that I think about one goal to work on during this first week. Then once the goal was decided, we would begin by offering stickers as a reward. At first, I was somewhat skeptical of this approach, because I didn't see how receiving stickers would be of any real interest to Marisa, but since Marisa, like most children, liked stickers, I decided to give it a try.

The behavior I selected to work on first was ending an outdoor playtime quietly rather than by kicking and screaming in disappointment. If Marisa could come in from the yard when she was told to do so, she would earn a sticker for that day. Marisa helped to make her chart with Dr. Taylor, which seemed like a good way to get her involved. At home the next morning, I reminded Marisa about the chart which was clear to see on the refrigerator door. We spent time outside and I was surprised to see how well Marisa responded when she was reminded about the sticker chart. We were off to a good start.

Meanwhile, at school the teacher made a *School Day* book for Marisa in order to help her transition from one activity to the next. By seeing a visual plan in book form with simple pictures and corresponding words, Marisa would be better prepared for what was to happen next. She was able to read through the book with full understanding, which prepared her for activities out of the classroom that had previously disturbed her such as gym, library, art or even a special performance.

Similarly, the teacher created written instructions with pictures for learning to take turns with her classmates at computer, cooking, and playing games. These clear and concise visual clues helped Marisa cut down on her outbursts, because she knew what was expected of her.

At home, I decided to add the school goal of waiting her turn, so that she could earn a sticker on her home chart for an activity she also practiced at school. I was starting to realize the advantage of visual cues for Marisa, and because the *School Day* book was working so well, I decided to make a book about an upcoming trip Dan and I were going to take, entitled *Mommy and Daddy's Trip to Bermuda*.

We were going on a four-day trip and would have my parents stay with the kids. The trip book would help Marisa understand what was going to happen and alleviate any fears that we might not come back. The teacher suggested I make a calendar to correspond with the book, showing the days we were to be away and the day we would return. Marisa watched as I made the calendar for her, and we hung it up so she could check off each day we were gone.

Although the book and calendar did help Marisa while we were gone, when we returned, we were confronted by a very angry, frightened Marisa. She cried for an hour, repeatedly saying, "Why did you go away?" Though it was upsetting to see how disturbed she was, it was also nice to know that she missed us so much. I also realized that she had become more capable of expressing her feelings, as compared to her reaction to our trip the year before.

As time went on, Marisa had more surprises for us. We were always delighted by her expressions and observation of things happening around her. When we had a second refrigerator installed in our kitchen, Marisa looked back and forth between the two refrigerators and then commented with a smile, gesturing with raised hands, "Crazy, it's CRAZY!"

Another time, it became very clear that Marisa was growing very conscious of her self image. One morning as she pulled up her pants, she remarked, "I'm getting fat!" I was surprised that she would say such a thing, but thought perhaps that her pants felt a bit tighter because she was growing. Nevertheless it was wonderful to see our special little three-year-old using comments spontaneously.

Because the idea of a visual schedule of the school day in book form worked so well, the teacher carried it over to planning for school trips. She made a book about an upcoming trip to a pumpkin farm so that Marisa would be able to transition through the day's activities. The trip to the farm went well as a result of the teacher's efforts.

Marisa was starting to show more interest in her classmates through turn-taking games and make-believe play. These activities, too, were improved through the use of a picture book of social rules. The book contained simple and basic rules as sharing, turn-taking and helping a friend, and there were pictures to illustrate each rule. I was able to plan play dates with some of the classmates since Marisa was still only attending school for a half day. Since school was from noon to three I had the whole morning available for get-togethers.

During a session with Dr. Taylor, we decided that it would be beneficial to practice taking a trip out into the community to shop for one item in a store. The plan was to inform Marisa ahead of time that she would be allowed to select one item to purchase. It was frightening and anxiety-provoking for me because I didn't know how she would behave. I was still worried about impulsiveness. Marisa frequently darted at things that interested her such as a crying baby or a dog, not considering the consequences. I also was concerned about whether she would be able to select one item in a store full of so many temptations. The day of the planned trip the three of us walked a block down from the doctor's office to the store. There Dr. Taylor and I patiently followed Marisa up and down the aisles as she scanned the toys available to her. After cruising the aisles, looking over all the possible selections, she carefully chose a plaster and paint magnet-making kit. Marisa was delighted and happy to be able to purchase it and bring it home to work on. All in all, it was a good lesson for both Marisa and myself. I had to remember to set the limits in advance of the planned activity. In this case that meant informing her that she could select just one item.

Marisa's behavior improved on short trips. We could pick Deborah up from activities and successfully took occasional trips to the store for art supplies and workbooks, without always expecting Marisa to make a scene over some item she wanted or some area of someone's house she insisted on exploring. Over Thanksgiving vacation Marisa worked in her activity books that were filled with color-by-number, beginning consonant letter sounds, matching pictures by category, and completing pictures by connecting the numbered dots, among other things.

I started to see the clear advantage of the sticker reward system, and I continued to find other goals for Marisa to earn stickers for. When Marisa started to scream and squirm in her seat one day while waiting for assistants to escort children off the bus at school, the teacher suggested that I give Marisa a book to keep busy with while she was waiting. I also felt that along with some activity to do during waits, it might be beneficial to add a "bus" goal to her home chart. Earning a sticker each day for staying in her seat created an incentive: when she earned five stickers, she would receive a special little reward. I made sure each day that Marisa was aware of her goal chart and what was expected of her. I also told Marisa that her teacher would let me know each day if Marisa had earned her sticker for staying in her bus seat. This plan worked well.

Chanukah came in early December that year, and Marisa enjoyed participating in lighting the candles and receiving gifts for each of the eight nights. This year she received talking books and Sesame Street books with audiocassettes so that she could follow along in the books. Marisa enjoyed all her gifts, but when I asked her what she wanted most of all, her reply was simply, "School!" I was surprised by the response but really thrilled, too, because I knew that being at school meant being with other children—her friends were clearly the thing Marisa wanted most of all. It is clear to me as I look back now that, at the age of four, Marisa's personality had taken a distinct direction. Marisa was becoming a sociable child with autism, which in her case meant she was so eager for friends that she was likely to invade the space of others in order to seek their friendship.

On our next visit to Dr. Taylor, she decided to end our sessions before the upcoming Christmas vacation. Marisa had shown steady improvement with the use of the sticker chart. The doctor and I felt that continuing the sticker and reward system would help her make additional positive gains. Since Marisa was doing so well, there was no longer a reason to continue the sessions.

I had started with one goal only but over the course of the months we had been meeting with Dr. Taylor, I gradually expanded the idea into a goal chart that Marisa could earn stickers for multiple goals at the same time. I knew that the stickers themselves were not of great value to Marisa. If she earned a set number of stickers, however, she could earn a prize of her choosing. The stickers quickly took on new meaning for Marisa. Behaviors started to change rapidly. Earning a desired prize became a strong incentive to do the right thing.

I realized that there were so many little things to accomplish. As I eagerly sat down to record the possibilities, the goals seemed to flow forth like an explosion. I couldn't write down the ideas fast enough. For example: using a tissue to blow her nose, walking with her heels down, looking at the person talking to her, taking turns in play, listening to instructions, showing concern for other people, controlling screaming, using words to ask for things, going to bed on time, sitting still in the car, answering questions with "yes" or "no." The list was endless. Marisa would not be a toddler forever. I realized as I watched Marisa grow that each goal was important in helping her get one step closer to fitting in to a world where there is little tolerance for those who are different. As sad as that may seem, it was nevertheless necessary if she was to make her way successfully as an adult in the society in which we live.

Because of the improvements Marisa was making, we were able to go on little trips to the store and go for outings to Burger King, but Marisa was still showing very impulsive behaviors. For example, on one trip to a neighborhood Burger King, Marisa suddenly darted into the restaurant's kitchen. She frightened the manager to such an extent that he rushed out looking like he just had a heart attack. I had to apologize and explain to the manager that Marisa had autism, which at times meant she would do very impulsive, unpredictable things. I had not ever tried to explain Marisa's behavior to anyone before, but in this instance, I felt it was appropriate because Marisa's behavior was so extremely invasive that it would have been negligent and unfair not to explain it.

It was upsetting not to be able to go places and be more relaxed, but I needed to keep reminding myself that things were improving. Marisa was talking in sentences most of the time now. She was reading. She was playing appropriately with her toys. At home she enjoyed dancing to a children's exercise video, mixing colors, painting beautiful pictures, and listening to audiotapes while reading along in her books. Likewise, at school she seemed to enjoy interacting with her classmates with peek-a-boo play, pretend play, and outdoor playground activities. She was sweet, adorable, and so loveable, but I knew she still had a very long way to go. Nevertheless, I had to remain encouraged, as I continued to stick to my plan of working on each of the small but important goals I set down for Marisa.

During the Christmas break, Marisa set up her stuffed animals in a make-believe game of school. With the animals she would play out the school day. This was interesting to listen to, because I could hear her talking to and for the animals. From this I derived a great sense of pleasure, because Marisa was attempting to engage her animals in conversation. This make-believe play was actually good practice for her.

After the vacation, I sent a list of Marisa's goals to school and asked the teacher to try to reinforce some of the things we were working on at home. For example, at home if Marisa did something nice for someone else, like picking up something someone dropped, or noticing if someone else was sad, she would earn a sticker in the category for *caring for other people*. I noticed that Marisa would frequently check her chart during the day to see what she could work on to earn stickers. She skipped over the goal for staying in her car seat one day, when she knew she wouldn't get a sticker in that category because she hadn't been in the car that day. Not only was she enjoying the prospect of earning stickers toward some special gift, but also she was getting practice in reading in a very functional way.

Although many good things were happening, there were always new problems evolving that needed attention. Marisa was having difficulty going to gym, and it occurred to me that perhaps we could try creating a goal for this at school. According to the teacher, Marisa seemed disturbed by the loud noise in the gym. I suggested that it might be worth trying the sticker system to motivate her to go to gym class, and I informed the teacher that I would add the gym goal to her home chart. The teacher wanted to know what kind of stickers to use on the chart for school. I assured her that it wasn't the stickers themselves that would motivate Marisa but the prize she would earn with a set number of stickers.

The plan was to start Marisa off by earning a sticker for just spending five minutes in the gym, and the teacher would gradually increase the amount of time required to earn the sticker. This technique worked well, and after a few weeks the teacher and I were happy to find that Marisa was able to spend the full period in the gym each day.

At home, Marisa was developing her own unique sense of humor, which took me by surprise. She often came up with mischievous ideas. One day she put a big *M* in magic marker on her headboard and put a big *D* on Deborah's headboard. I was angry until I realized that she got the idea from the kids' educational show *Sesame Street*, in which Bert and Ernie had initials on their headboards. As I cleaned off the marks from the headboards, I couldn't help but marvel at Marisa's logic and initiative. I was happy that she had so cleverly come up with the idea of doing what she had seen on the show. I reprimanded Marisa for what she had done, and I told her that, though I understood why she had done it, it was not acceptable for her to write on the furniture again.

I started to notice other incidents that indicated Marisa was becoming very much aware of her surroundings. One day she came home and informed me that her teacher was out sick. She seemed disappointed and sad to tell me the news. I also noticed that she started to treat her Mutsy dog in a motherly fashion; she would dress the stuffed dog each day after she dressed herself. She would match a hair bow of Mutsy's to her own and took him on outings with us during the day. At night she put Mutsy into a pajama.

I was also beginning to take Marisa on more trips into the community. She would go to the supermarket, to Home Depot, and to a local variety store. The trips to the stores went reasonably well at most times, though I was still having difficulties with her impulsiveness.

I had read about a new technique called "social stories" in *The Social Story Book*, written under the direction of Carol Gray by some 250 psychology and sociology students at Jenison High School in Michigan. The idea originated when Ms. Gray "was observing a child with autism who was confused and disoriented by a game his class was learning in gym." Ms. Gray wrote "a story describing the rules to the game, and the responses of the other children to the game. The child read the story once each day, for the following week. Upon returning to the gym class the following week, the child understood the rules, played the game, and enjoyed the activity. The results were so positive and immediate that stories were written for several other situations which were giving the child difficulty." Gray 1994, Preface. From this beginning, guidelines were set up for the psychology and sociology students at the Jenison High School to write about many different kinds of social situations, and because the stories were usually socially based, they were called social stories.

Social stories could be written about a number of different situations; it is basically a technique for planning an event by writing about what will happen and what should be expected. Reading such social stories gives autistic people some understanding of what is expected on the outing and how they should try to behave.

The social stories consisted of four types of sentences: *descriptive sentences,* which could consist of three or more, a couple of *perspective sentences,* no more than one *directive sentence,* and perhaps a *control sentence.* The structure of the social stories originally started out with these four main types of sentences in 1994, which I used in my planning of social stories for Marisa. Later the social stories evolved to include other types of sentences, which can be found in Carol Gray's updated version of *The Social Story Book.*

In this technique, it was important to give lots of descriptive sentences about the event. Descriptive sentences might describe the kind of place the child would be going and what it might look like. It might tell how many people to expect. In other words, it would prepare the person for the unexpected. The perspective sentences would give other people's points of view about a place or situation. For example, in writing about a trip to the supermarket, the story might state, "The people in the store are busy shopping and are not really interested in talking to strangers." A third type of sentence, the directive sentence, explained the desired response of the person with autism. The book suggested not including more than one directive sentence because it is best not to make too many demands on the person needing the story. The goal should be to try one's best, not to be overwhelmed by demands. For example, the directive sentence might be, "I will try to stay close to my mom." Finally, the control sentence could contain strategies that the autistic individual might find helpful for remembering how to behave. For example, such a sentence might be, "If I follow the rules, I may be rewarded by an ice cream cone."

I started to use social stories before my outings with Marisa, being careful to include a directive sentence that suggested trying to behave a certain way. This was a challenging activity that could not be done spontaneously; I had to plan it carefully in order to get the best possible outcome. For example, a story about a trip to the supermarket might contain many sentences about other people going to the store for things they need and not being interested in being bothered by an inquiring stranger. The story could also list the order in which things would happen, such as getting in the car, putting on a seatbelt, and staying near the car when getting out in the busy parking lot. Perhaps the story would mention how much time we would spend at the supermarket. The story could include the desired way to behave, which might be, "Stay near mom and keep my voice down." A control sentence that could serve as a helpful reminder might be, "I don't like when other people get too close to me, so I will try to remember not to get to close to other people." It was also helpful to mention that a successful supermarket trip would result in the choice of a special reward for proper behavior.

I started to write these little stories for all our outings. Whether it was a trip to the store, a visit to a relative's house during a holiday, or a school trip, I took the time to plan a social story. I found that it brought order and understanding to Marisa's perception of her world.

It was February of 1995 when I received Marisa's psychological report from the psychologist at her school. I was told that Marisa had a varying range of weaknesses and strengths from 1.5 years receptive ability to 6.2 years in written ability. The 1.5 year receptive ability meant Marisa had the ability to understand what was spoken to her as if she was only a year and 5 months old. However, her fine motor coordination which affects her ability to write letters and words and her drawing ability was that of a 6 year and 2 month old. Considering that Marisa, at the time of the test was 4 months short of being 6 years old, it is clear to see that she was lagging far behind in her ability to understand the spoken language. In spite of the results, I felt that Marisa still could have a good prognosis, if I could bring her areas of weakness up to an acceptable level and build on her strengths.

I had also just finished reading *There's a Boy in Here* by Judy and Sean Barron. It was the honest, down-to-earth thoughts and feelings of a mother struggling through the years as her autistic son, Sean, grows up. This book was refreshing to me, because the author didn't claim that any specific technique was a cure-all. As Sean gets older, he is able to explain his thoughts and feelings to his mom, which she then included in the book. As I read through this book, I felt I was acquiring an insight into what a person with autism may have to deal with on a daily basis. I felt, with this insight, that I could tolerate my daughter's strange behaviors with renewed energy and understanding. The insight I gained from the story would help me in planning how to approach and deal with problems that might arise.

During the February vacation, Marisa played nicely at home. Mutsy had become like her baby doll. She continued to put him in pajamas at night and dress him in the morning when she dressed herself. She would go through the motions of feeding and bathing him, she would put his jacket on him to go outside, and she would talk to him as if he were a real playmate. In a way, I saw this as a good thing, because she was playing out her daily routines with him, and the make-believe conversations with the dog were good practice for real life.

By March, I noticed that Marisa was getting increasingly frustrated by her inability to express her needs with the right words. From what I had read on the subject of autism, I was sure that she believed I could read her mind without actually hearing what she had to say. She would scream and throw things when I couldn't understand what she was thinking. It was difficult to explain to her that I didn't know what she was thinking if she didn't tell me with words.

When Marisa was upset, I began to encourage her to use the words she knew to tell me what was wrong, so that I could write the words down. The distraction of watching me write had a calming effect on her. Over time, she realized that if she could tell me what she was thinking, I could write it down. I would write down the words she was trying to use, and then I would put the words into a sentence that I read back to her. Then she would read it back to me, and I would ask her to say it to me without reading. By following this routine, she started to develop the ability to express herself better in sentences. At times I would hear her practicing familiar phrases and sentences to herself. Then she would store the information in her memory bank to use at a later time.

Marisa seemed to understand many more things that I would tell her. I realized that I could write out rules for her to follow, have her read them, and then practice the rules. I put some of these rules in to a little reminder book for her to refer to.

I also started to give her practice with verbal instruction, as I saw that her receptive language skills were improving. I was able to give her simple instructions to carry out with occasional physical prompts, and this, I felt, would help improve her ability to listen and carry out a request. For example:

> *Close the toilet seat cover gently.*
> *Put your clothes in the hamper.*
> *Bring your dish to the counter.*

Following simple instructions at home was good practice for following more involved commands in situations where self-control would be necessary. I hoped that this, along with social stories and her goal chart, would all contribute to helping Marisa control impulsive behaviors while she was out in the community. For example, if a rabbit were to run across the street, could Marisa resist the temptation to run after it into the road? I was becoming increasingly aware of addressing issues related to safety.

With my growing concern over safety, I started to think of what I would do if Marisa were to ever wander off without me. When I heard a story in the news about a little boy with autism in Florida who had wandered away from his parents, not to be found for many days, verbal prompts and commands took on new meaning to me. Fortunately, the little boy was found relatively unharmed, but this story made me realize that I needed to teach Marisa to respond to the question "Where are you?" I started to practice calling to her, both in the house and outdoors in the yard, as a kind of practice drill.

We played a game in which I would call out, "Marisa, where are you?" I taught her to respond by yelling out, "I'm by the swings," "I'm upstairs," or "I'm in my bedroom" so that she would have lots of practice in answering and hopefully be able to prevent herself from ever becoming separated from her father or me for any length of time.

I found that social stories also were very helpful in dealing with safety issues. I was able to write stories about outings and point out the dangers Marisa would encounter if she did not follow certain steps.

The social stories also helped a great deal at school. The teacher was using the stories at lunchtime. For example, Marisa wanted to eat dessert and not lunch. By reading the rule to "Eat lunch, then Oreo," Marisa would get the information she needed to create order in her schedule and help her stay in control of her own behavior. The teacher also used the social stories at recess time outside, where there were three playgrounds for varying ability levels. For example, Marisa only wanted to go to the gated playground for the older children and would stand by the gate and sadly watch beyond. Once the teacher wrote a social story about this situation, Marisa would follow the steps in the story. She would go on the yard equipment mentioned and even approach a friend to play with. The teacher wisely wrote three rotating stories to use, so that the routine would change according to the story written for that day. By following the social story, Marisa would be distracted from the urge to go in the older children's playground.

Another technique I continued to find very helpful in teaching many skills was the use of videos and songs. I purchased two new videos on table manners and phone manners. Though these videos were only ten minutes long, they were good lessons for Marisa, who asked to watch them a number of times. I also bought a set of audiocassette songs on self-esteem that were fun to listen to and sent a "feel good about yourself" message.

The remainder of the year went well for Marisa. With the use of social stories at home, Marisa remained calmer and much better able to handle new situations. She also got much practice in reading about the things that she was going to do, and the written stories helped her stay within the boundaries of what was required of her. The social stories and her sticker goal chart were making life in our house a little less stressful. Everyone was happier and more relaxed and we even started to go on family outings to a fast food restaurant for dinner occasionally.

However, planning does not always help when unforeseen events arise. We were reminded of this when we took a weekend trip in July to visit Deborah, who was up at ice-skating camp in New Hampshire. We were able to plan a social story for the long ride up, which was a good six hours, as well as the stay in the motel. We also promised Marisa that if she was well behaved on the trip, she would be rewarded with the Pocahontas doll she had asked for. However, having never visited the camp before, we had no way of knowing what was to happen once we reached our destination.

We arrived at the camp at 9:45 on Saturday morning. A bus was to pick up the parents and siblings and take them the last half mile to the camp meeting grounds. Marisa waited patiently for the bus while coloring. When the bus arrived, she climbed on, eager to get to the camp and see Deborah. However, once the bus reached the campsite, everything went wrong. She saw Deborah and then started running aimlessly from one cabin to the next, checking everything out. We finally walked back to the main meeting area with the idea that Marisa might be more cooperative if Deborah would give us a tour. After a very rushed tour, Marisa saw another bus arrive and started to scream and pull me toward the bus. We went to the bus and got on. Marisa was content with that, and so it was clear that she had enough of the camp and the visit. It was a frustrating day for me because I couldn't give Deborah my full attention and Deborah was somewhat embarrassed in front of her camp friends in spite of having explained her sister's disability to them.

In the meantime, the director of the camp talked to Dan about Marisa, asking if perhaps she had ADD (attention deficit disorder) and needed medication. Dan said, "No, she has PDD." The director said, "What's that?" and Dan replied, "Pervasive Developmental Disorder, or Autism." The director had a very sympathetic look on his face and responded, "Oh, we don't allow that here." This was a sad reminder about the need for spreading awareness about autism. Autism is not a disease; it is a neurological disorder of the brain involving difficulty with social skills and the processing of language. That doesn't mean that people with autism cannot achieve; people with autism may have skills and talents just like anyone else. This man's remarks gave me the impression that he considered Marisa incapable, diseased, or dangerous. It saddened me to know that there was such ignorance all around us.

The rest of the visit went well enough. We took Deborah out to lunch and attended the camp skating performance, through which Marisa sat reasonably well. We returned Deborah to camp at the designated time of 5:30, and Marisa cried to have to leave her sister. However, she did earn a Pocahontas doll on the ride back to the motel; we told her that she earned the doll for good car and good motel behavior, which were the things we had been able to write social stories for in advance. We also reminded her that she needed to use her words to ask for things instead of screaming, as she had done at the campgrounds. We knew that the camp situation must have been very overwhelming, and without any previous knowledge of the campgrounds or planned activities, it made it very difficult for us to foresee problems that would arise.

Back at home, Marisa enjoyed having company. We had some friends over with their two children, a boy of seven and his sister, age thirteen. Marisa went to put on lipstick and tried to kiss the boy. When he wasn't willing, she settled for pushing him on a roller racer instead. Marisa also styled his sister's long, red hair.

The school year and summer session came to an end on August 14. It had been another productive year for Marisa, and I felt we had made many positive gains in the course of the year. During the couple of weeks at home Marisa was sad, because she missed the school routine and the closeness of her classmates. On a more positive note, she managed to be content, filling the days with swimming, crafts, and casual outings. Because of the goal charting and social stories Marisa seemed less impulsive, more content, and happier. For the first time in five years, I took pleasure in the calmness of the lazy summer days.

Chapter Five

THRIVING

The new school year at Variety Preschooler's Workshop started on September 6, 2005. Marisa would have a new teacher, and because Marisa was now in kindergarten, she would be attending school for a full day. Marisa was excited to know that she would be with her friends from 9 to 3. Once again I sent a letter with pertinent information that I felt the teacher would find helpful. It is important not to assume that a new teacher has the information.

> *I don't know how much you know about Marisa, so I'll give a few pointers.*
>
> 1. *Marisa rarely asks for help but will be sure to help herself. This includes leaving the class if she thinks she can find a better place.*
>
> 2. *She's a terrible eater, usually needing an incentive, like dessert, to finish her meal.*
>
> 3. *She likes to color, read books, play with water, and play with her Barbie dolls and animals.*
>
> 4. *Mutsy is Marisa's favorite stuffed dog. She brought him to school every day last year. I think this will continue.*
>
> 5. *Writing social stories helps Marisa transition through activities on the daily schedule and class trips.*

Things started out well at school, which I felt was partly due to the sensitivity of the teacher and carrying over the social stories from the previous year. I continued daily correspondence, which also helped smooth over any problems that arose before they got out of hand. Marisa started to eat her lunches better at school. I attributed the improvement to adding a school lunchtime goal to her home goal chart.

At home, Marisa had the advantage of her older sisters as role models. Deborah, who always wanted to play school with Marisa, now had the opportunity to teach her little sister some simple board games, because Marisa was understanding so much more. Marisa was delighted to get the attention and Deborah was finally so happy to have a willing pupil.

Marisa's growing awareness of many things forced me to re-think the way I was leading my life. Marisa was starting to understand that there were holidays, like Thanksgiving, that everyone celebrated. She realized that other children were having family parties at home for such occasions, and Marisa wanted to know why we didn't have parties too. It was then that I started to see that I was depriving my children of the joys of family gatherings, and I knew that the time had come to make a change.

Because Rebecca always came home from her residential school over the holidays, I found it too difficult to plan a big dinner party or travel to someone else's home. This year I gave this some serious thought. Since Rebecca would return to school on Saturday after Thanksgiving, I would be able to plan a Thanksgiving dinner on Sunday instead of Thanksgiving Day. Though Rebecca did get to participate in holiday celebrations at school, I was saddened to think that I couldn't include her in a family gathering. However, I realized that I was not only depriving Rebecca, whose understanding was limited; I was depriving my other children as well.

Though I felt a sense of loss about excluding Rebecca from the family Thanksgiving celebration, I was happy that Marisa yearned for these special occasions. It wasn't long before I saw how fully she embraced the holiday gatherings. How ironic that it was my child with autism who made me realize the deprivation I was imposing on my family. Shoshana and Deborah had always been able to understand and accept the reason why we didn't have big family get-togethers. Because they were so understanding, I failed to see their own sense of loss. Marisa's desire for celebration ultimately changed all that.

As I prepared for our first big family gathering since before Marisa was born, I realized what an advantage it was for Marisa who eagerly watched and joined in helping prepare the Thanksgiving foods and decorations. She anticipated the arrival of family guests, eagerly greeting each of them. I realized the important part family holidays could play in helping Marisa to practice some of her social skills in an accepting and safe environment.

For Chanukah that year Marisa received gifts that I felt would be helpful to her emotional development. The Seven Dwarf Dolls, which I felt would help teach emotions through visual facial expressions, The Good Behavior Game, a board game from a special needs catalogue, and a feelings chart to hang on the wall. Of course, I included a few other toys that any five or six year old might enjoy.

During this third year at Variety Preschooler's Workshop, I could see that Marisa was better able to convey some of her feelings. The teacher felt that using a mirror to see her own facial expressions would help Marisa learn to show how she felt. Another tool the teacher put together was a communication book just for Marisa that would enable her to refer to the pictures and things that she might need to ask for. Many tantrums could be avoided if she were able to identify what was bothering her through the use of this personal communication book. Although it couldn't cover every problem, it was a good way to resolve many difficulties.

Around the middle of the year, I was informed by my school district director of special services, that there was a chance that my school district would be pushing for mainstreaming Marisa into the district school, or if she was not ready for the school, moving her to a BOCES (Board of Cooperative Educational Services) program similar to Variety. I decided that it would be a good time to look at the BOCES program, which was designed for children who needed a smaller class size or who were not yet ready to participate in a school district program.

Marisa's teacher and I went to visit the BOCES school, which was housed in an elementary school about twenty minutes from our home. The BOCES elementary school seemed like a well-run program and seemed to have the nurturing environment I was looking for. The class ratio was more than adequate, with one teacher and two assistants to either nine or six children in a class. It was something to think about for the future. Nevertheless I was hoping to persuade my school district to allow Marisa to continue for one more year in the program that she seemed to be thriving in. By law, the school district must provide an appropriate educational setting for all children with disabilities up to the age of 21. It should be understood that when school district budgets have to include the funds necessary to pay for the education of children with disabilities in their district, there has to be clear documented need for such programs chosen. All decisions are presented to the board of education in each district and must also be approved by the state, because some state funds may help pay for a percentage of the program for the individual child. Since Marisa was doing so well in her current program, I was not ready to take all that away from her, so I was grateful when my school district agreed to let her stay.

During the February vacation, Marisa spent much time working at the computer, which we had moved into the kitchen. There I could help her use the read-along books and other educational programs. *Sitting on the Farm*, an I Learn program, *Franklin's Reading World*, a pre-reading program, and a variety of *Living Books*, stories with interactive pictures, all opened up a whole new world of activities for Marisa to explore.

One day in April, Marisa came home from school crying for a friend named Chris who she met during school hours in the playground. She was sad because he was graduating from the school and moving up to BOCES. To mitigate her feeling of helplessness over his leaving the school, I had made an effort to make sure the friendship wasn't lost. Before Chris graduated from Variety Preschooler's Workshop, Marisa cried and told me he was leaving the school. I helped Marisa compose a letter to Chris about getting together outside of school. She included her phone number, and I had Marisa's teacher let Marisa deliver the letter to his class at the end of the summer. It paid off, not just because she was able to eventually get back together with him, but also because it made Marisa happy to know that we did something to hold on to a friendship that was important to her. She didn't have to feel powerless in a world that seemed so confusing. It also paid off because his mom eventually called, and we got together for many play dates. To this day, Marisa has remained friends with Chris. In fact, she recently said to me, "It's my ten-year anniversary with Chris!" I had to ask what she meant, and she said, "It's been ten years since we became friends." To me that's amazing, coming from a child diagnosed with autism, a condition in which one is often more interested in doing things on their own.

At the end of the school year, Marisa participated in a graduation ceremony, even though she would stay at Variety Preschooler's Workshop for the first grade. As a rule all kindergarten students were included in the graduation, which delighted Marisa. Her new friend, Chris, whom she had met during class playground time, was graduating from the first grade class and going on to BOCES after the summer session. At the end of the graduation ceremony, Marisa and Chris smiled at each other and embraced for a photograph. This would be a wonderful memory for Marisa, who would remain friends with Chris through the years.

Along with the excitement of graduation, Marisa had a sixth birthday party, which was filled with activity. We had face painting, a pizza lunch, a sand art project, a limbo, a marching band, and a lollipop hunt. We also had parachute game activities, followed by birthday cake and party favors. Marisa was delighted to share her birthday celebration with her friends, and everyone went home happy! After the party Marisa enjoyed opening her gifts, something I preferred to do once the party was over. I did not think it would be a good idea to open gifts at the party because Marisa was too honest about vocalizing how she felt about the things she received as gifts. I did not want her to blurt out anything unfavorable that would make another child feel badly. For example she might have said she didn't like something or that she already had it.

With the opening of our pool for the summer months, it was time to get Marisa back into her bathing suit. Unfortunately, she didn't want to go in the pool, and finally I realized it was because she didn't want to wear the special bathing suit with built-in floats. I decided to give her a beach bag containing a regular bathing suit and arm floats as a special gift. When she still wouldn't put on the bathing suit, I packed some crayons and computer printouts in her beach bag, so she could sit by the pool and color while hopefully getting hot enough in the sun to want to use the pool. The first day she spent thirty minutes coloring before she started to show interest in the water.

Finally she was willing to try on the bathing suit and arm floats. She went in the pool and tested the floats. At first, all went well, until she decided she didn't need the floats. She pulled off both arm floats and went in the shallow end of the pool to check out how far she could still stand. As I stood in the water nervously watching, she changed direction and started to swim out to the deep end. She swam across the length of the pool to the ladder, at what seemed to me as I swam along side, a rather fast pace.

How amazing that was! Over the course of the previous summers, Marisa had learned to swim by watching her sisters and practicing with her training bathing suit. Now she was taking off on her own, swimming naturally and with ease. It was so thrilling to watch this accomplishment!

In the meantime, during the school summer program Marisa became even closer to Chris. The teacher realized how much the two liked each other and arranged for them to get together at each other's classrooms for shared activities. I was happy that the teacher was encouraging this friendship, even though these children were not in the same class. I felt that any opportunity to share similar interests would make Marisa's conversation flow more easily and naturally. It was also a wonderful opportunity to use her social skills, an area in which she greatly needed practice.

Toward the end of July we took a trip to visit some colleges for Shoshana and then went to visit Deborah at her skating camp. The tours through Vassar and Skidmore went fairly well. Marisa enjoyed moving around the campuses and seeing the scenery, pretty buildings, and even the artwork in the halls of Skidmore.

We then traveled up to Vermont, where we stayed overnight. This was difficult for Marisa, who, anticipating the visit to the camp, was too excited to sleep well. We continued on the next morning to Deborah's camp in New Hampshire, where Marisa actually showed great improvement from the year before. This time around we knew what to expect, which enabled me to write an appropriate social story about the camp visit. She was even able to sit through a one-and-a-half-hour skating show! This was a great relief to us all.

With the end of the summer program approaching, I asked the teacher to send home some worksheets for Marisa to do along with her other play activities. At this time Marisa was enjoying a Wee Sing songbook that she followed along with her tape recorder. Sometimes she would even create dance steps for some of the songs. She was enjoying her computer programs and swimming. It was a happy, productive, and peaceful summer. What more could I ask for? I was feeling blessed!

Chapter Six

MOVING ON

Marisa returned to Variety Preschooler's Workshop on September 4, 1996, in a new classroom with a new teacher. Once again, I sent a note to the new teacher to inform her of the things that Marisa enjoyed doing and the techniques that I felt worked well for Marisa. I suggested to the teacher that she would be able to help Marisa through difficult moments by writing about her feelings. If anything, this technique created a distraction from the problem. By watching the teacher write out what she was saying, Marisa was able to focus on the words that would tell about the problem rather than the problem itself. I informed the teacher that Marisa also liked to read, draw, write, and work at the computer.

Marisa was a bit sad that her friend Chris was no longer in the program. I let the teacher know about this, too, so she would understand if Marisa should mention her friend. Though Marisa was missing Chris, things were going well at school. The new class was exciting to Marisa. There were now twelve children in the class, as opposed to six to nine children in the younger classes.

Things were not going quite so well on the bus. Marisa had developed an aversion to the bus radio dispatch system. Each time the dispatch unit went on, she would cover her ears and scream out, "No radio, no radio!" Though Marisa was sensitive to noises in the school hallway, the bus radio dispatch system had never been a problem before. The teacher made some changes that helped Marisa overcome her fear and annoyance of the radio: having the bus driver lower the volume of the dispatch unit, giving Marisa a book for the bus ride, and allowing her the opportunity to say good-bye to the other students on the bus once she arrived at her home. All these changes did help Marisa.

Marisa's sisters continued to be excellent role models for Marisa, who would imitate them when it came to doing homework. She would take her work, go in her room, and close her door to work quietly by herself. Marisa expressed her contentment with her new class by making beautiful, colorful pictures of all her teachers to present at school.

I noticed around the time that Marisa became sensitive to the loud dispatch unit on the bus that she also seemed to be developing sensitivity to background music in stores. The sensitivity was severe enough to make it impossible to go in to the supermarket or a bookstore without having her scream and cover her ears. Because of this sensitivity, it was difficult to take her into any public places anymore. I decided to try writing a social story to see if it would help. Over time, Marisa seemed to make an adjustment. Her teacher decided to play music at a low volume in the classroom to see if it would help desensitize Marisa. She also noticed that Marisa was less agitated by classical than other types of music.

Marisa also developed other fears out of the blue. She suddenly became afraid to sleep in her bed, claiming there might be a bug there. I decided to offer her a reward for staying in her bed. If she earned three stars for staying in her bed for three nights, I would reward her with new Play-Doe, which she expressed a desire for. To help her earn her stars, I tried changing the position of her bed, which I thought might motivate her to try out the new arrangement in her room. Marisa was so excited about the change that she immediately overcame her fear, quickly earning her three stars and her Play-Doe. This seemed to put the fear of bugs in the bed to rest. I had to wonder if every obstacle could be overcome this easily, by offering rewards that were appealing to Marisa.

Although it was only October, the teacher informed me that representatives of my school district were coming to visit Marisa at school to consider her placement for the next year. The school psychologist from my school district was thinking that Marisa would do well in a twelve-one-one ratio (twelve students to one teacher and one assistant) in the school district's self-contained, special needs class. Although Marisa was in a class of twelve students this year, it was staffed with one teacher and four assistants, making the ratio of care nearly one teacher to two students.

I was not too happy about the possible school district class placement for a number of reasons. By law, autistic students are entitled to a class ratio of six-one-one. I also felt that Marisa would have a limited number of children to interact with, thereby reducing her circle of friends, because in the regular public schools, the only friends she would have to socialize with would be the limited number of students in her self-contained class. On the other hand, if Marisa was included in a regular classroom, and even given a one-to-one aide as is usually suggested by the district director of special services in such situations, she would be too distracted by the large number of students to benefit from such a placement. Because of her distractibility, the possibility of mainstreaming her into an inclusion class (a regular class with a regular teacher and a special education teacher to assist the 3 or 4 special needs children included in the class) would not be beneficial to Marisa or the other children. Besides, such a placement was unlikely to be considered because of Marisa's behaviors.

I felt that if Marisa could not be included in a regular classroom, I didn't want her in the regular schools at all. I therefore was planning to advocate for the BOCES placement, where Marisa would at least be able to mix with the general population of the whole school she was to be placed in. BOCES programs gear their entire program to the needs of the children they serve. Children participate in school choirs and performances. There are after-school and evening activities planned for the children and all the students in BOCES are equal to one another. In a regular public school, Marisa would not feel like an equal participant to the general population of the school. Knowing how important Marisa's friendships were to her, I was determined to fight for the BOCES placement. I also felt it was important for her self-esteem to feel like she belonged to a group as an equal participant.

This same year, we continued looking at colleges for Shoshana. We were planning a trip to Boston to tour Brandeis University and Boston University. Although I had written out numerous social stories to cover this trip, there was much that happened that I could not have been prepared for.

We left home on a Thursday evening in a torrential downpour. It was quite late at night when we arrived at our stop-off point in Waterbury, Connecticut. Unfortunately, once we had settled in our room, we discovered there was a problem with the toilet. It was sluggish at first and then became clogged, and it overflowed into the bathroom and beyond. Although Marisa was tired and waiting to take a bath, she found the overflowing water to be very funny. We waited for maintenance to come fix the toilet, while Marisa spent the time laughing and standing out of range of the advancing water.

After a restless night, we spent our morning touring Brandeis, which went well, before we headed for Boston to tour Boston University. The tour was to be in the later afternoon. We didn't know where to wait and Marisa became uncooperative, as she started to cry, making it impossible to take the tour as planned. Rather than push our luck at getting through another university tour with a cranky, unpredictable child, we thought it would be best to explore the surrounding area by car and then perhaps visit a museum. Though we didn't get to visit Boston University, Shoshana felt that it didn't matter too much since the school was so spread out over the city anyway. We felt that Marisa would find a museum visit to be more interesting. However, we gave up the museum idea after thirty minutes in stand-still traffic, as we realized it was getting to be late in the afternoon. We decided the best plan would be to check in to our hotel.

After we checked in to our hotel at 5:00, we decided to settle down for the evening with room service and a movie. Our room was not exactly comfortable, because the air conditioning wasn't working properly, but we were too tired to report it. At about 10:30 that evening, in the middle of watching the movie, the fire alarm in the hotel went off. We all jumped up in alarm and Marisa's reaction was as surprised as the rest of us. As we checked out in the hall, we were asked to evacuate. There we were walking down six flights of stairs in pajamas and sneakers. Fortunately, it was a breezy, mild evening. As we stood outside, Marisa enjoyed a close-up view of fire engines. I believe she thought this was one of the attractions on our list of things to do and see. After the fire fighters gave us the all-clear (the alarm had been set off by cigarette smoke), we had our air conditioning checked. When the air conditioner could not be repaired, we packed up our things and moved to a new room. I was amazed to see how well Marisa had handled all the confusion of the day. Finally things settled down, and everyone went to sleep.

We traveled home the next day, Saturday, to Marisa's great disappointment. "What about Hershey Park?" she said. Though we had not planned on a visit to Hershey Park, Marisa apparently had other ideas. She was thinking about Hershey Park because we had spent a day there when we had taken a weekend trip. Since it was a fun experience for her she assumed we would be going back soon after. She seemed to have an unending thirst for adventure, and once Marisa tried something she usually assumed she would be doing it on a regular basis.

Back at school, Marisa enjoyed dancing in the gym and making new friends, while at home, she had fun at the planned get-togethers I arranged for her. She was excited to attend her friend Chris's birthday party at a disco party place, where she danced the afternoon away. She was so happy to see him once again! She was delighted that she was able to keep in touch with him even though he had graduated the previous year and was no longer in the school. I was glad that I had pursued the friendship that seemed to mean so much to Marisa.

Along with her growing interest in school friends, Marisa developed a strong interest in dolls. This year for Chanukah, we gave Marisa a doll named Allison. This doll, like the American Girl dolls, comes with a storybook and clothing. I felt that the doll gave her a chance to focus on grooming and caring for the doll's clothing and hair. She spent a great deal of time styling the doll's long hair and changing her outfits.

I also hoped that she would be interested in hearing the chapter book about Allison, but the story was too long for Marisa, who did not, at this age, have the patience to sit for extended reading of a story with very few pictures. It was several years before she wanted to read the book. At six, Marisa played with the doll, but it wasn't until she was thirteen that she was willing to read the Allison storybook with me—a long time, but it was worth the wait. Though her interest in the doll had long passed by that time, she developed a new interest in the story about Allison; Marisa was finally ready for this, and because she was ready, her interest was strong.

During the Christmas vacation, Marisa enjoyed playing with Allison and her Madeline doll, painting, writing, and dancing to music. Marisa became very excited to celebrate the New Year. We had our own little family celebration as we decorated with balloons and Marisa made her own *Happy New Year!* banner to hang. Marisa also had a make-believe party for her dolls.

After the vacation, Deborah decided to devote extra time in her woodworking class at school to making Marisa a beautiful, handcrafted bed for Allison. Deborah was so anxious to please her little sister that she devoted many early mornings to the project. She was rewarded by the overjoyed look on Marisa's face once Deborah presented the bed to her. It was a happy time for us, and all seemed to be going well.

Then, around the middle of January 1997, Marisa did the unthinkable. At least it was unthinkable until it happened. One of the guidelines for dealing with autism is to expect the unexpected, and with this in mind, I sadly had to accept what had happened. Marisa had enjoyed playing with Allison and brushing and styling the beautiful, long, golden hair. Then one day she cut off all of Allison's hair. Not only was I angry about what she had done, but also I was bothered by her reaction; she found it very funny to look at the doll with all the hair chopped off.

After my initial anger passed, I questioned her about the incident. Like most little girls, including myself when I was about that age, Marisa had the great desire to cut hair. In her eagerness to cut the doll's hair, she failed to realize that the haircut was final; doll hair does not grow back! I decided to give Marisa a second chance. Fortunately, the doll company made allowances for such unexpected mishaps. For a fee, I shipped the doll off to the doll hospital in exchange for a replacement head, and I warned Marisa that she was not to do any more hair-cutting on the new Allison.

However, I had not told Marisa that she shouldn't cut off other dolls' hair, which is exactly what she did. She managed to chop off the hair on many Barbie dolls, and because of that, I was forced to temporarily remove the dolls from her room. So I did manage to put a stop to Marisa's haircutting episodes on dolls, but in her eyes that didn't mean she shouldn't cut her own hair. After all, her hair would grow back.

Over the years there were quite a few of these unexpected hair-cutting episodes. Once, when she was fourteen, Marisa cut her hair to match the style of a boyfriend. Another time she shaved her eyebrows, making herself look like something from another planet. Her excuse was that a boy she was fashioning herself after had no eyebrows. Upon viewing his picture, I could see that he had blond eyebrows, which I had to explain to Marisa. Then another time she shaved her arm hair, thinking it looked cleaner, and even went to the extreme of shaving pubic hair, though I didn't quite understand her reasoning.

Around the time Marisa showed so much interest in her dolls, her teacher decided to purchase some Barbie dolls for the girls to play with at school. She planned to use the dolls as tools to teach social and simple conversational skills. This did seem like a good idea. The teacher would play along with Marisa and her classmates, helping them make the dolls respond in appropriate ways to various situations. I tried to do the same at home.

At school things were comfortable and settled, but it was also once again that time of year when my school district would be looking into programs for the next year. Marisa would be turning seven in June and could no longer stay at Variety Preschooler's Workshop, because she was aging out of their program.

The previous year, I had taken the time to tour a program for students with autism at NSSA's (Nassau Suffolk Services for the Autistic) Martin C. Barell School in Levittown, Long Island. This was an experimental program fashioned after the Ivar Lovaas method, which is an ABA (applied behavior analysis) approach. In ABA, learning is broken down into small steps. Students work individually on their own education plan. There may be many skills being worked on at the same time, but the learning is very specifically geared to the individual student. As the student works on each step, the teacher frequently rewards good results with reinforcers. This approach to teaching children with autism had gained popularity after the publication of the book *Let Me Hear Your Voice* by Catherine Maurice. It is the story of two autistic children who make incredible strides in overcoming their autistic behaviors with the aid of a skilled teacher who used the Lovaas method. The heartwarming story spread hope across the country. I wanted very much to place Marisa in the Martin C. Barell School, but the twenty-four spots in the program were filled, so there was a very long waiting list. I knew that I had no choice but to find, at best, a similar alternative.

I decided to go with representatives from my school district to check out another program for children with autism. It consisted of two classes of students with autism housed within a regular public school building. The educational director at Marisa's school had recommended the Dinkelmeyer program; apparently at least one Variety Preschooler's Workshop student had gone on to succeed in this program. The educational director at Marisa's school thought that it might also work well for Marisa. I waited for an appointment to visit this special program.

In the meantime, on February 17, 1997, we took Marisa for an evaluation with Dr. John Pomeroy, a psychiatrist who was very knowledgeable in the area of autism. I felt it would be helpful to have a specialist make recommendations about Marisa's schooling. When planning the education of a special needs child, it is always helpful for parents to have documented medical reports to back up their requests for services. It not only helps the parents acquire the services their child needs, but also makes it easier for the school district to justify the need when applying for approval from the school district's Board of Education and the State, both of which may be funding the services.

I was anxious to hear what recommendations Dr. Pomeroy would make, and I was willing to remain open minded to his suggestions. We spent two hours with Dr. Pomeroy. He suggested that we have Marisa psychologically evaluated by a clinician who regularly tests children with Pervasive Developmental Disorder. This evaluation would help in planning an appropriate placement. His report also suggested we look into "programs with a small class size with a strong emphasis on communication and social skills." He emphasized that whatever program we placed Marisa in "should continue speech and language services, a social skills training program, and an academic program that utilizes multiple media for education with an emphasis for Marisa on visual mediated material and clear expectations." He also stated that "it is possible that Marisa will require an aide to assist her in attending and socializing in the class." And, finally, he suggested that we might try "assessing the benefits of psycho stimulants, such as Ritalin, to reduce the symptoms of deficits in attention, distractibility, and restlessness."

Unfortunately, we were not able to try any medication, as suggested by Dr. Pomeroy, because Marisa refused to take any pills. She would not even take simple liquid vitamins, because she didn't like the taste, and because of her heightened sense of smell and taste, attempting to sneak medication into her food was not an option since I had tried such tactics with vitamins previously. Though I was disappointed not to be able to try medication at this time, I knew that Marisa might become more receptive at some point in the future.

Marisa's psychological evaluation was done by a very knowledgeable psychologist within our home school district. She performed a Developmental Test of Visual-Motor Integration, the Wechsler Preschool and Primary Scale of Intelligence, and a clinical interview. Although the testing was difficult, due to much distractibility (Marisa frequently attempted to wander around the room and at times attempted to leave the testing area) the testing was eventually completed. Because of Marisa's lack of verbal skills, however, a large section of the test remained incomplete. The test report stated "there was a significant discrepancy between Marisa's performance and Verbal IQ's. Due to her expressive language deficits Marisa's verbal IQ does not appear to be a true nor valid representation of her cognitive ability. However Marisa was able to demonstrate her intelligence nonverbally in response to visual concrete stimuli." Fortunately, the testing provided the information needed to plan for Marisa's educational goals. Based on the testing the recommendation was made to "provide consistency in classroom routines with individualized visual daily schedules. Visual cues should accompany auditory stimuli and there should be a balance of independent work and social interaction. Also, whenever possible allow Marisa to make choices concerning daily activities."

I made an appointment to take Marisa for a screening at the Dinkelmeyer School on March 19, 1997. I hoped that this screening would help clarify what was best for Marisa. I was very optimistic that this program would be the right place for Marisa but was concerned, because I had heard that the school only accepted those students with autism who were well behaved. That seemed odd to me, since children with autism can be so unpredictable, and outbursts are not uncommon. Nevertheless, that was a prerequisite for admission.

At around this time, Marisa's sensitivity to noises started to increase. Marisa's teacher told me that she had become fearful of walking in the school hallway because of the noises there. She insisted on walking in the halls with her hands firmly planted over her ears. The teacher decided to try to offer Marisa the reward of listening to music with a walkman in the classroom if she would walk through the hall with her hands down, away from her ears. However, the intervention did not work; it was too difficult for Marisa to keep her hands away from her ears when the hall noise seemed so disturbing to her. Looking back, it might have been more beneficial to allow her to listen to the music while she was in the hall. Perhaps over time, she would have relaxed and become less sensitive to the noises around her. However, this never happened, and Marisa continued to walk through the halls with her hands over her ears for much of the remainder of the year.

Marisa's screening day at the Dinkelmeyer School arrived, and I brought her to the designated classroom. Upon entering, Marisa and I saw that the children were seated on the floor for a morning discussion. The new room excited Marisa, and though the teacher asked her to come and join the group, she failed to comply; she preferred to eagerly explore the classroom. I brought her over to the group, and the teacher asked me to leave. As I was leaving, I heard the teacher continuing with the lesson. I had a strange feeling about this, because it seemed to me that it would have been more appropriate to introduce Marisa to the children and perhaps explain the activity before resuming the lesson. I felt this was insensitive and rigid. In spite of my feelings, I had no choice but to leave Marisa in the care of the special education teacher.

Later that morning when I returned to pick Marisa up, I noticed that she had been crying. Her eyes were all red and blotchy. Without even being told, I could see that things appeared not to have gone well at all. However, I felt encouraged, because a boy in the class named Ricky said he knew Marisa from Variety Pre-schooler's Workshop. Apparently Marisa had given this boy a flower the previous year while they were out in the playground, and Ricky remembered this. Ricky appeared to be doing well in the class, and I felt that since Marisa was happy to see him there, it might have had a favorable effect on her behavior. Although the teacher told me about Marisa's friendly encounter with Ricky, the staff did not indicate whether Marisa would be accepted to the program.

The next morning, Marisa seemed excited, because she thought she would be returning to the Dinkelmeyer School; she did not understand that the visit the day before had just been a screening. She wanted to go back and see Ricky!

In the meantime, my district director of special services came to visit Marisa in her Variety Preschooler's Workshop class. In spite of the fact that I was actively observing out-of-district programs for Marisa for the next year, my school district was still considering an in-district placement. Although Marisa's teacher was pleased with Marisa's behavior during the visit, the district psychologist and director were not pleased at all. At the end of the visit, they informed the teacher that because of Marisa's distractible behaviors, they would not be bringing her back to the district program.

Though I wasn't upset to hear this, I was quite disappointed to find out that the Dinkelmeyer program was also rejecting Marisa as a student in their program for the coming year. They explained that they were not happy with her sometimes out-of-control behavior and stressed that she had been unable to participate well in any of the group activities.

I was angry to think that a special program for children with autism would reject a child because of her unexpected behaviors. It seemed ironic that only well-behaved children with autism were to be part of the program. It seemed to me that such a program should be designed to teach, through a positive behavior modification plan, behaviors that would be more appropriate. Since there was not much I could do, I resigned myself to the two choices that remained. The Rosemary Kennedy School and the Fern Place Elementary School were both BOCES programs. Marisa still had to be screened by Fern Place. I was favoring the Fern Place School and was hopeful that there would be a placement for her there.

I felt very discouraged and sad to think that after all the goal charting I had been doing at home, Marisa had still not shown any gains in the area of controlled behavior and group participation. I expressed my concerns to Marisa's teacher, and she wrote back to me, "We have faith in Marisa, and we have seen the many gains that she has made. Yes, there continue to be areas of need, which we are working on, but we must also look at the progress. We are all so proud of her." The teacher also expressed concern at the prospect of Marisa going to the Rosemary Kennedy School. She felt it was not appropriate for Marisa, since the children there were more impaired (lower functioning) than Marisa, and my school district director felt much the same way. Marisa's teacher and I were hoping that Marisa would be accepted in the BOCES elementary school at Fern Place, which was a warm and nurturing environment. I was hoping the same.

Near the end of March, I visited the Rosemary Kennedy School with Marisa; we toured their program, and their staff screened Marisa. I did not find the ABA (applied behavior analysis) approach at the Rosemary Kennedy School to be as fine-tuned as the Martin C. Barell School and was disappointed with the program. Students were working on their individual skills but I did not see the one-to-one supervision that was present at the Martin C. Barell School. My own instincts were telling me that the ABA approach was harsh, and I felt it stripped a child of his or her spirit. In spite of Marisa's difficult behaviors at times, she was a happy, creative, curious, and friendly little girl. I didn't like the idea of putting her in a program that might discourage such positive personality traits in favor of working on only the ABA goals. I had always preferred to have Marisa's interests determine our curriculum plan at home, and I felt that Variety Preschooler's Workshop had also used gentle guidance when working with Marisa.

In the beginning of April I received a phone call from the Rosemary Kennedy School psychologist. Knowing that I was not happy with their ABA class, she informed me that they would be willing to place Marisa in their new pilot program. It would consist of twelve children in two adjoining classrooms with a full-time speech teacher, a regular teacher, and assistants for the two classes. It was to be a class of high-functioning children with autism and some children with other special needs, so it would not be in the same category as the ABA class setup. This sounded as if it might be a better option for Marisa. However, I told the psychologist that I needed to see the program again before I made a decision. She sensed my hesitation and stressed that Marisa had been very uncooperative at her Rosemary Kennedy screening; she expressed doubt that Fern Place would even consider taking Marisa once they screened her for a placement. She also felt that although Fern Place might be a pleasantly nurturing environment, their staff wouldn't be able to address Marisa's critical behavior issues and distractibility. I was upset to hear what she was telling me but set up an appointment to go back to visit the Rosemary Kennedy School again. I invited Marisa's teacher to come along for the tour; she planned to attend, but she was unable to go along when the appointed day arrived.

Marisa's teacher and school psychologist at Variety Preschooler's Workshop were concerned with the discouraging remarks of the Rosemary Kennedy School psychologist concerning Fern Place being unlikely to accept Marisa. They reminded me of all the positive gains Marisa had made at Variety, and they helped me put in perspective the fact that Marisa's behaviors were also exacerbated by her unfamiliarity with the school she was visiting. At this point Marisa had displayed uncontrolled behaviors at both the Dinkelmeyer School and the Rosemary Kennedy School; I had to wonder if being screened at Fern Place would also cause Marisa to show her worst behaviors. I was curious to see how the school would handle those behaviors. Marisa's screening at Fern Place was scheduled for April 16 at 10:00. The social worker told me that Marisa and I would also get a tour of the program at that time.

The subsequent screening at Fern Place was uneventful, which I considered to be a good sign. Marisa and I were given a tour by a social worker who then brought Marisa to a classroom for screening by a teacher, while I expressed to the school psychologist my concerns about Marisa's impulsiveness and difficult behaviors. When we left, the psychologist and social worker did not give us any information as to their decision, but more importantly, Marisa left happy and without incident.

The next day, I received a note from Marisa's teacher telling me of the terrific day the children had had at school. The children built a stage out of blocks, then each child took turns using a toy microphone to sing a song. Marisa took the American flag and sang "A Grand Old Flag" very beautifully, the teacher said. This was the kind of learning experience that I so strongly favored. The teacher was following the lead of the children and made good use of the stage the class had built. What a marvelous teaching opportunity the setting had created!

After the Fern Place screening, I visited the Rosemary Kennedy School again. I observed the classes of children that would most likely be with Marisa. I felt that although the children were busy doing well-planned individual work, Marisa would be way above the levels of most of the students I observed. I felt she would be bored focusing on the individual work assignments that seemed somewhat repetitive, and I wondered how often the assignments were changed to hold the child's interest. Also, there was not likely to be any real good peer role models, because the children appeared much lower functioning than Marisa. I also did not see signs of a strong, positive behavior plan to make this setting beneficial to Marisa's growth.

In the meantime, at home we were planning a Bat Mitzvah for Deborah. It was to culminate with a party at the catering hall of the Cresthollow Country Club. I did not want to busy myself during the party with the task of watching Marisa, so I asked the social worker at her school if anyone at the school would be able to baby-sit for Marisa at the party. The search began, and to my great relief a psychology student who worked at the school, Joelle, was interested in the job.

After speaking with Joelle, we decided that she would visit Marisa at her class and then come for some babysitting at the house so that she and Marisa would become comfortable with each other. The babysitting and school visits went well. I was pleased and relieved to know that I would be able to relax during the Bat Mitzvah celebration, and Marisa would be able to participate in the festivities as well.

In preparation for Deborah's Bat Mitzvah, we had discussed with Marisa's teacher the plan to have Marisa spend some time with Joelle at school. Marisa really liked Joelle and seemed to want to spend more time with her than was planned. To help Marisa accept a limited visiting time with Joelle, the teacher made a written script that included Joelle's once-a-day visits to the classroom. Marisa was much more accepting of this plan once she knew the set schedule.

At the end of April the whole family was invited to attend an engagement party in a restaurant. Although I was concerned about how Marisa would behave at this event, the host assured us that it would be a rather informal party with a buffet luncheon and dancing. It would also be a good opportunity to see how Marisa handled a party setting. As it turned out, Marisa had a blast of a time dancing to the DJ's music. She also enjoyed collecting balloons at the party. It was a good experience for all of us.

I received a notice from my school district that they had scheduled a CSE (Committee on Special Education) meeting for Marisa on May 21, to discuss her program for the following year. I was also pleased to receive news that Fern Place had accepted Marisa with the provision that she receive a one-to-one aide paid for by the school district and included in her IEP (Individualized Education Program). The one-to-one aide would stay in the IEP as long as he or she was needed. I was very excited to hear the news and informed Marisa's teacher immediately.

In the meantime, the teacher had come up with a new plan for helping Marisa walk through the school halls with her hands down. She brought a book of flags from home, because she knew how interested Marisa was in flags. She also brought in an empty photo album. If Marisa would walk in the halls with her hands down from her ears, she would be able to draw a picture of one of the flags and place it in her photo album. Marisa was very excited and motivated by the idea of drawing flags. She walked down the hall clutching her pants with her hands, trying desperately to keep them away from her ears. Drawing a flag was her reward. What a terrific idea this turned out to be! I applauded the creativeness of this teacher.

At Marisa's CSE meeting the director of special services decided that she would stay at Variety Preschooler's Workshop for the summer and start Fern Place in September with a one-to-one aide. I was greatly relieved that we had finally come to a decision about the upcoming year. I was also happy that Marisa would spend the summer in her familiar classroom. It was nice to know that all the children in the class would be together for the summer session.

The Bat Mitzvah day arrived, and Marisa was able to enjoy the festivities with the family with Joelle at her side. Marisa enjoyed dancing with Joelle and was happy to be participating throughout the entire evening. As tired as Marisa was, she was sad to see Joelle go at the end of the evening. Joelle did, however, come to our house to babysit for other occasions, and Marisa was always delighted to see her.

The school year came to an end, and Marisa participated in her second and final graduation from Variety Preschooler's Workshop. It was a bittersweet occasion, because Marisa had done so well at this school for four years. I didn't know if the new environment would be as nurturing to Marisa and as receptive to my input. The graduation went well, and I was proud to see how nicely Marisa sat and how patiently she waited during the announcements and calling of names to accept diplomas.

Marisa's seventh birthday party also went well. It was an exciting day for Marisa. The party was outside this year for the first time. In previous years I would have been afraid of her wandering off the grounds, but now I felt Marisa was controlled enough not to leave the backyard party area. The children ate pizza, painted caps with fabric paint, and danced through the sprinkler to music. She was thrilled and kept busy all week with her birthday gifts.

Marisa enjoyed her summer at Variety Preschooler's Workshop with all her familiar friends. She was happy at school and happy at home, swimming in the pool for hours at a time. It was a happy and carefree summer. When Marisa's teacher talked to the children about moving on to new schools, Marisa's response was to call out "Fern Place!" The teacher was surprised and asked if we had been discussing the new school at home. I informed the teacher that we had. Marisa said at home, "Variety's a mess. I'm going to Fern Place." I interpreted that to mean that she thought Variety was used up like old crayons because whenever Marisa's crayons broke or were worn down, she would say "The crayons are a mess."

Although Marisa had done well at Variety Preschooler's Workshop, she still had a long way to go in learning social skills and refining her behaviors into socially acceptable and appropriate form. There was no better reminder than the day we spent with friends at their home for a barbeque and swim.

At the barbeque, Marisa was anxious to be accepted by the other visiting children, a four-year-old boy and his sister, who was Marisa's age. The two children seemed to prefer staying away from Marisa, who approached them too closely invading their space, as she stared at them intensely. The little girl, uncomfortable with Marisa's advances, made faces at Marisa most of the afternoon. I didn't think Marisa noticed or cared until she suddenly picked up a water gun and squirted the girl and boy in their faces. It was very embarrassing as I quickly removed the water gun and reprimanded Marisa for her behavior with an angry "No!" When they left the party, Marisa stood in the driveway eagerly waving and yelling, "Good-bye, good-bye!" She threw kisses at them till they were out of sight. I think she was happy to see them go, since they didn't seem to want to play with her anyway.

Later, in the pool, Marisa attempted to climb on the homeowner's back. She thought he would enjoy swimming under water with her. She didn't have the words to ask, but rather assumed he knew her thoughts, which is sometimes typical of children with autism. He did not enjoy having his head pushed under water by a seven-year-old child. Marisa did not understand that she was doing something dangerous, even though she was doing it to an adult, who gave me very disapproving looks as I pulled Marisa off of him. This was an embarrassing incident, which I attempted to explain since I felt that I knew what Marisa was trying to do. Unfortunately, it is extremely difficult for people to understand something that they have no experience with and as much as I understand Marisa, I also try to accept the difficulty others have understanding Marisa's behavior. Shoshana, Deborah, and Dan were also embarrassed by Marisa's behavior, but they, like myself, are so much more tolerant of Marisa because we understand why she does what she does, and because we love her and she is a part of our family.

Needless to say, these friends never invited us to their home again. In spite of the fact that I tried to monitor Marisa's behavior, Marisa did too many things that the friends disapproved of. Unfortunately, since Marisa was the one with the strange and unfamiliar behaviors, she was the one blamed for all things that went wrong. For instance, the child making faces at Marisa was never reprimanded for her behavior, which was in itself unfortunate.

As I reviewed the events of the day, I thought about how ordinary people could play an important part in helping those with social difficulties gain acceptance. Because parents of a child with a disability often feel vulnerable, it is very hard for them to be assertive in helping others accept their child's differences. How wonderful it would be if people could be more understanding of the differences of others. It could conceivably relieve the burden on the overwhelmed parent.

If given the chance, the special needs child could learn from more socially appropriate peers. That is the goal of school inclusion, and that is also why siblings are so helpful to their special-needs family member. Empathy, compassion, and tolerance toward the child with somewhat unconventional behaviors could greatly help smooth the way for learning socially acceptable behaviors.

Things are hard enough for us "neurotypical" people, as Carol Gray (the creator of the social story concept) calls those of us who are so-called "normal." Think how hard it must be for the child with autism, who lacks the natural ability to learn the social order of the world we live in. Rather than shunning those that are different, what a beautiful thing it would be if neurotypical people could make the effort to meet them halfway and help this vulnerable population of people find a place in the world we all must learn to share.

Chapter Seven

NEW CHALLENGES

On September 4, 1997, Marisa entered the elementary program at the Fern Place School in Plainview, Long Island. Once again, I corresponded with the teacher, as I had in her previous school. The first day Marisa arrived home from her new school, she said, "I want to go to Variety." I explained to her that she could go back to visit, but she needed to be in a more grown-up school now. The teacher wrote a note telling me how the day had gone, and the name of the one-to-one aide who would be working with Marisa. There were three girls and four boys in the class. I asked Marisa the names of the girls in the class, and she told me Erinn, Meghan, and Ariel. I asked the teacher if this was correct, and I was pleased to learn that it was.

Though Marisa was quick to learn the names of her classmates, she had difficulty transitioning from one activity to the next. I suggested to the teacher that they use a written schedule so Marisa could see the order of events in the day. The second day of school I received a note from Marisa's aide. She informed me that she had written out Marisa's schedule on a card attached to her desk. The schedule also included all her special classes outside the classroom, such as speech, art and music, etc. I was happy to know that she had followed my advice in using a written schedule for Marisa.

As recommended by the school, I decided to take advantage of the breakfast and lunch that the school provided, since Marisa wasn't eating breakfast at home, because she was still quite fussy in selecting foods. I was hopeful that she might expand her food preferences if she ate with her classmates. I suggested that the school menu for each week be attached to Marisa's desk so she could review what foods were on the menu. It also seemed like a good way to get Marisa to learn some new words. Marisa's aide liked this idea. Although I thought Marisa might become less finicky, according to her one-to-one aide, Marisa did not find the school lunches as appealing as I had hoped. Nevertheless, I continued with the lunch program for the year, in the hopes that she would learn to try the foods her classmates were eating.

Things appeared to be going well at the new school. According to Marisa's aide, Marisa earned stickers for completing work assignments. However, I was not surprised to learn that during outdoor play time, Marisa ran away from the class. She was not able to resist exploring the large outdoor area. The aide had to run after her many times to bring her back to the group. I suggested that it would be a good idea to come up with a list of acceptable activities to replace Marisa's urge to run across the open field. Such activities as blowing bubbles, flying a kite, jumping on an outdoor trampoline, riding a bike or scooter, playing with a hopping ball, and running on the track would be good replacement activities.

One afternoon, Marisa had difficulty ending the outdoor kite-flying activity. To ease her back to the classroom, the aide took her for a walk and then brought her to the music room. There she enjoyed playing the drums and listening to other children play their instruments. I thought this was an excellent way to ease her back indoors. Realizing that it wouldn't always be possible to have Marisa play music every time she didn't want to return to the classroom, I suggested a rotating list of fun transitioning activities, such as having a special snack, taking a quick walking tour of the school, or watching music for a few minutes, to be followed by reading or whatever else was on the regular schedule.

I also suggested that it would help to be firm but sympathetic to show understanding of Marisa's disappointment, always stressing that she could do other fun things later. I explained to the teacher and aide that I would help create an incentive for Marisa. I informed Marisa that for every day she earned 100 percent of her stickers at school, she would get an added bonus star on her home goal chart. I also explained that for every fifty stars on the home chart, Marisa would earn a special gift of her choice. I was hoping that the incentive of the sticker rewards would put an end to her difficulty transitioning from outdoors to classroom work.

Since Marisa enjoyed the music room so much, she was earning a lot of extra drum-playing time for good behavior at school. This reminded me of the time when Marisa was three years old and she had attended my parents' fiftieth anniversary party, where she was mesmerized by the band and attempted to play the drums.

As the year progressed, there were lots of bumps in the road. One such problem occurred on a bus ride home. Marisa was having difficulty getting off the bus after school; she wanted to linger and say good-bye to each and every person on the bus, as she had done the previous year. Because she was seated in the front of the bus and had to walk to the very back to say good-bye to everyone, the routine became time-consuming and annoying to the bus driver. To help alleviate the problem, I wrote a social story to explain why it was important to get off the bus promptly and how to say good-bye quickly. Saying good-bye to the other children on the bus seemed like a very sociable and acceptable thing to do, and in order to make it possible for Marisa, she was moved to the back of the bus. Her new seat enabled her to say her good-byes as she walked down the aisle to exit. This was a sensible solution that was satisfactory to the bus driver and fulfilled Marisa's desire to be sociable.

To overcome any difficulties Marisa had focusing on and completing her work, the teacher set up video games as special rewards. The video games were an incentive to finish work assignments and a way to encourage interaction with other children. This seemed like a good idea for Marisa, since she was familiar with video games at home.

Although earning special activities was a good incentive, Marisa's behavior became problematic when she was unable to earn a special activity. For example, when she failed to earn extra gym time one day, her disappointment made her unmanageable. She would start to scream and cry as she angrily would jump up and down shooting her fists in the air. Her aide had to take her for a walk and remove her to a quiet room until she could regain control. The aide discovered that working with Marisa in a quiet area away from the other children at these times was quite beneficial.

During the year the class took many trips out into the community. In October they visited a pumpkin farm, and the trip was a huge success. Marisa enjoyed the hayride and the lunch at McDonald's, though she had difficulty leaving the restaurant's playground. However, an ice cream treat did help ease her away from the playground activity.

Things seemed to be going very well at Fern Place. Marisa was beginning to socialize and interact well with her classmates. I was pleased by the nurturing, caring manner of Marisa's aide, who always seemed to find lots of opportunity for Marisa to release her excess energy, through bike riding on the track behind the school, roller skating in the gym, and roller racing. The aide even brought her own skates from home to join in. All in all, Marisa was adjusting well and was happy in her new school.

Then one day in early December, I became concerned when, by chance, I came across some information that I had not been informed of. While speaking to one of the other parents, I learned that the class was to take a trip to Manhattan to see a holiday show. I was concerned because I had not received a permission slip for this outing. I thought that perhaps by mistake, the teacher had not given Marisa one. I quickly called the school to inform the teacher that I hadn't received the notice regarding the trip.

I became upset when the teacher told me that the she and the school psychologist decided it would be best for Marisa to skip this trip and spend her day in another teacher's class. The teacher reminded me that Marisa's behavior was very unpredictable; the staff was concerned that the trip would be too over-stimulating for her. She apologized for not informing me, insisting that she had planned to do so. I thought that perhaps she recognized how wrong this decision was, so she didn't know how to go about telling me.

I informed the teacher that I would discuss this with my school district director of special services. I was angry because given the fact that my district was paying for Marisa's one-to-one aide, I felt the purpose of the aide was being wasted. The director of special services was also not pleased to hear that Marisa was being excluded from a trip.

While discussing the problem, I learned from the director that it was now the law that a new technique called a functional behavior assessment (FBA) be conducted for children with serious behavioral problems. The assessment includes looking at events leading up to the behavior (antecedents), identifying the reason for the behavior itself (whether for escape, attention, or for a more tangible reason), and reviewing the consequences of the behavior—necessary steps in formulating an acceptable plan for change. Once the evaluators identify the unacceptable behavior, more acceptable alternative means for achieving the same purpose the problem behavior serves are put in place. For example, "Teaching the individual specific forms of communication that serve the same purpose as the problem behavior is one way of providing an alternative to problem behavior. When a problem behavior such as head banging and a communicative behavior such as saying, 'I have to go to the bathroom,' serve the same purpose and both are successful in getting the individual displaying the behavior to the toilet, then we say that the two behaviors are functionally equivalent. The technical term, 'functional equivalence,' simply means that two behaviors serve the same purpose (function) and are therefore equivalent to one another" (Carr 1994, 125). I was pleased to know that functional behavior assessments were now considered necessary by law in situations where behaviors were severe enough and frequent enough to be warranted.

However, because this was a new procedure, unfortunately not too many schools were familiar with the long process of performing FBAs properly. Probably for this reason, Marisa had not been considered for an FBA. Therefore despite all the precautions that the teacher and aide had used to keep Marisa's day running smoothly at school, they had made no effort to plan for the long and potentially difficult trip into the city.

Marisa's exclusion from the trip was an eye-opener to me, and I was determined to make sure it would never happen again. The director of special services also made it clear to the school that they should only schedule outings that all the children could participate in.

Though I was greatly disappointed by the teacher's behavior regarding the trip incident, I continued to receive encouraging notes from Marisa's aide. One day she wrote asking if it would be all right to do nail polishing at school, since Marisa seemed interested in painting her nails. I thought it was a nice idea as a reward and a good way to share a social activity with other girls in the class. This seemed to be a good alternative to other reward activities and could be considered a special treat.

The teacher decided that during special performances by theatre groups that visited the school periodically, Marisa would be taken to meet the performers ahead of time. She would get to talk to the performers and see some of their props to become familiar with them, with the idea that it would be easier for her to sit through a performance with the class. Over the course of the year, previewing the performances worked well for Marisa most of the time, and she did well with keeping her impulsiveness in check during the actual show.

During the winter recess I tried scheduling play dates with Marisa's friends. She got together with her old friend Chris from Variety Preschool and also saw two other friends from her new school and her after-school social skills class. These play dates were becoming increasingly more important; Marisa was seven years old now, and I could see from her maturing process that she needed more peer interaction. She was extremely anxious to get together with friends, and I tried my best to arrange more visits.

In March, the teacher sent a letter expressing concern about an upcoming trip to the Queens Science Museum. She knew that she was not going to be able to exclude Marisa, so she wrote to ask if I had any concerns regarding elevators or anything else that might present a problem at the museum. I responded that I did not feel there would be a problem. I prepared Marisa as best I could with a social story and a trip point incentive. When the trip day arrived, all went reasonably well, to my great relief.

This outing was soon followed by one to a matzah factory, which was a huge success. All the children were given baker's hats, a ball of dough, and a rolling pin to roll out their matzah before baking it in the oversized oven. Marisa's one-to-one aide wrote a note to let me know how delightful an experience this trip was for Marisa.

Although Marisa was managing to go on trips with the class, she still displayed much impulsive behavior at school and at home. She would frequently run out of her seat on the bus, and at school she continually jumped up to check noises in the hallway. Walking down the halls in line was also a problem, because Marisa would frequently run off the line to look into classes she passed by.

One evening at home gave me a frightening reminder of how important it was to keep tabs on Marisa at all times. It was six in the evening, and I was on my way to pick up Deborah from an overnight school trip. Marisa wanted to come along for the ride, but I refused, knowing I might have to wait in the car for a while, since the actual arrival time of the bus was only approximate. I had been waiting at the school for about half an hour when I started to feel that something was terribly wrong at home.

I decided to drive back home, just two minutes from the school, to make sure everything was all right. When I walked in the door, my greatest fear had come to pass. Dan had just realized that Marisa was missing and was about to drive out to look for her. Apparently she had wandered out an unlocked door while her dad was watching the news in the next room. By the time he realized what had happened, she was out of sight.

He got in the car and drove around the circle of homes where we live. As he drove down the road slowly, looking all around, he spotted Marisa ahead of his car in the distance. She was walking down the middle of the road with Mutsy dangling from her hand. He was greatly relieved to find her, but we realized that Marisa was now capable of letting herself out of the house. Dan and I were frightened by the prospect of new problems that could arise from her ability to open an unlocked door, and we knew that the time had come for serious re-evaluating of Marisa's goals.

When they arrived home safely, I asked her why she had left the house. She said, "I wanted to see Deborah come off the bus!" Apparently, Marisa decided to attempt to walk to the school on her own. I realized then that it would have been wiser to take her with me; feeling left out, she put herself in a potentially dangerous situation. I decided that from that point on I would always use cues from Marisa before making a decision about what to do with her.

As time went on, I continued to communicate with the teacher and aide. One day the teacher sent a note about an incident that occurred while the children attended the school store. Apparently Marisa wanted to purchase a camera with the points she had earned in her class. However, because she did not have enough points, she became unruly and angry, pinching and lashing out at her aide. They took Marisa to the time-out room to regain control.

I saw this as an opportunity to suggest that perhaps it would be a good idea to use social stories to help Marisa prepare for the school store. I hadn't mentioned social stories to the teacher before this because the one-to-one aide seemed so sensitive to Marisa's needs. However, because of the difficulty the teacher and aide were having at this time, I thought this information might be helpful to them. I told the teacher how successful this technique had been with Marisa in her previous school. I explained the concept of the social stories and how helpful they were for children with autism. In the case of trips to the school store, the social story would remind Marisa that she could use her points immediately or choose to save up for a bigger, more expensive item to purchase at a later time. It would also be a written reminder of the behavior expected of her. Providing a social story for this situation certainly could not hurt.

But to my disappointment, the teacher became defensive at my suggestion of using social stories for this or any other situation. She insisted that Marisa knew the rules and that she and the aide prepared Marisa for all new experiences. She was unwilling to try the technique that had worked so well for Marisa in her previous school and was having promising results for her at home. I was angry and frustrated by her response but did not respond to her remarks because I did not want to antagonize her any further.

Soon after the incident at the school store, Marisa had another major tantrum at school when she was not allowed to select a candy, which was the goal for the class fifty-point behavior chart. Marisa did not understand that the class as a whole had not received the fifty points yet. Again, I felt that a social story could have prevented a misunderstanding that resulted in a tantrum. Although the problem was occurring at school, I decided to write a social story for Marisa at home. I encouraged her to remember what she read and tried to assure her that I had faith in her ability to carry out the goals at school. Although this was a tall order, I felt it was important to help Marisa realize that she needed to develop some responsibility for her own actions. I hoped she would try to follow what I had written out for her.

Although Marisa's aide developed a strong bond with Marisa, the teacher did not share the aide's faith in Marisa's abilities. This was clearly obvious during the end-of-year performance that the parents were invited to. Marisa's aide expressed to me that she was very excited for Marisa and had prepared her for her part in the show. As we watched the small group during their presentation, we patiently waited to see what role Marisa would play. Then, to our great surprise, the little performance came to an end. We looked at Marisa's aide for some confirmation that something was wrong. She, too, was disturbed, and she had to remind the teacher that a part had been inadvertently forgotten.

Needless to say, it was disturbing enough that Marisa was forgotten, but when she finally stood up to do her part, I was even more disappointed. I realized that the "big part" Marisa was given was to point to pictures. She had not been given the opportunity for a reading part, as had the other children. When I later asked the aide about this, she said that although she had asked for Marisa to have a speaking role, the teacher was uncomfortable about giving her that responsibility. Shoshana and I were both upset by the oversight of the teacher during the performance and by the teacher's lack of faith in Marisa's ability to do more than point to pictures. However, I did not feel it necessary to discuss it further with the teacher since the year was nearly over. Instead, I knew that I would have to express my feelings, concerning Marisa's ability, to the teacher at the beginning of the new year.

As the end of the school year approached, I held a party for Marisa's eighth birthday. Unfortunately, bad weather caused us to plan our party indoors. I cleared out our large atrium and set up the party table and balloons. The children had pizza, painted T-shirts, and enjoyed a candy hunt while a torrential downpour and thunderstorm were going on outside. The children actually enjoyed watching the rain through the skylights above. It was a successful party in spite of the awful weather, and everyone had a nice time.

This was confirmed when the teacher sent me a note letting me know that the children came in to school talked excitedly about the party they had attended. Many of them were also wearing the T-shirts they had made. I was happy to receive the teacher's complimentary note and realized that, though she didn't seem to like receiving my suggestions when it came to school activities, she was showing appreciation for my efforts at home.

Though Marisa and most of her regular classmates stayed on for the summer session, which was a full day program with the same hours as during the regular school year, many of the teachers took a summer break and were replaced by different teachers. She was in a class of six children with a new teacher just for the summer and a new one-to-one aide.

It turned out to be a wonderful summer experience. The children did reading and math skill work every morning and then participated in a wealth of fun activities in the afternoons. They went to a town park to swim once a week and even took trips to the beach. There were lots of gym activities, outdoor play periods, and water play experiences. Marisa also received her five days of speech therapy each week as written in her IEP(Individual Education Plan). The summer program had a nice balance of academics and fun-filled activities.

Because this teacher was very receptive to the use of social stories and written cues, I sensed that Marisa was having an easier time than during the school year. Whether it was because of the more relaxed atmosphere of the summer program or the way the teacher was handling Marisa, I was not certain. Nevertheless, it was something to think about.

When the summer program ended, Marisa was to be home for five weeks. We filled our time with swimming in our pool. I also arranged some get-togethers for Marisa with some of her friends that she had remained in touch with from her previous years at school. She saw Chris, her first boyfriend from Variety Preschool; Trevor, from her social skills class at Variety Preschooler's Workshop; and her friend Brittany. It was a pleasant and happy summer. Marisa, my daughter with autism, was thoroughly enjoying her friends.

Shoshana, Marisa and Deborah are enjoying a family vacation in the mountains, after Marisa's first birthday.

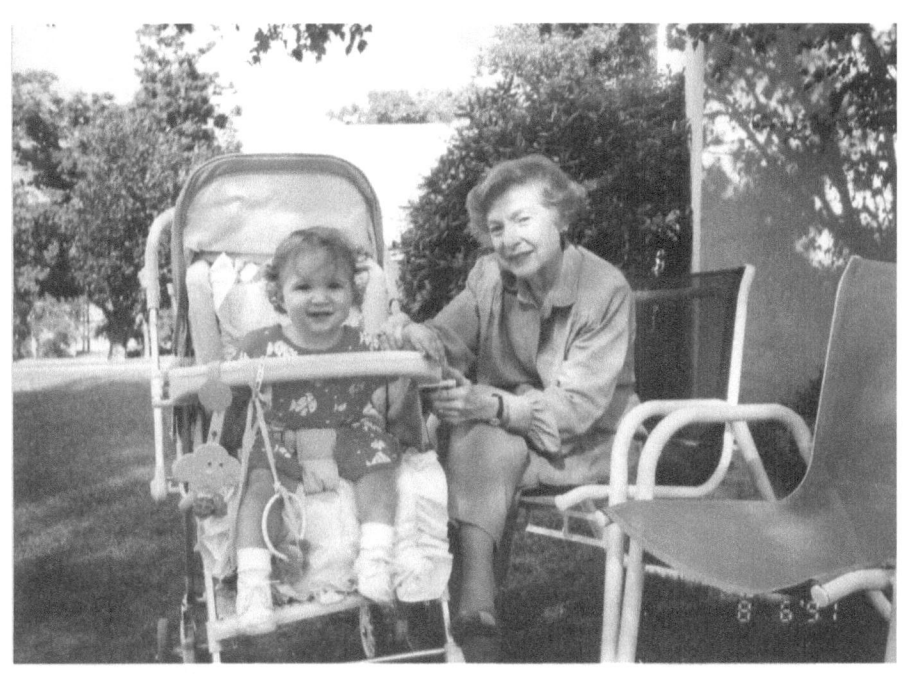

Marisa is with her grandmother at thirteen months.

Shoshana, Deborah, Marisa and myself are enjoying the beach. Marisa is too active to allow her out of the playpen.

Marisa, just before her autism diagnosis at 20 months.

Marisa at 21 months.

Marisa's enjoying her second birthday at home with Deborah and grandmother.

At Shoshana's Bat Mitzvah, she couldn't take her eyes off the candles.

Marisa at two years old, is with her grandfather, at the housewarming party for our new home.

Marisa and Deborah are enjoying a bubble bath.

Marisa is enjoying her third birthday party with the family.

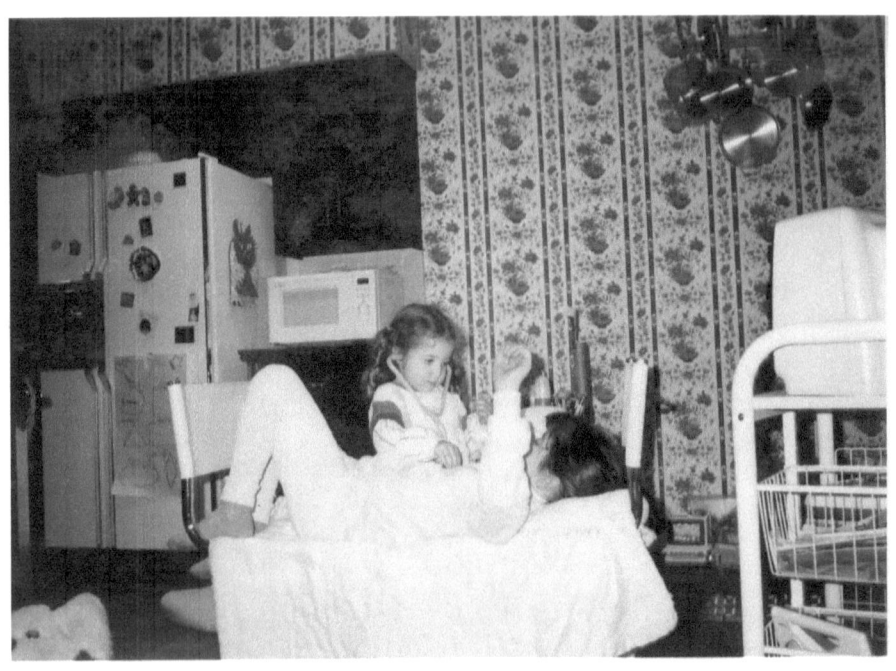

Marisa is playing doctor with her sister, Deborah.

Marisa at three years old is ready for a swim with her sister, Deborah.

Deborah is playing with the house we made for Marisa's third birthday.

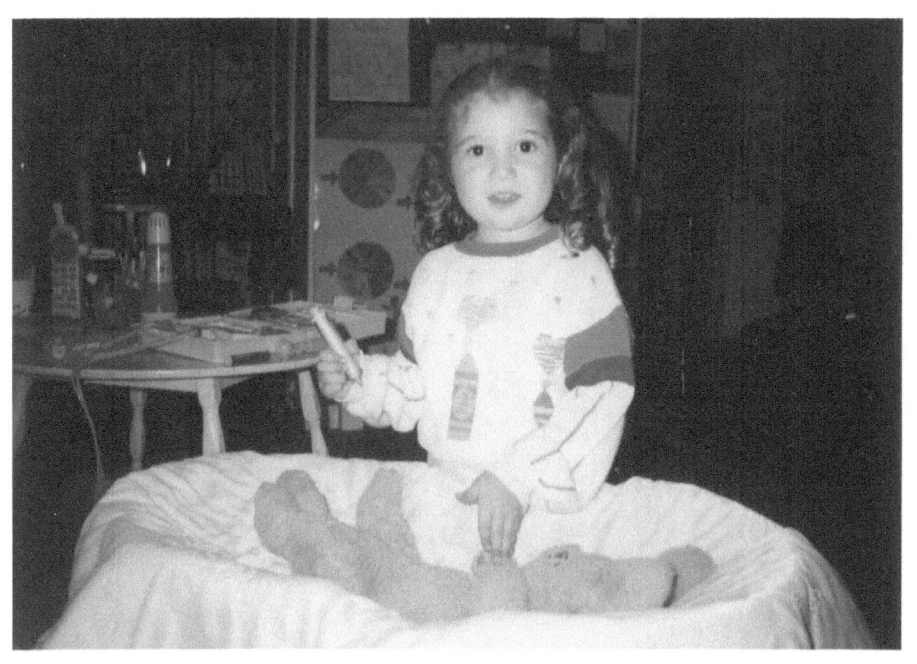

Marisa is playing doctor with her favorite stuffed dog, Mutsy.

Marisa is excited just before her fourth birthday party,
because it's her first party with friends.

Marisa is playing dress-up with a friend.

Marisa at age four, is enjoying an evening at home with Shoshana and Deborah.

Marisa, at age five, is participating at Deborah's birthday party.

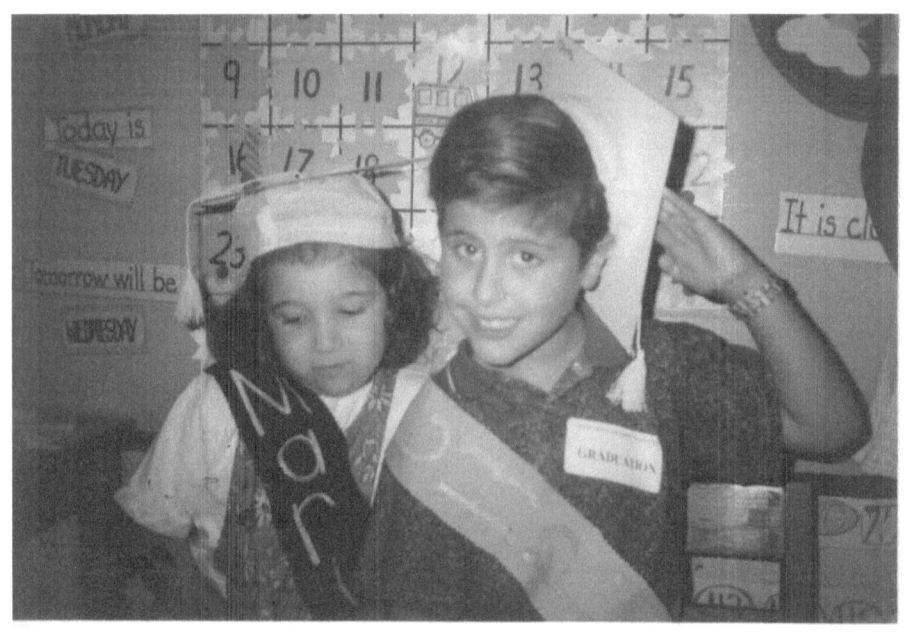

Marisa, age six, is with her friend Chris, at her first graduation from Variety Preschooler's Workshop.

Marisa is proud and happy at her graduation.

At six, Marisa is loving Deborah and Mutsy.

At seven, Marisa is loving Shoshana and Mutsy.

Marisa is excited to be celebrating Memorial Day and was happy to have a chance to sit in an antique car.

Marisa is happy to see her dad after his return from Arizona.

Marisa is graduating from Variety Preschooler's Workshop in 1997 at age seven.

Marisa is excited just before her seventh birthday party.

Marisa is enjoying an afternoon in the pool at home.

Marisa at seven, is helping her sister, Shoshana, move in to the Brandeis University dormitory.

Marisa is participating in lighting the candles at Deborah's Bat Mitzvah.

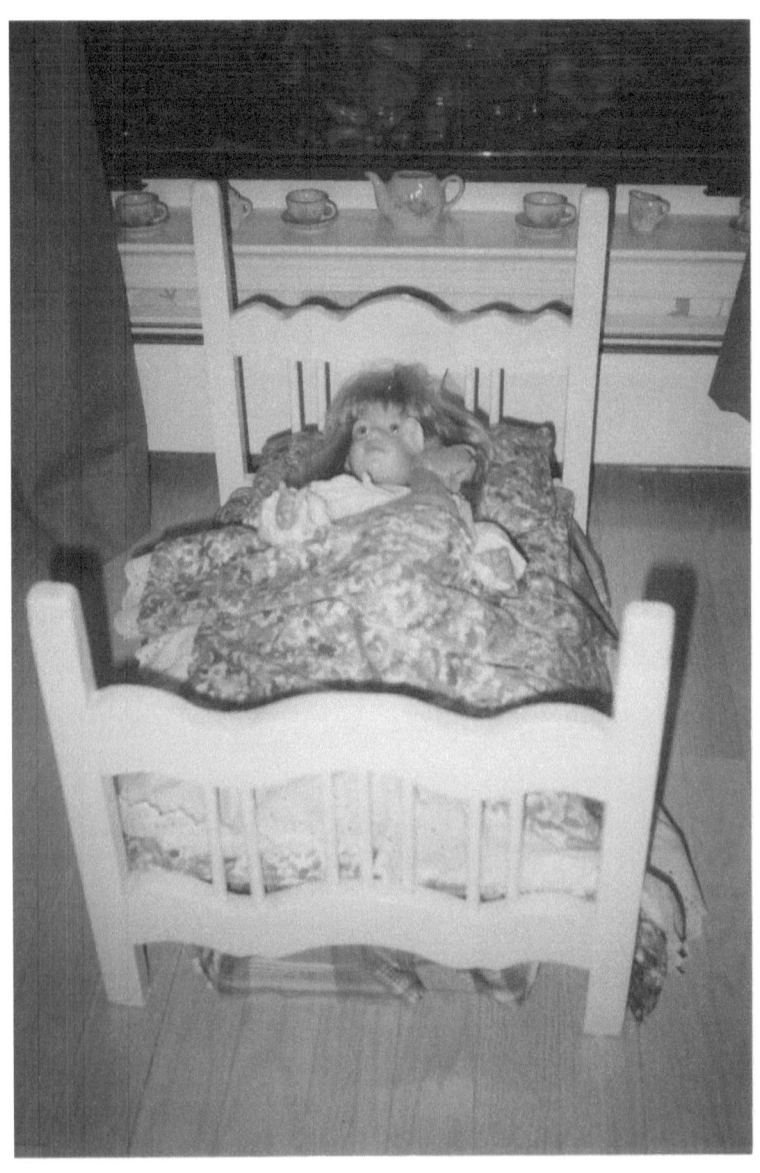

This is the bed Deborah made for Marisa's Alison doll.

Marisa, at nine, is visiting her Aunt Geri and Uncle Milt.

In the spring of 1999, Marisa posed with her sisters, mom and her Mutsy dog, before a ride to visit her grandparents.

In 1999, at nine years old, Marisa is enjoying the wedding reception at The Water's Edge Restaurant.

Deborah, Marisa, Shoshana and myself are seated at The Water's Edge Restaurant.

Marisa, with Deborah and Shoshana, is excited just before her tenth birthday party.

At eleven, Marisa was so happy to be invited to a party at her friend Peter's house.

Marisa is happy at her twelfth birthday party.

Marisa painted this album cover as a gift for a favorite teacher.

Marisa at tweve, is dressed for Halloween.

Marisa is excited to be participating in a horse-back riding competition.

At thirteen, Marisa is performing a solo at the GAP summer camp show.

Marisa with her sisters, is showing off the haircut she gave herself.

Shoshana, Marisa at thirteen, and myself are all ready just before my parent's sixtieth wedding anniversary.

On Valentine's Day, at age thirteen, Marisa is wearing the red skirt I had promised her the year before.

Marisa, age fourteen, is proud and happy on visiting day at Camp Northwood in 2004.

Shoshana and Marisa, age 15, are celebrating Chanukah at their grandparent's home in 2005.

Marisa is concentrating while playing scrabble with Uncle Eddie and Deborah.

Marisa at fifteen, feeling happy.

Marisa is enjoying the Camp Northwood reunion with her good friend, Alex, in 2006.

Kyle and Marisa are posing for a Newsday photographer for the September 11th Newsday story that appeared covering the Common Connections Event on September 10, 2005.

Chapter Eight

A BUMPY ROAD

At the age of eight, Marisa was ready to begin her second year at Fern Place. At the start of school, I did not know who her teacher would be, but it turned out to be the same teacher from the year before. Although I had some reservations, I was determined to start the new year optimistically. I was happy to know that Marisa still had the same one-to-one aide, and many of the children in the class remained the same as the year before.

I decided to start sending Marisa's lunch from home this year, since Marisa had been wasting most of the school lunches the year before. Marisa still had not learned to try new foods, and although she saw the other children eating the school lunches, it did not motivate her to want to eat what was placed in front of her. I sent in the poptarts and Hi-C that she requested. I wasn't happy about her choice but for the time being I had no other alternative. She needed to eat something, and if the school lunches were mostly thrown out, I assumed that she would do the same with a lunch she didn't want.

I received a warm welcome-back note from Marisa's teacher and "Thrilled to be back!" from Marisa's one-to-one aide. The year seemed to be starting off well, and my relationship with the teacher seemed to improve as a result of a situation that had developed at home.

When our neighbor died, leaving her adorable but short-tempered black-and-white Persian cat abandoned in the street, Marisa developed a curiosity about the animal. I couldn't help but feel sorry for the hungry and lonely cat that frequently stood outside our door meowing. This cat was not friendly in the least, and there was no way she would allow anyone to pick her up. However, Marisa seemed fascinated by the cat, and as we all grew concerned by her unfortunate circumstances, we decided to adopt her and call her Fluffy. Because the cat did not trust us, I needed to lure her into a carrier with food in order to take her to the vet for a checkup.

As soon as I informed Marisa's teacher of what was happening at home, she immediately responded by writing back about her own cats. At last I realized that I had something in common with the teacher, who had always seemed so defensive about things I suggested the year before. I was hoping that our common interest in cats would help improve the relationship that never seemed to progress.

One day the teacher sent an amazing note, which made me realize that perhaps I had hit on a really good idea; I was finally building a rapport with her. She wrote to me, "I am so pleased that you are adopting another cat. I love cats. We have one in the house and three outdoor cats that we feed. Please send pictures to share." I wrote back, assuring the teacher that I would take pictures of the cat once she returned from her full checkup in the animal hospital. I also asked for advice about how to keep Fluffy outdoors if she didn't get along with our cats, Pablo and Milo.

Over the next few weeks, the teacher sent much information about how to help the new cat adjust to the others. She also sent information on how to keep a cat outdoors through the winter months, if things didn't work out inside the house. There was a whole other side to this teacher that I hadn't known. I felt like I had at last made a connection that would perhaps be helpful for Marisa. I hoped that the teacher would become more receptive to some of my suggestions. The communication book was filled with cat stories in between brief notes about how Marisa was getting along at school.

At home I noticed Marisa being very attentive to the relationships developing between the cats. Fluffy was not very trusting of other animals; she had clearly been a loner and was not willing to let Milo or Pablo come anywhere near her. Marisa enjoyed watching how the three animals interacted. She also developed an appreciation for petting Pablo and Milo, because she knew that Fluffy was one animal she probably would never be able to get near.

Things were progressing well at home and at school. Then one day, I received an angry note from the teacher. Marisa had run off during a fire drill. According to the note, the teachers had escorted the children out to the football field. Marisa, being unable to resist the urge to run across the open field, took off, forcing one of the other teachers to run after her. I had to wonder where Marisa's one-to-one aide was and why another aide, instead of her own, was the one to run after Marisa.

Though this was a serious incident, envisioning Marisa running off in the large field struck me as a bit humorous. I couldn't help but see the situation from Marisa's point of view. In her eyes, she needed to take advantage of the open space. The teacher failed to see any humor in this and insisted that, if there were a fire, Marisa could have been hurt.

Of course, this was true, but what happened was caused by Marisa's impulsiveness. If the teacher was so concerned about keeping Marisa in line on a football field, she should have been prepared for the unexpected. Marisa was still quite unpredictable and still very impulsive at times, which was why Marisa was given a one-to-one aide in the first place. So why wasn't the aide right there holding on to Marisa during the fire drill? When I asked about this, the teacher said that the aide was at lunch and another assistant was with Marisa. Unfortunately the assistant wasn't as tuned in to Marisa's impulsiveness. This was unfortunate because if the proper precautions had been taken, Marisa would not have been given the opportunity to run off, and she also would not have had to be punished with a time-out afterwards. Marisa was definitely reminding her teacher and her aide that she needed to be constantly and closely watched, as future fire drills and trips out of the building would surely provoke other incidents.

In October the class enjoyed a trip to a farm, where they saw baby goats and pigs, got a chance to milk a cow, took pony rides, and went on a hayride. Fortunately the trip went well, as Marisa's behavior was closely monitored, and everyone had a wonderful time.

Shortly before Thanksgiving, I was abruptly reminded of my own warning to expect the unexpected. I was busy preparing the house for the holiday and wasn't keeping track of Marisa's whereabouts as closely as I should have been. I was in the kitchen, and I suddenly heard Marisa calling from some far-off place. I called out to her but couldn't quite place where her response was coming from. I called out to Deborah to see if we could figure out exactly where Marisa was. It was such a frightening moment, because she was nowhere in the house. It reminded me of a movie I had once seen in which a child disappears behind a wall into another dimension. Of course, that was a make-believe story; this was the real world.

Deborah and I frantically searched the house, listening for Marisa. We kept hearing her distant calls. She kept saying, "I'm in the tube. I'm in the tube!" Then it suddenly occurred to me! Marisa was in the attic crawl space. I remembered Marisa was always asking about the big, silver air-conditioner ducts. She always had asked if she could "play in the tubes."

As we ran back toward the kitchen, where the attic access was located in the pantry closet, we finally understood what had happened. There in the closet was a ladder on top of the filing cabinet. As I looked up at the attic opening, I saw that the two-by-three-foot board had been moved to the side, leaving the attic entrance opened. I was surprised that Marisa had been able to take the small ladder out of the coat closet, place it on top of the filing cabinet, and move the two-by-three foot attic opening to the side in order to climb up. What I suspected had been confirmed: Marisa had climbed up into the attic.

Suddenly there was a cracking noise behind us in the hall. We quickly turned to see Marisa's leg come through the ceiling, dislodging my main air conditioner vent and a square-foot section of ceiling. I had to calmly tell Marisa how to get back to the main opening with the greatest of caution, before she would fall through the ceiling. She needed to lift her leg back into the attic and climb carefully on the two-by-four-inch boards of wood between the insulation to get back to the opening she had climbed up through.

I was grateful that she was able to listen to my instructions and understand what I was asking her to do. It was imperative that she stay on the narrow boards, because the space between them was only Sheetrock, which she had already learned would not support her weight. It was a very scary couple of minutes as she made her way back some ten feet to the opening. Finally she appeared at the opening, and I was able to help her down with some difficulty.

I asked her what she was thinking. She said, "I wanted to climb through the tube." This confirmed what I had suspected: the air-conditioning duct seemed like a play tunnel to her, and she was fascinated by it. Once she had seen it by climbing a ladder to look into the attic while a routine air conditioning inspection was going on in the spring. She remembered this and couldn't resist the idea of exploring it. It occurred to me that Marisa had frequently asked to go play in the tube, and I had simply brushed it off as a silly request. I should have taken what she was saying a little more seriously. I considered the idea that at some point in the very near future, it might be a good idea to purchase a real play tube for Marisa, so she wouldn't have to be so interested in the air-conditioner ducts. It could even be an added activity for our next birthday party!

I knew this kind of event would inevitably happen again if I didn't take steps to prevent it. I removed the filing cabinet from the pantry closet so there wouldn't be something conveniently close to the attic opening for her to climb on again. I also added an extra warning to her goal chart: if it happened again,

Marisa would lose all her earned points. Though it might seem harsh to take away points that Marisa had earned, I felt that dangerous situations like this warranted drastic measures. Next time there might not be a second chance.

Meantime, at school, the teacher was planning a trip to Garvie's Point but changed the outing to a performance of *The Nutcracker* ballet. The teacher wrote, "I want to talk to you about this change, as I have some concerns. Please call me so that we can discuss the trip." I knew that once again the teacher was worried about how to handle Marisa's impulsiveness on a class trip to see a show. I knew that if this trip was going to work, we would have to plan for it together.

I spoke with the teacher about the trip to *The Nutcracker*. She knew I wasn't going to allow Marisa to be left behind, so together we would put a plan in place. We decided that the children would preview the show on video in the classroom so they would know what to expect. During the show, Marisa's aide was to sit on the aisle with Marisa just in case they needed to leave the performance in a hurry. I would also remind Marisa about the trip points she would earn if she behaved well and followed all the rules. In addition, I was to send in chewing gum to help keep Marisa quiet during the performance. Leaving the theatre would only be a last resort if all else failed.

At home we went over what was expected of her. I wrote out step-by-step instructions for her in a social story. It was all spelled out clearly enough; now it was up to Marisa to show that she could do it. During the classroom showing of *The Nutcracker*, Marisa kept saying, "I want to go on the stage. I want to go on TV!" This was something that we all were worrying about. Did this mean that Marisa would attempt to go on the stage during the performance? I wondered if my social story preparation and my trip points reward would be enough to prevent such a thing from happening. Or was Marisa's asking to go on TV simply a request to go to the live show? She knew that the class was going on the trip to the live performance, and she was excited and eager to get there.

The day of the trip, Marisa came in to school happy and excited. Then she became disruptive when she misplaced her weather calendar. Suddenly, she was crying and yelling, and it took several adults in addition to Marisa's aide to calm her down until the weather calendar was found. This unfortunate episode only made everyone more concerned about the trip. I can just imagine how anxious Marisa's teacher and aide felt after this seemingly benign incident in the classroom. In spite of all fears, the trip was on, and fortunately it went well enough. There were several trying moments, according to the teacher, but basically Marisa was able to hold it together. Marisa's aide was also kind enough to send a copy of *The Nutcracker* on CD for Marisa to enjoy at home.

After the trip, Marisa returned home crying for a Lillian Vernon catalog. The crying continued on and off for two hours. I was puzzled about the connection between the Lillian Vernon catalog and *The Nutcracker* show, but I knew there had to be some link. As I searched my mind for an answer, I realized that there were ballet costumes in the catalog. Most likely that was it! She probably was also exhausted from the day and tired from having to control her behavior through the performance.

Although Marisa did well on the Nutcracker trip, I sympathized with the teacher, who I felt was struggling through the year with Marisa. Early in January, I spoke to my school district director of special services. I expressed many concerns about the difficulties at school with handling Marisa's impulsive behaviors. We set up a meeting with the school principal, teacher, and psychologist. The director of special services decided that a functional behavior assessment (FBA) needed to be done. An FBA would mean gathering information on what was occurring throughout the day so that the evaluator could determine what preceded the unwanted behaviors, what behavior occurred, and how it was handled.

The school district director also felt that talking to an autism consultant would also be a good idea. Such a person could address many problem areas, such as transitioning from one activity to the next, helping Marisa learn self control, promoting socialization with peers, and encouraging Marisa's expression of feelings and use of language. Also, the director of special services felt that an OT (occupational therapy) evaluation would be a good idea. Although Marisa had completed OT services at Variety Preschooler's Workshop, the director felt that OT services now might be able to correct certain behaviors, and it was worth checking into it.

Although there was no problem arranging for the OT evaluation, which would be done by the BOCES staff, the BOCES administrator was not happy about an outside autism consultant being brought in. She offered to contact their own consultant. My school district director agreed that the BOCES autism consultant should evaluate the problems first, and if necessary, the school district would bring in another consultant.

In the meantime, the Fern Place School was in the process of moving to another location. The north shore students at Fern Place and the south shore students at The Ames School were going to come together into one school. The Jerusalem Avenue School in Bellmore, Long Island would be big enough to house all the students from both programs. Unfortunately, the move created a delay in Marisa's OT evaluation and autism consultation.

In February I received a note from the teacher informing me that the autism consultant had come for an initial meeting and that the classroom staff and psychologist would start collecting data to complete a functional behavior assessment. When I received the note I was infuriated. A whole month had passed, and the FBA data collecting had not even begun. Somebody should have been keeping a log of inappropriate behaviors throughout the day. This could easily have been done since Marisa had her own one-to-one aide. I wrote to the school psychologist expressing my concerns.

The school psychologist called to assure me that the staff was working as a team to collect the data and that they had a plan in place. However, he did not answer my questions about why it had taken so long to get started. I could only assume that because the FBA process was new, the staff did not know how to go about gathering the necessary data without the consultant.

In spite of my concerns, some good things were happening. Marisa was interested in playing with some girls in another class during lunchtime recess. The teacher decided that it might be a good idea to have Marisa spend time in the other students' classroom for social interaction. I felt this was a positive step in the right direction.

At the end of April I decided to call the school psychologist to find out how the FBA was progressing and if the OT evaluation had been completed. I was hoping that all the information would be ready before my upcoming CSE (Committee on Special Education) meeting for Marisa on May 18th. I was happy to hear that the data was being gathered and the OT evaluation had been done.

The OT therapist made recommendations that would possibly reduce some of Marisa's problem behaviors. She noted that Marisa needed frequent break times to burn up some of her excess energy. It was also noted that she was sensitive to the sounds around her and the lights in the classroom. These difficulties were recorded in the functional behavior assessment, and it was hoped that the occupational therapy suggestions and services would solve some of the problems, thereby avoiding unnecessary disciplinary action against Marisa.

The autism consultant also suggested the use of script cards that Marisa could use to help her express her needs more clearly. This was one of the techniques that the teacher at Variety Preschooler's Workshop had used. I felt that this would work well with my suggestion to use written scripts to clarify the day's routine and social stories to help get through special situations. Once the autism consultant explained this to the teacher, the written script cards became a useful and regular classroom tool.

In the meantime, I noticed that Marisa was developing some new skills. She took an interest in maps and the globe and spent much time enjoying a map of the United States and exploring how to get to various places. She had also learned to tie her shoes at school, which I considered a major milestone.

Only two students from the class attended Marisa's ninth birthday party because, sadly, many of the parents didn't want to be bothered. Since the children attending Marisa's school came from many different school districts, parents would have to travel at least 30 minutes or more to get to our home. Some parents either didn't have a car available or just didn't want to take the time. However, three other friends Marisa had made over the years came to celebrate with us. It was a beautiful day, so we held the party outside. The children had pizza and did a stained-glass-window craft project. We had a peanut hunt in the grass, and children took turns on an air pogo that we hung from a tree. The air pogo, a bouncing swing, was a big hit as the children lined up to take turns trying it. Although it was a small group, it was a lot of fun for everyone. Once again, Marisa was so excited to have her friends come celebrate her birthday!

After the party, Ariel, another girl from the class, arrived. Her mother had gotten lost and finally found her way to our home. Marisa and Ariel played together for a while, and Marisa opened her gifts with Ariel. All in all it was a rewarding and fun day!

The school year came to an end, and Marisa spent a quiet week at home making jewelry and sand art, playing with her new doll, and swimming. Once again, Marisa enjoyed the full day six-week summer session at her school. She then spent a pleasant month at home swimming and getting together with some of her friends. Best of all, she was content and happy!

Chapter Nine

STANDING BY MY CONVICTIONS

On September 9, Marisa started school again. She was moved to a new classroom with her one-to-one aide. I had no way of knowing how fortunate Marisa would be this year to have a new teacher. Her new teacher was a warm and compassionate person, with what seemed to me like an ability to foresee problems before they could escalate. She always seemed to be one step ahead of Marisa. Though she took no credit for her insight and ability to prevent disasters, I felt she had the secret to bringing out the best in her students.

Marisa entered her new class that year with Mutsy, her stuffed dog, hanging on her arm. At the age of nine, Marisa had made Mutsy an extension of herself. She didn't leave the house without him and didn't go to bed at night without him. I informed the teacher that Mutsy would most likely be a regular along with Marisa's backpack each day.

The first day, the teacher sent me a personal welcome note assuring me that Marisa had a wonderful first day at school. Marisa's aide also wrote to tell me that Marisa seemed to have matured over the summer. She informed me that Marisa was consistently greeting people at school beautifully with a smile, a wave, and a "Hi!"

I continued to receive encouraging notes from the teacher. Marisa was choosing to play games with other students during "independent time," as the teacher called it. Marisa also was following directions with few reminders and playing nicely outside with the other children, taking turns and sharing appropriately.

The teacher was pleased to see how quickly Marisa had responded to the new class and new routines.

The teacher also informed me that she had changed Marisa's seat assignment, not because she was being difficult, but because the teacher noticed Marisa enjoyed interacting with another student, Joey. The teacher felt it was important to seat the students near each other to encourage their interaction, giving their friendship a chance to develop.

Another time the teacher noted that Marisa showed concern for another student who got hurt, asking, "Anthony, are you all right?" I was pleased that this teacher was sensitive to the positive little things that happened at school and always made a point of letting me know when something special happened.

Marisa's aide asked me to send in a brush and comb with hair bands, so she could help Marisa style her hair while waiting for the bus or during special break times during the school day. This was an opportunity for Marisa to develop rapport with her aide.

This year I enrolled Marisa in a social skills class at Variety Preschooler's Workshop on Saturday mornings. I felt it would be a good idea to have her socially engaged as often as possible. I also continued her in the Sunday program at Variety Preschooler's Workshop, which was held about once a month. Both these programs gave Marisa the opportunity for social interaction in a safe, controlled environment.

Early in October, Marisa started making a fuss over wearing pants to school. She only wanted to go in shorts, and seeing another student in shorts would only make her more stubborn. She fussed a great deal at school when she went in pants. Marisa's teacher suggested I send in a pair of shorts to leave at school. She felt it wasn't worthwhile to lose valuable work time at school because she was upset over not wearing shorts. I sent in a pair of shorts that Marisa could change into if she wanted to. I also decided to pick up some more fashionable pants for Marisa, hoping this would motivate her to wear pants, as the cooler weather would arrive soon.

I knew that Marisa was developing a very distinct style of her own. She was becoming extremely selective in her choices of clothing. She no longer would wear the hand-me-down hot pink jacket with leopard lining from the year before. I allowed her to browse the catalogs, and she found a blue, down-filled jacket that met with her approval. I realized that I could no longer buy Marisa clothes without her input. Actually, the purchase of the blue jacket was a turning point for Marisa; she needed to select her own clothes, or she just wouldn't wear them. I could see that Marisa was developing an interest in fashion, and had a definite opinion about what she liked.

At school the teacher started journal writing activities with the children; Marisa would get practice writing some of her thoughts down. This was a difficult but important skill for Marisa to work on. Because she was initially unable to write down her own thoughts, I gave her practice in putting sentences together. I had her fill in blanks in sentences I wrote, and sometimes I had her unscramble sentences I wrote for her; I would write the words on pieces of paper for her to move around till she could create a proper sentence. I hoped that in time, this practice would help her learn to create her own sentences in order to put her thoughts on paper.

Early that year we received an invitation to a wedding reception for my cousin's son and his wife, which was to take place at a restaurant called The Water's Edge in Long Island City. Marisa was excited to be included in the invitation to this afternoon event. Although I prepared Marisa for the event by writing a social story and reviewing what would happen at the party, I couldn't be prepared for the unforeseen.

When we arrived, Marisa became overwhelmed with the view of the water and the boat that was docked outside. The restaurant had a wall of windows and doors leading to a deck and boat dock. It was beckoning Marisa! She immediately ran off, vanishing in the crowd of people; we didn't even know where she had disappeared. As I entered the restaurant, I immediately thought it had been a mistake to bring her, and I panicked, not knowing where she had gone. Was she on the boat? Could she have fallen in the water? I couldn't even stop to say hello to any of the guests in our extended family, as thoughts of Marisa in the murky water flashed through my mind.

Then, as quickly as she had vanished, she suddenly rushed in from the outside deck. Before I could stop her to ask her where she had been, she was racing to the kitchen door. In an instant the swinging door opened toward her, knocking Marisa to the floor, where she was left crying. At that point I was able to help her up and escort her away from the door and to a seat, where I hoped to regain some control of the situation.

She didn't seem to be seriously hurt, and she was excited about the boat outside and could think of nothing but going for a boat ride. Unfortunately, I hadn't realized there would be a boat outside the restaurant, and I hadn't included anything about it in my social story. I needed to explain to her that the boat was not part of the party and that I was genuinely sorry I hadn't known about it. I tried to redirect her behavior, reminding her that this was a party, and soon we would hear dance music and be served food. I also reminded her about The American Girl Dress Designer computer program, a goal she was working toward on her home goal chart.

In spite of her screaming and crying for a boat ride, I prayed that she was in some small way still receptive to what I was telling her. Here we were at a family party in a restaurant an hour away from home. I had no real plan but to hope that Marisa would be motivated enough to pull herself together to earn the points toward the reward on her goal chart. Had I put too much faith in my point system? Had I expected too much from Marisa? We were counting on her to show she was mature enough to be trusted at this family gathering. Was this unreasonable? As I thought about the situation we were now embarrassed to be in, Marisa struggled to pull herself together. Then the music began.

Suddenly she was a new person, happy and bubbly and dancing to the music. A great sense of relief came over me as the party music swept Marisa away to join in the festivities on the dance floor. The rest of the party went well. Marisa ate a chicken nugget meal and danced away the afternoon. I let her use our camera to take pictures of some of my cousins.

Then, as the party was winding down, my cousin made a surprise announcement. There was to be a boat ride around Manhattan Island! What a special treat! I thought about how I had managed to help Marisa overcome her tantrum without the promise of a boat ride; I was proud that she had been able to regain control of herself. Now it seemed as though she was being rewarded for a job well done, but it felt more like we were all being rewarded for having given Marisa the chance to prove herself.

We all enjoyed the beautiful ride. As the sun set, casting its rays on the magnificent Manhattan skyline, I became pensive, yet hopeful, as I looked toward the future. I thought, what is life worth if one cannot venture out to be a part of all it has to offer? As daylight grew into darkness, the skyline changed; the lights from the buildings created a beautiful new scene. It was a wonderful ending to a partly nerve-wracking day, but it was fulfilling to know that we had given Marisa the chance to participate fully in this family event. Not only had Marisa earned her points toward her chosen reward, but I felt rewarded, too, that my whole family had been able to share in the joyous occasion.

At school, Marisa's speech was improving. The aide noticed that she would make comments and ask questions at various points in the day. At lunch Marisa would think about something she wanted me to buy and would say to her aide, "I hope Mom goes shopping!" She would also ask her aide at times, "What are you doing?" She was showing more interest in things and people around her and was using her words more to comment and interact.

Marisa's social skills class had not gone as well as in the group she had been in the year before. I was disappointed with the social worker who ran the group. It seemed to me that Marisa was always being used as a scapegoat in the class; the instructor used Marisa's behaviors to point out to the rest of the class what not to do. Surprisingly, at the end of each session, when I arrived to pick up Marisa, the instructor told me what she had done. She seemed to feel it was perfectly okay to use Marisa's inappropriate behaviors as examples for the rest of the group. This was very disturbing to me, so when the semester ended, I wrote a note to the psychologist in charge to let her know about my experience in this group. I felt that although the concept of the social skills class was a good one, much depended on the style of each group instructor. I knew that Variety Preschooler's Workshop valued parent input enough to take my concerns and comments into consideration when planning for future social skills classes.

Rather than enroll Marisa in another social skills class, I decided that I would start taking a more active roll in enforcing social skills on my own. I started to see every event out of the house as an opportunity for her to learn and grow. There could be no better classroom to practice social skills than the real world, and that was what I intended to do.

I started out by making five-by-seven-inch cards mounted in magnetic frames for the refrigerator so that Marisa could see the script I had written. I made a card with our address and phone number so she could learn and share the information with friends at school. I wrote out a phone script for Marisa so she could answer the phone and know exactly what to say and what information to ask. I also added phone messaging to her goal chart, offering her points for answering the phone and taking messages. Later I would expand this goal by adding a point for being able to carry on a phone conversation with someone that she knew, like a grandparent, sister, aunt, or friend. Much later on, as she became proficient at this, I would add the goal of taking written messages, too.

In the beginning I had to prompt Marisa to use the cards on the refrigerator when answering the phone, but with time, she would remember what to say and eventually did not need to refer to the cards. I also wrote scripts for how to have a simple conversation, by listing the way to begin and some topics that are good conversation-starters. I had a refrigerator door full of information, and I would go over the cards and then give examples.

Later, outside the house while waiting for the bus, I would try to engage Marisa in conversation about the weather, what was happening at school that day, or what we would be doing over the weekend. I would even talk about the ants and worms on the ground and the birds flying by. Anything that would make Marisa listen and respond became a topic for conversation. When the bus arrived, I would prompt Marisa to greet the bus driver and the kids on the bus, and when she returned, I would prompt her again to say good-bye appropriately with words such as, "Bye!" or "See you tomorrow!" rather than just a wave.

During the Christmas vacation, I made arrangements for Marisa to meet her old friend Chris at Pizza Hut for a lunch date. Marisa enjoyed sitting at the table with her friend while waiting for the pizza to arrive. Also that week, Marisa attended her friend Erinn's birthday party, which was held in a party place with laser gun shooting as the theme. Although Marisa was happy to be at the party and see Erinn, she was frightened by the laser gun activity and opted to sit it out at the video games, while the rest of the party group proceeded to shoot at each other. It did seem odd to have shooting laser beams at each other as a birthday party theme for nine and ten year olds.

At school, Marisa continued to do well. She participated well in group activities and enjoyed doing math and reading activities on the computer. She also did well on class trips to the farm in October, Safety Town in January, and later to the Garvies Point Museum. I was so pleased with Marisa's progress and assumed that Marisa would have another year in this class. So when I was informed that Marisa was to have her graduation picture taken, I was somewhat surprised.

Children generally move on to middle school at the age of ten, and Marisa was turning ten in June. However, I had hoped that Marisa would be staying at the Jerusalem Avenue School for one more year because I thought that children could stay in the elementary program through their tenth year if they needed more time to mature. I called my school district director of special services to ask her if Marisa could stay at Jerusalem Avenue the next year. I was even more disturbed when she suggested that she preferred to bring Marisa back to the district middle school instead of letting her go on to the middle school BOCES program. Here I was, concerned that Marisa might have to move up to the middle school BOCES, when I was then being informed that BOCES wasn't even being considered. The district director of special services was implying that Marisa was now ready to return to the district program, where she would blend in with the regular population of children.

I wrote to the teacher, who suggested that I find out what the district was offering in terms of services before jumping to any conclusions. I was scared for Marisa. I wanted her to have the advantage of another year with her wonderful teacher.

During the winter break I arranged for Marisa to play with her old friend Brittany from Variety Preschooler's Workshop, but since I was unable to fill every day with planned activities, Marisa got into lots of mischief. One afternoon she ran off onto a neighbor's property. Another time, without asking to do so, she attempted to bake by mixing ingredients together. Also during this vacation, she made phone calls to friends at odd times of the day, without asking. It was hard to keep up with her endless energy level and her growing ability to do things for herself as she strived for independence.

When school resumed at the end of February, Marisa's teacher let me know that my district was going to observe Marisa early in March. A special education teacher, a speech pathologist, and the school psychologist from the district middle school were coming for the observation to decide if Marisa would fit in to the district program. The district also informed me that the director of special services, whom I had known and worked with all the previous years, had retired and was going to be replaced by someone new. Though the position was still not filled, the director who retired had left instructions with the school psychologist to plan for Marisa's return to the district middle school. On the day of the observation, the visitors watched Marisa for thirty minutes and gave no information to the teacher. All I could do was wait anxiously to hear from the district.

In the meantime, I was eager to look at the BOCES middle school but was unable to obtain permission from my district, since there was still no director of special services. Obtaining permission was important since the funds necessary to pay for the BOCES program had to be made available in the school budget. Instead of waiting for a new director to be hired, I decided to try to obtain a tour at the recommendation of Marisa's teacher. I felt that since Marisa was already in a BOCES program, the middle school principal would find the teacher's recommendation to be adequate. I called the Seaman Neck Middle School BOCES and told the secretary that Marisa would be moving up the following year and her teacher recommended that I look at the school.

I managed to get an appointment with the principal to take a tour and answer my questions about the program. I was most concerned about whether there was a reward system in place like at the Jerusalem Avenue School. Although Marisa had difficulty saving up points for larger rewards, she enjoyed earning the points that she could use at the school store. The points charts motivated Marisa, and I was hoping that the middle school had a similar system. I also felt that when things got difficult for Marisa, she should have a safe, quiet place where she could go to calm down.

At the end of March, I visited the Seaman Neck Middle School and met with the principal, who gave me a tour of classrooms and showed me the quiet rooms where children could go if they were having a tantrum or being disruptive. There was even a padded room for children who were possibly angry enough to hurt themselves. The behavior plan was very similar to that of Marisa's current elementary program, so very little about the routine and goals would require any major adjustment. All in all, it seemed an equally nurturing environment to the BOCES elementary program.

Shortly after my visit, I received a call from the special education teacher who had visited Marisa at her class at the Jerusalem Avenue School. She informed me that she found the BOCES classroom to be inadequate, the teaching to be unproductive, and the class setting lacking challenge. I could not believe that she could be so critical of the teacher that I felt to be so gifted.

She suggested I call and visit the district middle school, where Marisa would be placed in the self-contained special education class. I grew angry as she told me that I would be better off getting Marisa out of the BOCES program, where she would only be around disabled children. She really believed that Marisa should be in the regular school, where she would be surrounded mostly by "normal" children who could be better peer models for her. I was quite upset by her abrupt manner, and I reminded her that Marisa, after all, did have a disability that couldn't be ignored. As long as she was going to be placed in a self-contained class of kids with special needs, in the district public school, she would spend most of her day around kids with disabilities anyway, since the opportunity to be included with the regular school population would be limited to lunch and recess and perhaps gym. I stressed that at the BOCES school Marisa had developed a nice network of friends, and she felt good about herself. What could be more important than that to a child who needed to develop social skills more than anything else? However, I agreed to look at the self-contained class at the middle school in my home town.

I spoke with the school psychologist to arrange for my visit to the self-contained class. I told him that if Marisa were placed in their program, I felt it was important to have her try out the new setting for a few days, so they could see what they would have to deal with on a regular basis. Though he understood my concern, the psychologist felt the director would be unlikely to grant my request.

In the meantime, the school district had hired a new director of special services, and I called her to ask permission to not only observe the middle school self-contained class (many of whom would be moving up into high school the next year), but also observe the children in the self-contained elementary school class who would be moving up to Marisa's prospective classroom. Unfortunately, the new director did not give me permission to observe the elementary school class, since it wasn't the class that Marisa would be going into. She did not seem to think there was a good reason for me to see the students that would be Marisa's new classmates. I disagreed, since so much of Marisa's disability was due to her lack of social skills. Interaction with her peers was of prime importance, if she was to make any progress in this area.

I was disappointed by the new director's abrupt behavior and unsympathetic manner. Nevertheless, I had no option but to move ahead with the observation at the middle school. I spoke with the psychologist on April 5 and arranged to visit the following Monday. I planned to bring a list of questions for the teacher and the psychologist. Some of those questions were:

1. *Marisa would require a 1:1 aide on the bus and at school. How were the aides trained for handling autism?*

2. *Marisa would need a twelve-month program. If she were in the district program (which was only ten months), how would the district prepare for the summer months, and where would the continuing education program be held?*

3. *An autism consultant would be a must. How often would the consultant come to visit Marisa in class and offer help to the teacher?*

4. *Could it be arranged for the autism consultant to observe Marisa before a decision was made about her placement in the district program?*

5. *Would it be possible for the autism consultant to make recommendations in advance of placement in the district program or elsewhere if necessary?*

6. *What would be the class size of the self-contained class in the district?*

7. *What was the teacher's background in autism?*

8. *Was there a social skills program in place within the district?*

9. *How would out-of-class specials be arranged, such as speech and occupational therapy?*

10. *Marisa was receiving speech five times a week. Would she still receive these services, which are an entitlement for children with an autism diagnosis, or would scheduling make this unlikely?*

11. *What experience did the speech therapists in the district have with autism?*

12. *What was the age variance of the children in the classroom?*

I showed my list of questions to Marisa's teacher and asked her if she had any to add to the list. She informed me that at BOCES, the age range within a class was no more than two years, though the maximum New York State regulations allowed for a three-year span.

She also added the following questions to my list for the teacher and psychologist:

1. *Is there a Behavior Management Program in place? If so can Marisa self-evaluate since she responds so well to this?*

2. *Is there a structured schedule posted for the children to see?*

3. *Are the children mainstreamed for gym, lunch, etc.?*

4. *What provisions will be in place when Marisa becomes upset, behavior escalates, behavior is out of control, and she has emotional outbursts?*

5. *Do they have an area where she will be able to calm down?*

6. *If mainstreamed, will the levels of academic work be appropriate for Marisa?*

When I visited the school, I brought copies of my list of questions and concerns which I gave to the psychologist and the teacher. Later, I was lucky enough to meet the new director of special services and gave her a list, as well.

During my visit, I was to observe the self-contained class between 9:30 and 11:30 AM. The classroom size was small; there were seven children, but one was absent. The children's range in age was three years, which kept within the guidelines of New York State law.

As I knew, some of these children would move up to the high school for the next year. The psychologist told me that there would be two new female students moving up from the elementary program; these were the students that I wasn't going to get to meet, because the new director of special services would not allow it.

As I sat down to watch the classroom lessons, I continually thought about how Marisa could fit in to this setting. The lesson I observed first was an oral reading lesson. The teacher read a story from a textbook reader, and the children sat quietly, listening from their desks. Periodically, the teacher would stop and ask a question, and she gave the students a chance to record their answers. I envisioned Marisa getting lost during this type of lesson, since she is a visual learner. I could imagine her frustration level rising and see her bolting from the room. After she completed the story, the teacher asked the children for the answers to some questions, and they went over them all together.

The next lesson followed immediately with no physical break time between. I saw this as a potential problem for Marisa, who needed to move around more than these children were. In spite of my concern over the lack of a break or stretch period, I liked the next lesson, which allowed for some play of the imagination. It was a lesson on dialogue, visual cues, and the purpose of quotation marks around what people are saying. The teacher handed out comics for the children to look at and see the bubbles with the dialogue written in. Then she gave out copies of pictures with empty bubbles so that the children could write their own dialogue based on what they saw in the pictures.

At the end of the lesson I checked the clock and realized that the two lessons had taken a total of one hour. The reading and language arts activities were immediately followed by a brief math lesson. Once again there was no break time between the lessons. The math lesson was a review of geometry terms the class had been working on. The teacher and students reviewed the material, and the teacher informed the class there would be a test on Wednesday. It was 11 AM when the teacher told the class to study on their own while she spoke to me. Then at 11:30, the class went out on their own to various "specials" such as gym and music. There were no aides to escort anyone.

I left the room to meet with the psychologist, to whom I expressed my many worries.

I was concerned about the lack of space in the room, the absence of breaks for stretching, the lack of a place to handle unpredictable eruptions of problem behaviors, and the teacher's lack of training in autism. I did not see any problem behaviors with any of the six children in the class, consisting of one girl and five boys. They were all well-behaved children but slow in academic areas, and many of the children appeared to be Hispanic, so I wondered how many of them were there because of language barriers.

As I was talking with the psychologist in the hallway, the new director of special services was walking by, and I was fortunate enough to be introduced. This was a lucky break! I felt it was fortunate to have this unexpected opportunity to meet and talk with her. I expressed my concerns to her about how much integration into the mainstream Marisa would actually be getting in this setting. It didn't seem to me that she would have much of an opportunity for mixing with the general population. I also didn't see her as a candidate for mainstreaming for lunch, which would probably be overwhelming because of the noise and large numbers of students in the cafeteria at once. I then expressed my concerns about the lack of space and Marisa's need to release excess energy periodically. I told her that it was unlikely that Marisa would be able to sit quietly for one and a half hours of straight work. I let her know that Marisa would need a safe, quiet place to go if she was having a difficult time or was exhibiting out of control behaviors.

The director remained insensitive to my concerns and chalked them up to my fear of a new environment. Yet she did not know Marisa, had never even met her, and I knew she was treading on dangerous ground. She had no idea how Marisa's autism could affect her behavior and how difficult it could be to manage an outburst once it occurred. I suggested to her that she go visit Marisa for herself and if possible bring an autism consultant with her. I told her that she might also benefit by visiting the BOCES middle school to see for herself what provisions they had for children with difficult and sometimes out-of-control behaviors. I suggested she consider the BOCES program for Marisa's special needs.

She looked over my list of concerns as we stood in the hall. She seemed to appreciate the effort I had put in to expressing my concerns. She then assured me that no matter what happened, Marisa would stay at BOCES for the summer. I later realized that she offered that to me only because the district didn't provide a summer program anyway. She ended her conversation with me by saying, "Let's not worry long term, because a lot happens in one year, and Marisa may not need a summer program next year." When I heard that, I was sure that she had made up her mind to bring Marisa back to the district no matter what. I was worried and annoyed; this woman didn't even know my daughter and had made the baseless assumption that she wouldn't need a twelve-month program next year.

At this point I was determined to fight for Marisa to stay at BOCES. This was my child, and I knew that she was not a good candidate for the in-district, self-contained class. Surely this could not be the most ideal setting for a student with autism who was bright but greatly lacking in social skills. I went home to write a letter to present at the CSE meeting. The director of special services remained noncommittal about Marisa's placement, and was leaving a final decision for the CSE meeting at the end of the year. I knew that if I didn't have my case prepared well for Marisa to stay at BOCES, I would most likely find Marisa placed in the district with little if any classroom support. I also was going to insist that Marisa be given a trial period at the district school if the committee decided to place her there.

I waited till after the spring vacation to call the district office for follow-up. I was anxious to know if any steps had been taken in planning for the next year. The director called me back early in May. I was relieved to hear that she was going to arrange to see Marisa for herself but wanted to try to get the district autism consultant to go with her. She informed me that she did not have a date set yet. I reminded her that I was concerned about Marisa being in the district self-contained class, because I didn't think Marisa would have many opportunities for integrating with the regular kids, since she still had many difficult behaviors to deal with. She did not agree, though she hadn't met Marisa yet. Nevertheless, I was relieved to know that she was planning a visit with an autism consultant.

The district visit was arranged for May 9. The day before, I watched Marisa sit quietly on a pool tube, as she seemed to be deep in thought. Then she announced, "I'm weird!" I wondered where this was coming from and assumed that she must have overheard talk at school regarding the upcoming district visit to see Marisa. Still, I wondered how she had come up with this word to describe herself, though I couldn't believe she could have heard it from the caring staff at her school. I was somewhat bothered by this but realized that she could have picked up the word from another child on the bus. Though there was a driver assistant on Marisa's bus, the other children on the bus who attended area private schools, were intolerant of Marisa's differences, frequently making fun of her and provoking responses from her. Marisa interpreted such behaviors as friendly, because her autism prevented her from having a clear understanding of what the other children were doing.

The day of the visit I received a notice from Marisa's teacher. She informed me that the visit lasted from 9:30 to 11:30. The teacher had spent time speaking to the director from my district and the consultant she brought with her. They observed Marisa during an individual lesson and a group lesson. They had an opportunity to speak to the BOCES school psychologist and the speech teacher who had been working with Marisa for three years. The classroom teacher expressed the importance to them of actually viewing Marisa in the district setting, since it would give them a better idea of how Marisa functioned.

I was happy to know that the observation was over a two-hour period and that the autism consultant had been there. This seemed like a much more thorough observation than the one that had been done previously for thirty minutes by the special education teacher and psychologist from the district.

While all this was going on, Marisa continued to do well and remained happy at school. She enjoyed greeting friends in the hallway, could be seen walking hand in hand with girlfriends on the playground, and was enjoying participating in the school show, the book fair, and school entertainment events arranged for the students.

Around the middle of May I spoke with the director of special services. She remained undecided, though she still seemed to think Marisa would have better socialization opportunities at the district school. I still strongly disagreed, mainly because they were planning to place Marisa in the self-contained class, not in an inclusion class. If Marisa had been a good candidate for an inclusion class, perhaps I would have felt differently about the district placement, but because of her distractibility and angry outbursts at times, I knew this was not to be an option.

She suggested that we would have to "brainstorm at the CSE meeting," which was to be held on May 30th at my school district's administration building. I wanted to be sure that Marisa's teacher would be able to attend rather than participate by phone conference, so I got in touch with her immediately. I felt that her presence was important, although I was planning to write up my own presentation as well. I was happy to hear that the teacher had arranged to come to the meeting with the assistant principal to back up what she had to say regarding Marisa staying in the BOCES program. I was grateful to know that two representatives from BOCES would be in attendance at the meeting. I almost felt like I was preparing for trial in a court of law.

In the midst of this very anxious time, I received a note from Marisa's teacher that was sweet and touching and made me smile.

> *I have to share a dialogue I overheard between Marisa and Joey: Marisa went over to Joey and gave him a hug. She then said, "I like your shirt, Joey!" "Thank you!" Joey said. Marisa waited for Joey to comment on her shirt. When Joey didn't comment, Marisa said, "Do you like my shirt?" Joey said, "I like your shirt." Marisa said, "Thank you!" Then Marisa said, "I like your shoes!" Joey said, "Thank you!" Then they hugged.*

This was such a cute story. It was nice to know that Marisa was using compliments to engage herself in a conversation, and I was sure that the scripts I had placed on the refrigerator at home had some influence on this interaction. I did suspect, though, that Marisa was also very envious of Joey's Pokemon shirt and shoes, which she had informed me Joey had. Marisa had become a great fan of Pokemon and wanted Pokemon apparel just like Joey's.

The teacher continued to send encouraging reports in regard to Marisa's use of words to communicate with her friends in a spontaneous way. She was becoming more comfortable in her use of language to convey her thoughts and feelings with her classmates, and she was learning to engage in conversations with those around her.

At the end of May, Marisa was asked to participate in the Color Guard for a special assembly. In the past, when asked, she had been hesitant, but she was more willing to participate in the practice sessions now, and I was told she did beautifully during the final ceremony. The twenty-five participants walked to the front of the auditorium, some holding flags and singing a song. Marisa did well following along with the other students involved. I told Marisa that I heard she did a great job, and we were all so proud of her. I grabbed every opportunity I could to compliment Marisa on a job well done; I felt this was important for building self-esteem. The year Marisa had spent in this class had provided so many positive experiences and opportunities for Marisa to feel good about herself. I feared that all this was about to come to an abrupt end.

Memorial Day weekend was quite successful from a socialization standpoint. Marisa enjoyed participating in Deborah's sixteenth birthday party, eating and swimming with Deborah's friends. The next day we took a trip out to Walden, New York to a barbeque at Dan's cousin's one-hundred-year-old farmhouse on fifty acres of land with a pond, a pool, walking trails, and a huge trampoline. Marisa had a terrific afternoon, swimming, jumping on the trampoline with other kids at the party, and even going on a boat ride.

At this time we were also getting ready for Marisa's tenth birthday party. We got the invitations ready, and Marisa distributed them at school. She invited everyone in her class and also invited other students from outside the class that she had become friendly with. I had always thought that the list of friends would dwindle with age, but Marisa was showing me that she had actually increased her scope of friendships by using her newly acquired conversational skills.

When May 30 arrived, I attended Marisa's CSE meeting with copies of a letter I had composed to hand out at the meeting. I walked in and distributed my letter before anyone had a chance to speak. I waited and watched the faces of the people around me at the meeting. The district psychologist was smiling and shaking his head. The director of special services read my letter with great concern on her face. The letter I composed was direct, to the point, and too true to be ignored:

> *My only real concern is for Marisa's well-being. Her emotional, social, and educational needs are primary in where she goes to school. I know that we are all interested in the same things, but being closest to Marisa, I feel that she will be best served in a well supervised, protected environment that is nurturing and will enable her to have the greatest opportunity for mingling with her peers.*
>
> *Because Marisa has a serious social deficit, she will be open to dangerous situations, where she is likely to be victimized by her peers. Marisa is totally unaware of the social cues from others that would help her to be better accepted, and the result*

is that she has been subjected to kicking, punching, biting, and verbal abuse from others on her school bus, much of which has been provoked by her own behaviors. In spite of it, Marisa does not understand what these behaviors really mean and interprets them in her own way, as acceptable social interactions.

Marisa also has sensory difficulties, which will draw much negative attention to her. Lights and sounds will cause her to walk through halls shielding her eyes and covering her ears. Hallway noise may cause her to jump up unexpectedly to check on things going on outside her classroom. She may also proceed to touch and check over other children's clothing. These behaviors will inevitably lead to a quick rejection of Marisa by all the other students in the school, and will place her in a very isolating environment.

Marisa also does not understand potentially dangerous situations. She may dart in front of a bus suddenly, approach strangers, walk off at will, and be taken advantage of by others. Although I myself have a strong background in teaching, with a Master of Science in Early Childhood Education, and many years experience in being cued in to dangerous situations, even I could not prevent the things that occurred over the years that placed Marisa in harm's way. Methodically sneaking, flashlight in hand, into the attic crawl space and falling through our ceiling, pouring cooking oil into the fireplace, thinking all she needed was to find the matches to start a fire, quietly leaving the house to walk down a main road to wait for her sister's return from a trip, are just some of the things she has done that are not surprising and are so typical in the life of this autistic child. Marisa is extremely self-reliant, and the result is that she will pursue whatever plan of action she believes makes sense to her. In Marisa's mind, there is always a very logical reason for what she wants to do, but usually the dangerous things she does are things that the rest of us would not even consider until it is too late.

Because of all these concerns, I believe that Marisa's best interests can only be served in a carefully guarded environment that is nurturing and peer friendly. The public schools are a wonderful place to be, if you are a typical kid. I presently have one daughter in the high school who is happy and doing well, and one daughter who has graduated and is currently a senior in college. Marisa, however, would best be served in a program where there is some choice of class placement that would be more likely to meet Marisa's social and emotional needs. This is not possible in the district school if Marisa is placed in the one and only self-contained class available to her. Marisa also would have a greater opportunity for varied social interactions in a program where she has more choice for mixing with her peers. The goal should be to broaden her social circle, through careful social-skill planning incorporated into her other educational goals. It is highly unlikely that this will occur in the district classroom, where Marisa will inevitably become the school outcast because of her many social, sensory, and emotional difficulties.

After everyone read my letter, the rest of the committee members were given an opportunity to talk. Marisa's teacher and the assistant principal spoke in support of my concerns. At the end of the meeting, the director spoke, addressing everyone in the room. I could barely breathe as I listened to what she said. "The school district is not mandated by law to provide the best education, but is only required to provide an education that adequately is able to meet the needs of the student. From what I have gathered, I do not think that the school district will be able to do so at this time."

She also informed me that the school district was not prepared to give Marisa a trial period at the school to see how things would go, even though the autism consultant felt that it would be a good idea.

After taking all the information into consideration, she decided that the BOCES program would best serve Marisa's needs. She also decided that Marisa would start the summer program at the middle school BOCES, so there would be less of an adjustment to deal with in September. Marisa would continue to have a one-to-one aide, five days of speech services, and two days of occupational therapy at her new school. I left the meeting greatly relieved, feeling a heavy burden had been lifted off my shoulders, and Marisa's teacher agreed that the decision was a good one, greatly influenced by the "powerful words" of my letter.

Marisa was happy and attentive during this time. She was excited about her upcoming tenth birthday and was more talkative and spontaneous with her classmates than ever. One boy in the class told Marisa that he couldn't come to the party because it was too far. Marisa looked at him and replied, "I'm sorry!" When Marisa's aide was out one morning and arrived at noon, Marisa greeted her by saying, "Hi, Mrs. G., I missed you so much!"

Marisa's school made many preparations for the transition to the Seaman Neck Middle School BOCES. A school psychologist came to observe and meet Marisa. It was an opportunity to gather information and plan for her arrival in the summer. Another step in planning for moving up to the middle school involved making arrangements for the graduating students to visit the new building to hear what the principal had to say and take a tour of the building. I thought this was a wonderful opportunity for Marisa to see what her new school would be like. Marisa, however, did not want to go on the visit, because she didn't want to miss a day of school at Jerusalem Avenue. To alleviate the problem, the teacher introduced Marisa to another girl who was also going on the trip to tour the new school. This made Marisa feel more comfortable and willing to participate in the activity.

At home, Marisa continued to do surprising and disturbing things,which just made me think about the letter I had written for my CSE meeting. I realized how very frightening and real the things I said were. One day, Marisa walked out of the house twice, once disappearing into a neighbor's yard. When she returned, she said, "No one was home. I missed you! I lost myself!" She thought this was funny. I looked at her and thought she must have been ringing the neighbor's doorbell or looking in the backyard door and then she realized how alone she was. Perhaps she knew how strange it was to have been away from the house and not have a soul in sight.

I knew that scolding Marisa didn't seem to help in these kinds of situations. Marisa would just look at my angry face and start to laugh at my expression. In her eyes, the angry expression on my face would be funny. I found that the only way to impress the seriousness of the situation on her was to remove all her points on her goal chart. Marisa needed to learn that some things were just too dangerous to do again, and this was one of those things. Marisa's increasing ability to do things was placing her in greater danger. Marisa was able to open the door that did not require a key. I needed her to learn that just because she could open the door, it didn't mean she should do it without asking.

Another day, Marisa decided to spin the brightly colored Tiffany lamp hanging low over the kitchen table. I could only assume that she wanted to see how the colors would blend as it turned. I quickly stopped her. She then disappeared out of the kitchen, though without my knowledge, she had headed for more trouble.

I had failed to foresee the impending danger in spite of always reminding myself to expect the unexpected. It hadn't occurred to me that she might do something similar in another room. Unfortunately, that is just what happened. Marisa had climbed up on a chair to spin the heavy, thirty-six-inch diameter crystal chandelier. All of a sudden there was a deafening crash.

Dan and I rushed into the dining room to find Marisa standing open mouthed on the chair with the chandelier on the dining room table, a smashed bowl beneath it. Crystals had fallen off and dispersed, and glass was all around from the bowl that had shattered. There were huge gashes in the wood dining room table where the enormous chandelier had fallen. Fortunately, Marisa appeared to be unharmed. I tried to move the chandelier, but I realized that I couldn't, because it was enormous in size and weight.

After removing Marisa from the room, I cleaned up as much glass as I could. Later Marisa laughed while thinking about the incident, which didn't seem to have alarmed her in any way. She found it funny, and the more she thought about it, the more she laughed. Even two hours later, she went off to bed laughing. I couldn't be upset about this, because I understood that Marisa had no concept of how much she could have been hurt; she was most likely replaying the scene over and over in her mind and apparently found this to be quite humorous.

We took the chandelier to a welder to fix one of the arms that had broken off in the fall and then called an electrician in to hang it much higher up on the ceiling, so that Marisa could not reach it. The electrician informed us that the thread for such a heavy chandelier had been dangerously inadequate. That was the reason why it had fallen, though he warned us that even with a good thread, a chandelier should not be spun around. He added an attachment to ensure its future safety.

Early in June, Marisa snuck out of the house, once again going across to my neighbor's backyard. This time the neighbor was home and was upset to have Marisa in her yard. It didn't occur to her to pick up the phone and call me, as I frantically ran around calling out for Marisa. Then she heard me and appeared from her yard with Marisa following. She was angry and insisted that I was going to eventually sue her when my daughter drowned in her pool. We stood in the middle of the road as she went on and on about how she shouldn't have to deal with kids anymore since hers were now grown up.

I didn't understand why she was so upset but attributed it to the fact that Marisa was not a typical kid and probably appeared strange to her. I tried to reason with her; I told her that Marisa was a good swimmer and wasn't going to drown in her pool. I asked her why she didn't just call me to tell me that Marisa was in her yard, but she wasn't willing to listen to anything I had to say. Then she went so far as to suggest I have an invisible fence company for dogs install an invisible fence mechanism in Marisa. Marisa, in the meantime, just stood there laughing at the neighbor, because the angry face she saw just looked funny to her. I tried to explain this to my neighbor because I didn't want her to think Marisa was deliberately being disrespectful, but I was angered by the remark she had made as well, and I realized how ignorant and self-centered this woman was. The situation was going nowhere, so I finally said I would do my best to prevent a recurrence in the future.

At around this time, I was extremely nervous about the weekend Dan and I were planning to spend at The Plaza Hotel in Manhattan; I was desperately afraid Marisa would leave the house while in Shoshana's care. I promised Marisa that if she was very good and stayed away from the neighbor's yard, I would reward her with the Eloise doll that she had requested. Fortunately, all went well, and Marisa was happy to receive her new doll.

We celebrated Marisa's tenth birthday on June 17. Marisa had another terrific day for her party, which we held outside. The eight children who attended had pizza and decorated doorknob signs, listened to music, had a candy hunt, and enjoyed the sprinkler. It was a fun day for all the kids. I enjoyed watching the children interact and felt saddened by a message Shoshana had taken for me earlier that week. One child's mom had called to say she wouldn't bring her daughter, because she hadn't taken her to any other parties and didn't want to start now. How sad it was to think that the little girl had lost an opportunity for socializing in a natural setting.

Another child, whose mom was nervous and hesitant to come, attended the party only to start out by having trouble getting her son to leave the car. As he sat in the driveway, he could hear the voices of the other children and see them moving around. Something must have clicked for him, and he finally left the safety of his car and decided to join the group. His mother was so happy that he was able to participate in the activities and had a good time. She felt it was a successful day for her son and later called to thank me. I fully understood how she felt as I reflected on memories of both my own failed party experiences and triumphs.

Graduation day came, and Marisa participated very well with the other students. It was nice to see how patiently she was able to stand through the long ceremony. It was sad to say good-bye to Jerusalem Avenue School, but because of all the BOCES preparations for students graduating to the middle school, Marisa seemed happy, excited, and willing to be moving on.

On July 6 Marisa started the summer program at Seaman Neck Middle School BOCES. I wrote a note to the new teacher, as I always had done before. I informed the teacher about Marisa's stuffed dog companion; I said that although Mutsy would be fine spending his day in a cubby, it was imperative that he not get lost or left at school. I dreaded to think what kind of reaction Marisa would have if he didn't come home with her one day. I also informed the teacher that Marisa did well with written scripts and schedules and that she self-evaluated (was able to keep her own record of points she earned for good behavior) well on a behavior plan.

In the meantime Marisa had developed a crush on a boy named Conan at Jerusalem Avenue Elementary School. She had been sad that he was going to be attending the south shore BOCES middle school. Marisa was attending the north shore BOCES middle school, which was decided, based on where the students lived. When Marisa realized that the south shore students were going to attend the north shore school for the summer program only, she was so excited, because she knew she would see her friend Conan.

When Conan came to Seaman Neck, Marisa became so preoccupied that all she could think of was seeing him. She would run out of her room to find him, chase after him during a fire drill, and, in general, ignore all rules if he was within her view. The aide devised a plan to help Marisa control her impulsiveness to run after Conan every time she saw him. The chart the aide devised required Marisa to earn ten stars for working well between Monday and Wednesday. After earning the ten stars, Marisa would get to spend time with Conan on Wednesday afternoon, and if she earned her ten stars for working well on Thursday and Friday, she would get to spend time with Conan again on Friday afternoon. This chart seemed to work well for Marisa, who was able to check her progress and look forward to reaching her goal. It was nice to see how quickly Marisa's summer teacher and aide had come up with such a successful behavior plan. I was happy about their solution.

Marisa seemed to adjust to the idea that she could look forward to seeing her friend Conan two afternoons a week, but something positive evolved out of the limited times they spent with each other. Conan drew pictures and wrote notes to Marisa, and she did the same for him. Marisa drew beautiful cards and was able to write simple notes with my quidance. She would tell me what she wanted to say and I would write it out for her to copy. This was great practice in letter writing. The correspondence continued through the summer.

During that summer the class took trips to Garvies Point, Cedar Creek, and Fun Zone. They also went bowling, took walking trips to the ice cream parlor, and went to a town park for swimming on a weekly basis. The trips went well and were basically uneventful. It was a full and happy summer for Marisa. She had reading, math, speech, and OT in the mornings and enjoyed afternoons filled with special events, trips, and hands-on projects. The summer program was bursting with activity! It was a wonderful way to transition in to her new school.

Chapter Ten

DISAPPOINTMENT

On September 7 Marisa went off to her new school with a note I had written for the teacher. Although Marisa spent the summer at Seaman Neck Middle School, the summer staff was not the same as the staff during the year. The note I sent was somewhat long, showing signs of being an overly concerned mother.

I thought I would include some information that may be helpful in as brief a way as possible:

1. *Marisa has always taken her stuffed dog Mutsy to school. To this day she cannot be convinced to leave him home, though she usually leaves him in her cubby. She may periodically ask where Mutsy is for reassurance.*

2. *Marisa has become obsessed with a boy she met during graduation rehearsal at the Jerusalem Avenue BOCES. His name is Conan, and he was in the summer program at Seaman Neck with Marisa. The summer teacher found it helpful to create a point system, where Marisa was able to earn visiting time with her new friend twice a week. If he is in the school, this technique may be helpful to you also.*

3. *Visual cues, activity schedules, and social stories work well for Marisa. She will be better able to maintain self-control if she knows her own schedule or plan written for her to follow.*

4. *Marisa is set on wearing shorts until the weather doesn't permit. I did buy her new pants that she likes, and hopefully she will come around and wear her pants like everybody else.*

I did not receive a response from the teacher the first day, and when she did respond, it was only to thank me for the information and inform me that she hadn't written because the first day was so hectic. I knew this had to be true, but hoped that the teacher had not just glanced at and then forgotten my tips.

As time went on, I suspected that the teacher had not taken what I had to say seriously or given my advice the least bit of consideration in planning how to deal with Marisa's difficult behaviors. I strongly believe that because of this, Marisa's behavior took a turn for the worse.

Every day at lunch she wanted to search the lunchroom for Conan. When she was not allowed to leave her seat she became angry, jumping out of her seat and punching the air. Rather than having the one-to-one aide help Marisa navigate in the lunchroom to find a friend to hang out with or bring some after-lunch activities from the classroom, the teacher opted to have Marisa escorted out of the lunchroom by the principal, to eat alone with her aide in the classroom.

This way of handling the problem was a big disappointment to me and was not in any way going to help Marisa meet new friends, thereby diverting her thoughts away from Conan. The teacher simply informed me that the target behavior of "social/emotional" adjustment came right from the IEP (Individual Education Program). However, it was clear to me that this way of handling the problem was not going to accomplish a healthy solution, nor was it going to help Marisa achieve the very general goal, "social/emotional adjustment," in any way. I could not understand how a special education teacher could not see this.

Although there was a general goal chart for all students, the teacher did not set up an individual positive behavior plan for Marisa, as I had suggested. I had hoped that the teacher would follow my advice to address Marisa's specific goals, so she could self-evaluate and be responsible for her own behaviors, as she had done during the summer and at her other school. I was deeply concerned, because I felt that the teacher was disregarding all the hard work from the years before. The teacher was ignoring my parental input as well as the recommendations of the teacher from the year before.

Not only was I frustrated, but I also sensed great frustration on Marisa's part. The one-to-one aide she had for three years was no longer with her, and all the positive efforts of the teacher from the year before now seemed lost at the new school. I wondered why things had gone so well in the summer and then turned so disruptive now. I knew the answer to that was simply because of the sensitive planning of the teacher during the summer session.

I realized that although Marisa was upset about missing her special friend, so many of the behavior plan techniques that worked before were being ignored.

Nobody was willing to help Marisa sort out her feelings. When she wanted to look around the lunchroom, she most likely wanted to confirm that her friend wasn't there, but she wasn't being allowed to do that. Considering that Marisa had her own one-to-one aide, she should have been given the chance to at least look around. The teacher did not understand what behaviors led up to the outbursts of anger, which was only going to result in creating more anger, thereby escalating the problems.

Although I made numerous suggestions, the teacher continued to disregard my ideas. When Marisa came home each day, I tried to learn from her description of the day where things were going wrong. Marisa told me that she wanted to sit on the other side of the lunchroom with a group of girls she knew. I explained to the teacher that Marisa's aide in her previous school frequently escorted Marisa to other lunchroom tables, where she could engage in appropriate social interactions with other girls. The teacher abruptly told me that Marisa was expected to eat and play at her own class's lunchroom table.

I realized that the school aides' time was being wasted on policing their students. Although I also tried suggesting the use of board games at lunchtime or gel pens to spend time drawing after lunch, the teacher insisted that she would not allow any classroom supplies to leave the classroom, even though Marisa had a one-to-one aide with her. This made no sense to me. As a result, the principal and teacher decided that the best way to handle the problems in the lunchroom would be to have Marisa eat her lunch in the classroom with the one-to-one aide on a permanent basis.

This made me angry. Marisa would be learning nothing about interacting with other students at a time of the day that was specifically meant for that. I did suggest that a functional behavior assessment be done to evaluate why Marisa was causing so much trouble in the lunchroom. I also suggested that an autism consultant would be helpful in planning a healthier solution. The teacher said she would talk to the principal about it. However, I never received any indication of follow up in this regard. Furthermore, the director of special services in my district didn't seem to think there was anything wrong with what the teacher was doing. I was not only angry, but at this point I felt helpless and alone.

In the meantime, I tried to be understanding of the way the teacher was handling things, though I continued to make suggestions that were ignored. I sent many notices about conferences on autism and handling difficult behaviors, because I hoped that the teacher would take advantage of them. Each time I did so, she would thank me and tell me that someone else in the school was already going.

One day, the teacher informed me about a problem they were having getting Marisa to sit with her feet on the floor. Because she was sitting on her feet, it was difficult for her to sit still at her desk. I suggested that perhaps the OT could make a recommendation. It seemed to me that there had to be a reason why Marisa was sitting on her feet. Fortunately, in this case, the teacher did take my advice. As it turned out, the OT found that Marisa's legs were too short to reach the floor comfortably. By simply adding a footstool, the problem was solved.

Although I was happy that a solution had been found for the sitting problem, other problems continued to arise that I felt were not handled in a healthy and productive way. For example, when the class went outside for a walk, Marisa would start walking faster and faster, until she would suddenly take off and run away from the class. I knew all too well how Marisa was capable of running off, a behavior that for a long time had prevented me from taking her to public places. I also knew that the way the teacher was handling this was doing nothing to correct the problem. When such an incident would occur, Marisa was immediately sent to the "Thinking Room" at school as a consequence for bad behavior. Unfortunately, sitting in a room with her aide did nothing to correct the problem, because when she was given the opportunity again, she would engage in the same behavior of bolting. Likewise, when Marisa was given a chance to sit in the lunchroom, and she would grab at another child's toy, the aide would again have her removed from the lunchroom rather than finding a way to redirect her. It was obvious to me that the Thinking Room was not solving anything, and being removed from the lunchroom didn't solve anything, either. Marisa was learning nothing from these isolating punishments, and I could not understand why nobody else realized this.

During that year, I rarely heard of a solution to a problem that was a positive, productive one. Instead of replacing a bad behavior with an acceptable one, as was the goal of a functional behavior assessment, the teacher and aide continued to handle Marisa's unacceptable behaviors by removing her from the situation and sending her to the Thinking Room. In the Thinking Room Marisa was expected to identify what she did wrong, and, with the aide's assistance, come up with a solution. The problem with this was that the aides dictated the solutions which were not student motivated. Like Marisa, it is also doubtful that any of the staff was willing to understand the underlying reasons for the problem behaviors of any of the students. I began to wonder if I was wrong to have placed Marisa in the BOCES program.

The problems at school only made me more determined to find a way to integrate Marisa more in community settings and to make things work better at home. I hoped that social outings would at least give Marisa some practice on how to behave better at school. I decided to take Marisa out to the mall for new shoes, but before we went, I wrote a short social story. I also wrote a list of rules on a card for her to hold and review before the trip. It was my own little experiment. As scary as a trip to the mall seemed to me, I was determined to see if I could somehow come up with a way to make it a success. The rules I wrote were very specific:

1. Stay with mother.

2. Walk, don't run.

3. Only talk to people you know, not strangers.

Marisa reviewed and read her rules again just before we got out of the car. Then each time I saw something that might cause her to run away from me in curiosity, I reminded her to stay with me. A baby crying in a stroller, a child the same age as Marisa, or apparel that she wanted a closer look at all had potential for causing problems. By prompting her to stay close to me, I was hoping to prevent an incident before it had the chance to occur. Knowing the kinds of things that were likely to provoke Marisa was helpful in this regard. The result was that the trip went well. Marisa knew the rules from her card, and I reminded her of the proper behavior throughout the trip.

In spite of the fact that the mall was filled with busy weekend shoppers, I was delighted that things went as well as they did. I wrote to the teacher, telling her what I had done, and I suggested to her that she write out a card of rules for Marisa before they took one of their walks outside the school again. I did not get a response from the teacher and began to feel that she resented my suggestions.

I was pleased with my new approach to community outings but was not at all prepared for what was to happen in the security of our own home. One weekend at the end of September, Marisa and I were baking chocolate-chip cookies. It was a fun activity, and I thought I had her engaged well. However, while I was mixing the cookie dough with the electric mixer, Marisa went off to the bathroom. So I thought. When I turned off the mixer a couple of minutes later, Marisa had still not returned. I went to check the bathroom, and to my dismay, I realized that she was not there.

I ran through the house calling and looking for Marisa. When I realized she was nowhere to be found, I checked the back door, the only one in the house that didn't require a key. My heart sank down to my feet when I saw that the door had been opened; I realized Marisa had left the house. Our house alarm, though off at the time, did have a warning signal for when doors were opened. However, I had not heard it because of the noise from the electric mixer.

I ran out of the house, calling to Marisa, and ran down the driveway to the road. I looked up the road and saw my neighbors standing at the end of their driveway. I asked them if they had seen a little girl. These neighbors were new to the neighborhood, and they didn't know us or who Marisa was, but they mentioned that a little girl had run through their house calling for Conan, and then ran out of the house and up the street. I had to wonder what these neighbors were thinking and how they must have felt as Marisa ran through their house. They seemed to be quite understanding of the situation and were just happy that they at least learned that we were her parents and were going out to find her. Dan went to get the car and managed to find Marisa walking down the middle of the road with Mutsy. When she saw him coming up behind her, she started to run, as if that would prevent him from bringing her home.

When she returned, I reminded her of our rule not to leave the house without permission. I realized that Marisa would very likely disobey this rule anytime she had a motivation strong enough to make her leave the house. I felt she needed to lose all her points on her goal chart because of her inability to recognize the dangerous position she was putting herself in.

Losing her points was extremely traumatic for her. Marisa realized that she was not going to get away with what she had done, and though she was very upset about the point loss, she knew there wasn't much she could do about it. She seemed to show remorse by apologizing and telling us that she won't ever do it again. To help ensure that she would not sneak out of the house again, I decided that for the time being we should always activate the alarm while Marisa was in the house. Hopefully this precaution would prevent a recurrence and therefore prevent any further loss of points on her goal chart.

In the meantime, the teacher let me know that Marisa was now eating in the classroom on a permanent basis rather than joining the rest of the class in the lunchroom and only removing her if there was a problem. I was angry that the teacher had literally given up on trying to work out a solution that would enable Marisa to successfully eat lunch with the other children. Although I wasn't happy about it, I didn't know what to do. I didn't want to complain to the director of special services in my district. After all, I had made such a strong case for wanting Marisa to be in the BOCES program, where I thought they had the ability to handle the difficulties that would arise. I had not taken into consideration that sending Marisa to the Thinking Room would be the staff's solution to most problems. Sadly, the staff were not analyzing problems that arose through the use of functional behavior assessments, which would then be helpful in finding appropriate replacement behaviors.

It was still early in the year, though, and I was willing to give the teacher a chance to get to know Marisa better. I hoped that things would improve, but every day Marisa came home crying to go back to the Jerusalem Avenue Elementary School, where she was understood so well. It became very clear to me that the good results at the other school were due to the teacher's sensitivity, a receptive one-to-one aide, and the teacher's willingness to include me as a team member.

More than ever, I started to realize that I would have to take more responsibility for helping Marisa with her difficult behaviors. Marisa was having some problems on the bus also at this point, frequently jumping out of her seat and distracting the bus driver. I decided to, once again, add a bus point to her home goal chart and asked the matron on the bus to let me know how Marisa was doing on a daily basis. The addition of the bus point seemed to alleviate any minor problems on the bus.

In order to give Marisa the opportunity for more social interaction out of the school setting, I set up an appointment to have her evaluated by the town program for children and adults with special needs, the GAP program. Marisa and I were to meet the evaluator at the local bowling alley where the Saturday GAP bowling group met.

When we arrived, Marisa appeared disappointed as she looked around at the people in the group. Suddenly she started running up and down the length of the bowling alley in front of the lanes. She remained unruly and disruptive, not listening to her sister Deborah, the social worker attempting to do the evaluation, or me. Within five minutes of my arrival, the social worker informed me that Marisa's behaviors were unacceptable for the group. Any person requiring a one-to-one aide to participate could not be accepted, because the program did not have the staffing for such a requirement.

I left the bowling alley angry with Marisa and frustrated with my predicament. How was I to find activities that Marisa could participate in and practice her social skills if I could not manage her behaviors? I thought back to the time we met with the pediatric neurologist who insisted that getting the behaviors under control was the single most important thing we could do for Marisa. At that moment, I knew just how right she was.

Once we were in the car, I sat and thought about what had happened. I started to think about what I had learned about functional behavior assessments as well as what had occurred in the bowling alley. Marisa had walked in to the bowling alley, browsed the group in attendance, and made a decision. That decision was that she didn't want to be with the people that she saw. Many of the participants that day were older teenagers and even adults. Marisa was just ten years old. She wanted to be with children, not adults! At that moment, I suspected that she had deliberately put on a display of bad behavior to get herself rejected from a group she didn't want to be in. I brightened at this thought! Look how smart my daughter was after all! Marisa was taking control of her own life. She was really making choices that made sense to her, not me. Though I was disappointed, I was also happy when I realized this. Then I knew that the GAP was out of the question for Marisa at that time and thought we would try again in a few years when she was older.

In the middle of October the "open school night" notices went home. I couldn't attend the evening meeting but arranged for a daytime meeting instead. When I arrived for the meeting, I learned that the class would soon take a trip to a local pumpkin farm—everyone but Marisa. I was shocked and angry to hear this. I thought back to the time when Marisa first started at Fern Place Elementary School, and her teacher had tried to exclude her from a trip because of her fears of handling Marisa's impulsive, unpredictable behaviors. But that trip had been to a show, which was a much more difficult situation. I let the teacher know how unacceptable her decision was, and I assured her that I would help come up with a plan for making the trip a successful one. I realized then that she had ignored all my notes regarding written scripts, social stories, and goal charts.

I told the teacher that I understood her fears but encouraged her to give Marisa a chance and insisted that she write out the rules for Marisa to review. I also told the teacher that I would give Marisa three bonus points on her home chart if she was good on the trip. I stressed that Marisa should be reminded of the bonus points frequently on the trip. I assured the teacher that with the support of the written rule card, backed up with the promise of bonus points, Marisa was likely to do well. The teacher agreed reluctantly, and I was happy that she was listening to me. The trip did go well, and Marisa came home happy that day, because she knew she had done a good job. It was a rewarding experience for Marisa, her teacher, and her aide.

Although that first trip of the year had gone well, the teacher continued to send me disturbing news. For instance, she had removed Marisa from a show that the children had attended at school, because she was being disruptive by calling out and making noises. Once again, there had been no plan in place to prepare Marisa for attending the show. I wrote to the teacher to explain how Marisa's one-to-one aide in her previous school would take Marisa to meet the performers ahead of time. I reminded her that she should prepare a list of rules for each occasion. I felt that the purpose of the one-to-one aide was being wasted. I once again suggested that an autism consultant from my school district or BOCES would be beneficial in helping to come up with solutions for handling special events. However, the teacher continued to ignore my remarks.

On picture day Marisa had become upset because some of the girls were wearing skirts; she realized she would be having her picture taken in pants when other girls were wearing dresses. Fortunately, in this situation, the teacher realized that simply getting Marisa into a skirt would solve the problem. Once getting our permission by phone, one of the assistants, who lived close by, was able to go home and pick up a skirt that Marisa was happy to wear for the picture. I was pleased, when the teacher informed me that Marisa was satisfied to wear the skirt, and I was glad that a simple solution had prevented a complete meltdown.

The school was preparing a holiday show for December, and Marisa was eager to participate in it. The school needed my permission to have her return to the school for the evening show that was performed for parents to see. However, because Marisa's behaviors during rehearsals remained unpredictable, the teacher decided that she would participate in the day show only, which ordinarily was for the rest of the school to see. I told Marisa that only the older students participated in the evening show, because I didn't want her to know that her teacher did not have faith in her ability to cooperate.

At around this same time, Marisa was being tested each day in speech but was having trouble focusing on the testing material. I decided to offer her bonus points on her home chart if the testing each day went well. I told the teacher to remind Marisa of the bonus points for good listening during the testing and was anxious to see what effect the bonus points would have on her. Because Marisa was motivated to earn the bonus points, she easily remained cooperative throughout the testing period. Then she was happy to receive the extra bonus points as her reward. I was pleased that this plan had worked so well.

It became very apparent to me on the day of the school show that Marisa understood her teacher and aide much better than they understood her. I had sent in a white shirt for the show, as the music teacher had requested. Marisa was preoccupied with Pokemon at the time, and insisted on wearing her Pokemon shirt for school that day, though she agreed with me early that morning to change into the white shirt before the show. When I arrived for the morning show, however, I saw that Marisa was wearing someone else's white shirt. I asked the assistant why Marisa wasn't wearing her own shirt. Her reply was that Marisa said she didn't have one. "What do you mean she doesn't have one?" I said. "I put the shirt in her backpack this morning!" I realized that Marisa had deliberately fooled the aide, because she knew her shirt was in her backpack. The aide went back to the classroom to look in Marisa's bag, and sure enough, there was her white shirt. Marisa apparently thought she would be able to wear her Pokemon shirt. I don't know if she was disappointed when the aide presented her with an extra white shirt, because I wasn't there at the time, but Marisa seemed fine when I saw her. The performance went well, and Marisa was happy and proud to be participating with the theatre group.

One afternoon I received a note from Marisa's aide that Marisa had left the building without supervision to go to her bus. The aide informed me that she had reprimanded Marisa for going out unassisted and was to be punished the next day by losing Learning Center time. Learning Center was a "special" during the day for computer programs, and I was angry to think that a day after the infraction, Marisa would have an educational program denied her as a punishment. I wasn't sure that Marisa would understand that this punishment was for something that happened the day before. Reprimanding her at the time with a warning of punishment if it should happen a second time would have been more appropriate, in my opinion. However, the teacher insisted that this was the only subject area in the day that would have an impact on Marisa as a punishment, because it was a favorite for her. I couldn't understand why exclusion from any subject area had to be used as a punishment. Surely not earning points toward the school store, removal of Mutsy, or even denial of snack would have made an impact on Marisa as appropriate punishments. I also felt that any punishment a day late was inappropriate.

Almost half the year had passed, and I was not happy with my communication with the teacher. Although I continued to write suggestions that I knew would be helpful in controlling Marisa's behavior, she ignored much of what I said, and she continued to send negative notes concerning the things Marisa was doing wrong. None of this had happened the year before, when Marisa received much praise and was doing a great deal of self-evaluating.

My director of special services set up a meeting so that I could share my concerns with the teacher and the principal. The director of special services from my school district also attended. At the meeting, the teacher said she was sorry that I felt there was a lack of communication. She said that she hadn't been writing notes because Marisa's behavior had improved, and she didn't feel she needed to let me know. The fact remained that I wasn't hearing about any improved behaviors. To her way of thinking, good behaviors were not worthy of mentioning, and this was a major problem for me. I was a strong believer in rewarding good behaviors, and I wasn't even being told when they occurred. How could I then reinforce them by complimenting Marisa for a job well done?

I informed the teacher that all communication was important to me, whether positive or negative. I also expressed concern that because Marisa was a child with great difficulties in communication, it was important for me to know what was going on each day, so that I could have something to discuss with Marisa about her day. I wanted to be able to ask her about specific things that were happening at school, and I couldn't do that unless I had information about what went on. If there was an assembly, for example, I could ask Marisa what she saw. If she went to Learning Center, gym, or had a fire drill, I could have something to question her about and hopefully be able to initiate some kind of conversation with her. I also needed to know what good things happened at school so that I would be able to apply the points earned for appropriate school behaviors to her home goal chart. There was a whole area of learning to be taken advantage of, and this teacher was stifling it. The teacher then agreed to communicate daily with me.

Although the teacher had insisted that Marisa's behavior had improved, she kept sending notes that Marisa needed continuous refocusing to stay on task. I again suggested that the teacher give Marisa small incentives. An extra bonus point, a special note of a job well done, or even a special activity like polishing nails could be good motivators. This didn't seem to make any impression on the teacher or the aide. I realized how serious the situation was when I received a note about the new sticker system the teacher had devised for Marisa.

Rather than reward the good behaviors, it seemed the teacher was giving more attention to the bad behaviors. Marisa would start out with ten stickers each day, and for every distraction she caused, she would lose a sticker. Marisa was also being given pennies as rewards for each period of the day that she worked well. I could not understand why the "reward" system should focus on the negative instead of the positive. It seemed to me that it would be more appropriate to give a sticker for good behavior rather than take one away for bad behavior. Also, the penny rewards were not a very strong incentive, since pennies could not be traded in for anything of value to Marisa. Marisa quickly lost interest in the penny reward and continued to be distracted, running off hall lines to check on friends in other classes and generally remaining unfocused during classroom time.

I did try discussing the problems with Marisa at home. I decided to try to turn the negative reward system into a positive one for Marisa. I informed her that if she received her full ten stickers for each day, she would earn a bonus point on her chart at home. Our home chart was very important to Marisa, because a set number of points would be rewarded with a gift of her choosing. This incentive had a tremendous impact on her school behavior, and she started to walk beautifully on line in the halls at school, even receiving numerous compliments.

In February a new boy, named Peter, came to the school, and Marisa developed an interest in him. She would try to hug him at school and had to be continually reminded that saying hello and waving would be a more appropriate greeting. She started to talk about this new boy a lot at school, and at home she enjoyed creating pretty greeting cards to give him. I didn't really think much about this at the time. Marisa was just being Marisa. She always liked boys.

Marisa was so infatuated with Peter that one day she came in to school with his name written on her arm in gel pens. She had drawn a design using his name the evening before, and I thought it actually looked quite artistic. Her teacher reprimanded her in a loud voice for writing on her arm, insisting that this was unacceptable. Marisa could not understand this, because the year before, her one-to-one aide encouraged Marisa and her friends to decorate their arms with gel pens during lunchtime recess. Marisa just looked at her teacher and yelled out, "Fuck you!" She then laughed at her teacher's angry reaction. Cursing was not something that Marisa had ever done before. It came as a surprise and caused quite a commotion in the front lobby of the school, as everyone turned to see who said the curse word. Marisa continued to laugh at the teacher's angry expression and yelling. I knew all too well that expressions of anger and loud yelling did not frighten her but rather appeared humorous to her. Marisa's teacher did not understand this; she interpreted it as disrespectful and quickly took action.

She then escorted Marisa to the Thinking Room as a punishment, where she spent the first part of her day. She later had to miss art, because she needed to make up the class work she missed while she was in the Thinking Room. She continued to laugh as she thought about the incident and the chain of events that had followed. The teacher told her that if she continued the behavior, she would miss ice cream. Marisa seemed to be on a laughing spree for the day, so she did miss ice cream.

When she arrived home and I read the note about what had happened, I was extremely upset. I called the teacher. I had seen what was written on Marisa's arm that morning. The fact that she wrote Peter's name with gel pens in an artistic manner had not bothered me. Why had the teacher made such a fuss over this? I asked her about it. It's not as though Marisa wrote curse words on her arm. To make such a fuss over such a silly thing as writing a friend's name was unwarranted and left Marisa confused.

This incident had set off a chain of unfortunate events. The trip to the Thinking Room, the loss of art, and the loss of ice cream all could have been avoided if the teacher had ignored the harmless writing on Marisa's arm. I expressed my annoyance to the teacher, letting her know that if writing a name on one's arm was a problem to the school, then Marisa should have been told in a quiet and nonaccusing way, which most likely would have resulted in a completely different outcome. The teacher actually agreed with me, but I think the curse word took her off guard causing her to over react. When I said to her "Don't you think Marisa was actually right to be angry enough to curse at you?" "Yes," she answered as she then laughed and agreed that it was kind of funny. I wasn't particularly concerned about the cursing because Marisa had never done it before, but I did let Marisa know that it better not happen again if she didn't want to lose a lot more points.

Later in March, Marisa managed to squeeze a phone number out of Peter. She came home all excited and rushed to the phone. Marisa spoke to Peter's mom, who said that Peter was very shy about the idea of talking on the phone. However, his mom didn't seem to mind that Marisa called, and when I spoke to her we decided that it would even be a good way for them to practice phone conversation.

I wrote to the teacher to let her know that Marisa made a phone call to Peter and spoke to his mom. Because Peter was turning sixteen and Marisa was not yet eleven, the teacher suggested I discourage the friendship. Perhaps she felt Marisa would get into trouble with an older boy. It seemed odd to me since it wasn't like they were going on a date or anything unsupervised. I was not going to discourage the friendship; it seemed that the relationship was having a positive effect on Marisa's behavior. Marisa and Peter had a common interest: they were both big Pokemon fans. Marisa's friendship with Peter was giving her a motivation to practice social skills. She was creating decorative cards with written messages to mail. She was starting to learn the skill of phone conversation. I was not about to put a stop to such positive learning experiences.

In the beginning of April the school planned a trip to a farm. Marisa's class and Peter's class were both going on the trip, and Marisa was so excited when the morning of the trip arrived. When she came home later that day, upset to tell me that she had missed the trip, I immediately checked her communication book for an answer, but there was none. I had to wait till the next day to hear from the teacher. Apparently the classes arrived back late in the day, and there wasn't enough time to inform me of what had happened. The next day I received this explanation:

We had been going over the rules for the trip that Marisa had to sit with her class on the bus and stay as a group when we got to the farm. It was time to get on the bus, so Marisa's aide sat with her and the others in the front of the bus. When Marisa saw Peter get on the bus she wanted to sit with him. She began pushing her way through everyone to get to Peter. When she wasn't allowed to go down the aisle, she started to climb over the seats. She was getting more and more upset as we were saying that she had to sit with her class. Peter did not want to sit with her either, because he was already paired with his classmate. We gave her several chances to get herself under control. She began to scream and get more upset, and she tried to bite her aide. At this time we took her off the bus.

I felt nothing but frustration and anger. Although I was told that there was a plan worked out for the trip, it seemed more like a plan to fail. Everyone knew how much Marisa liked Peter, and it seemed as though she had deliberately been set up to fail by having her sit as far away from her new friend as possible. There was no room for compromise at all; perhaps Marisa could have sat across from Peter. Or one class could have been seated one on the left side of the aisle and the other class on the right side of the aisle, rather than one class in the front of the bus and the other in the back. Knowing that the seating arrangement was likely to be a problem and a great disappointment for Marisa, the teacher could have taken steps that would have ensured a better outcome. Instead, the opportunity to use a friendship to foster social skills and appropriate interactions was lost in a struggle to maintain rules that were far too rigid and inflexible. The incident was a terrible blow to Marisa as she continued to talk about the trip she missed for days and even weeks after the incident. To this day, Marisa is saddened when reminded about the trip to the farm that she missed. I promised Marisa that I would help her to work on a plan to have successful trips in the future.

The teacher informed me that there was another trip planned with Peter's class for June, to Theodore Roosevelt's home at Sagamore Hill. A plan would have to be worked out so that there would not be a repeat of the behaviors of the previous trip. I fully agreed and hoped that the teacher would take some of my suggestions the next time around. Here we were in the middle of April, and the teacher still had not taken my suggestion to bring in an autism consultant. Even my school district failed to bring in their consultant to offer help.

I wrote to the teacher in an effort to initiate some change in how the next trip would be handled. Once again I suggested rule cards that Marisa could read while on the trip. I felt there was a need for compromise in terms of the seating arrangement for the next trip. I stressed that as long as Marisa liked her new friend and wanted to be near him, there would continue to be a struggle, unless the staff started to work with the problem rather than against it. Marisa's desire for this friendship was not going to go away.

Spring was in the air, and Marisa was upset one day late in April when she came home and complained that her friend Peter was wearing shorts to school. Although I didn't feel it was warm enough for shorts, I decided to send shorts to school in Marisa's backpack, so as not to create any unnecessary problems for the school staff. Marisa would be able to wear the shorts at school if the weather was warm enough, thereby preventing any unnecessary outbursts.

It was nearing the end of the year, when the teacher told me she had finally taped rule cards to Marisa's desk. I was happy to learn this while reading about a funny incident at school. The teacher wrote to tell me that Marisa had changed a rule card that read, "I will not touch Peter" to read, "I will touch Peter," crossing out the word "not." When the teacher talked to her about it, she just laughed at what she had done. Good for Marisa! At least she has a sense of humor. The teacher was so serious about the change on the rule card that she could not see the clever bit of humor in it. She could have shared a valuable moment with Marisa and possibly have gained some rapport with her student. Instead, she continued to maintain a serious, angry posture over what had been done, resulting in the loss of any bonding that could have occurred between them.

In early May, Marisa often seemed distracted by her friend Peter, jumping out of her seat to check the halls for him and occasionally popping her head into his classroom while walking down the hall. I reminded the teacher that she should use the upcoming June trip as a motivation for Marisa to stay focused on her schoolwork. The teacher had also notified me that she would be attending the autism conference I had recently sent her information on. I was so happy to hear that she would finally be taking advantage of such an opportunity; I thought it was better late than not at all.

After the teacher attended the conference, I noticed that she started using a more positive approach with Marisa. She gave Marisa more opportunities to interact appropriately with her friend Peter while in the gym. She was able to ask him to play basketball with her in gym class, and then later they rode on scooters together. At home Marisa asked to write an extra goal on her chart. The goal as she wrote it was, "I will not hug Peter." She really wanted to earn the point each day for this goal, since at school, hugging of students was not considered appropriate. I let the teacher know that I would give Marisa a point for the goal each day, unless she let me know that she didn't follow through. Marisa was really starting to appreciate the rewards of her goal chart. More and more, she was taking responsibility for her own behavior because of her motivation to earn her points.

In preparation for the upcoming June trip, the two classes had a trial run on the bus. The seating arrangements were made for the trip, and Marisa was to sit with a girl from Peter's class. This arrangement was made so that Marisa would get to sit near Peter but not with him. The rule cards for the trip were at this point being reviewed daily. I was hopeful that if the teacher and I could work together then Marisa would be able to have a rewarding experience.

The day of the trip to Sagamore Hill had arrived. I sent a note to the teacher that she should remind Marisa numerous times during the trip that if all went well, she would be earning the Red Version Pokemon game for Game Boy that she was working towards on her home goal chart.

Later that day, I received a super note from the teacher in regard to how well the trip had gone. Marisa's behavior was excellent! She didn't even bring Mutsy on the trip; that was a first! She spent the entire trip with Peter and kept herself in perfect control. What a big difference this was from the previous trip disaster. It seemed to me that this trip succeeded because the teacher took much of my advice, used the rule cards I recommended and compromising on where Marisa sat and who she spent her time with during the trip. Marisa and Peter, both having an interest in Pokemon, had things to talk about. On the trip, they had a wonderful opportunity to practice their conversational and social skills together. Marisa was also able to earn the game she was working toward on her home goal chart. It was a win/win event all around!

Marisa's eleventh birthday was approaching. We prepared invitations to the party, which Marisa distributed at school. When she received a call from her friend Peter that he would attend the party, she was so excited. She started to talk about how she was planning to leave with Peter after the party to go live with him, and she even joked around about it by saying she would miss us. Knowing how unpredictable Marisa could be, I decided to inform her that gift opening at the party would only take place once all the party guests had gone home. I felt this would be a good transition from having a house full of friends. And hopefully letting Peter leave would not become an issue.

Six children attended Marisa's eleventh birthday. We held the party indoors, because the weather was not cooperative. There was pizza for lunch, followed by painting T-shirts with fabric paints using stencils or original designs. Everyone seemed happy and engrossed in the activity. The small group seemed to enjoy working on their shirts and engaging in conversation. There was a camaraderie I had never quite seen before at Marisa's birthday parties; something was different.

I realized that Marisa was no longer a little girl. She was growing into a teenager, even though she was just eleven years old. The way she sat with her friends from school, some of whom I had just met for the first time, made me realize how important having this birthday party really was to Marisa. It gave her the opportunity to bring friends she liked together, and it was having such a positive affect on her. She was bright-eyed and attentive throughout the party and seemed fully engaged in all the activities. I had never quite seen her looking so animated, happy, and receptive.

After the party, I told Marisa how proud I was of her. I also realized that although not a single person from her class had attended the party, she still managed to draw together a group of friends who could interact well with each other and who all seemed to have a single common interest, Pokemon! This group of kids sat engaged in a craft activity and talked about the Pokemon games they all seemed to enjoy. It was amazing to watch them interact so naturally with one another as they all worked on their individual T-shirt designs. Some made their own Pokemon pictures on the tie-dyed shirts I distributed, and some used the stencils I provided. All turned out to be beautiful, original masterpieces!

I was also amazed to see how Marisa would hug her friend Peter. It didn't seem to me that there was any resistance on his part, which made me wonder about all the fuss at school to prevent hugging. Social interaction and the need for affection in all human beings had become such an issue at school. Considering that individuals with autism tend to have difficulty interacting with others, it seemed sad that an innocent hug was discouraged at school, where both Marisa and Peter were being taught that it was wrong and inappropriate.

As the year came to an end, I was hoping that the next year would provide us with a new teacher, a new aide for Marisa, and perhaps a fresh new perspective. I expressed my concerns to the principal.

The summer program went well. Marisa was fortunate and happy to have the teacher that Peter had had during the year. It was a fulfilling, stress-free summer session. During the summer, Marisa had many get-togethers with Peter, who had graduated and was moving up to the high school program. Marisa also had numerous play dates with other friends over the summer, including her friends Chris and Brittany from Variety Preschooler's Workshop. There were many swim dates, lunch dates, and video games played with friends during the summer weekends. Marisa and Brittany also enjoyed listening to music, singing, and dancing together. Most of all, it was encouraging and reassuring to me to see Marisa building so many new friendships as she also kept and cherished those from her earlier years.

Chapter Eleven

A FRESH START

Once again, as the year began, I sent a note to the new teacher so that he would have some background on things that work well with Marisa and things that were important to her.

I received a note back thanking me for my note and informing me that the school's behavior modification program would begin on the following Monday. The teacher also informed me that Marisa had a nice first day and had a new one-to-one aide working with her this year. However, Marisa came home sad and cried for the first hour after school. She cried for her old friends who she missed. She cried for Peter who had graduated. She cried for Brittany, who had been mainstreamed into an inclusion class in her school district. She also cried for Conan, the friend she had met during graduation rehearsals from her previous school, and although she had been separated from Conan for one whole year already, it was not unusual for her to have flashbacks from the past that would make her sad. She continued to cry as she said "I want to go to Variety with Brittany! I want to go back to Jerusalem Avenue with Peter and Conan!" I felt bad for Marisa to be missing her friends but I was glad that she had these feelings. I thought it might help if she could at least speak to some of them. That afternoon, I suggested to Marisa that she call some of her friends just to say hello. After she called a few of her friends, it did not take long for Marisa to get back to her usual happy self.

Marisa had come home with two boxes of Pokemon tissues the first day that she said she got from a boy in her class. I wanted to verify whether or not this was true, so I wrote to ask the teacher where the boxes of tissues came from. Apparently, another classmate knew that Marisa liked Pokemon, and he gave them to her as a gesture of friendship. I was happy that Marisa had given me the correct information, but I wondered if Marisa could appreciate the other child's efforts at friendship.

I was happy that Marisa had a new teacher and one-to-one aide. Judging by some of the early correspondence I received from the new teacher and aide, I sensed the teacher had more empathy and compassion for the children than last year's teacher had. He seemed to have a better understanding of each child's needs, and he made an effort to understand and reach out to each student on a more personal level. I also found that he had a refreshing sense of humor toward the children, which clearly showed his appreciation for their uniqueness.

From the beginning of the year, the teacher had Marisa eat lunch in the lunch-room with the other children. The aide worked well with Marisa, bringing games to the lunchroom to help keep her occupied, and she engaged Marisa in socially acceptable activities during the recess period. The teacher told me that the previous year he had been watching Marisa and wondering why the teacher had not found a solution that would enable Marisa to eat in the lunchroom. He felt it was inexcusable to have her separated from the other children at the time of day when children should have an opportunity to socialize. He had hoped that he would be given the chance to work with her this year, and he was happy that he now would be able to do so. I was relieved to hear that the new teacher agreed with me; I felt that perhaps things would start to improve as a result of his positive attitude and commitment to help Marisa eat in the lunchroom with everyone else.

When the teacher planned a trip in early October, he reviewed the rules for the trip with Marisa. He came up with a plan for bus seating that took into consideration the children's requests. Though Marisa was expressing an interest in sitting with a boy from another class named Chris, the teacher redirected her to select a partner from her own class.

I sent information to the teacher in regard to an autism conference that was coming up and was happy to receive word back from him that he would try to attend. It was nice to know that the teacher was open to new ideas and seemed willing to work with me.

On October 5, the class took their trip to a local pumpkin farm, where they went on a hayride. The temperature that day was in the high eighties, and although the children were told they had to wear pants for the trip, Marisa stood up in the middle of the hayride and pulled off her pants, revealing a pair of shorts underneath. Although the teacher was not happy to see what she had done, he realized that it wasn't going to be worth a major struggle, considering the high,

Indian summer temperatures. I was not pleased to read about Marisa's tricky stunt, but I was happy to know that the teacher was able to be flexible. Later, he said that Marisa was clearly the most comfortable one on the hayride, as she enjoyed the warmth of the air while everyone else was sweating.

Though the teacher was able to forgive the pants incident, he was disappointed that Marisa did not follow directions in regard to staying with the class during the trip, continually bothering the boy Chris, who was in the other class. He informed me that he would have to rethink his approach to future trips.

It was increasingly apparent to me that Marisa was becoming obsessive about approaching and hugging boys that she was interested in. This became more problematic as the year progressed; Chris clearly was not interested in being friends with her. I was told by the teacher that every time she approached him, he would run away or yell out "No!" Once she had actually pinned him against a wall as he cried out "No, not again!" and raised his arms in surrender. Marisa just laughed and thought it was funny.

During Open School Night, I met with Marisa's teacher to talk about ways of handling the problem. I told the teacher that I felt her behavior stemmed from the need for friendship and suggested that perhaps the teacher could encourage her friendships with girls in the school. It seemed that boys with special needs far outnumbered girls at this school, and there were very few girls in Marisa's class. The teacher decided he would check the enrollment of girls in the school to see if he could come up with a good match for Marisa, and perhaps he could even start a girls club as a last-period class once a week. I was pleased to hear such a refreshing and wonderful idea!

In the meantime, I began to notice that whenever Marisa got upset at school, the aide would take her to the Thinking Room for brief periods of time. I was concerned about this, particularly because I felt the Thinking Room had been overused the year before, but the teacher told me that it was only used for a ten-minute period. The aide would sit with Marisa, and together they would fill out a planning sheet for preventing whatever unacceptable behavior had occurred. I could understand using the room as a way to help an angry or upset child calm down, but I was becoming concerned by the frequency with which this approach was being used to change unacceptable behaviors. I knew this technique would not work for Marisa, because she could not understand the concrete thinking necessary to complete a planning sheet successfully. However, because relying on the Thinking Room was part of the school's behavior plan, I might once again be in for a fight.

At home, Marisa was discovering new ways to get into mischief. She managed to find a way to dial people's phone numbers on the Internet. She would call people on the computer and hear their voices when they picked up the phone. One evening Shoshana found Marisa sitting and laughing in front of the computer as a man's voice yelled back, "Don't call here again!" She was clearly enjoying the angry voice coming out of the computer.

The next thing I knew, the phone rang, and it was Peter's mom. She had dialed star-sixty-nine, and as she had suspected, it led her to us. She said she had received a number of calls with no answer on the other end of the line. I had just found out about Marisa's Internet activity and was able to put two and two together.

Marisa lost all computer privileges for a week and all her home goal points. As I had done before, serious consequences were necessary to make sure she didn't repeat this behavior. Marisa's teacher sympathized with me, and he suggested I use praise for good behaviors as much as possible. I tended to agree but knew that there was no other alternative for this particular dilemma but to take away Marisa's hard-earned points and computer access.

Marisa was eleven years old now and was showing increasing signs of wanting to be more independent. She wanted a phone and actually took the teacher's cell phone home from school with her one day. When she returned the phone the next day, she had to spend her lunch in Time Out as a consequence. The teacher said that Marisa actually seemed more upset about not getting to buy a snack than the idea of having to spend lunchtime in Time Out. I could see that the teacher was quite receptive to what punishments worked for Marisa and expected that, knowing what worked better than Time Out, would be a wake-up call to him. Maybe he was ready to re-think his approach to punishment.

Another scary problem developed at home as a result of Marisa's desire for independence. Before Halloween, Marisa had been talking about wanting to go to Chris's house. Marisa was disappointed that we didn't live in a neighborhood where kids could go trick-or-treating. I started to remember earlier incidents in which I should have foreseen trouble brewing. But once again, Marisa was a step ahead of me. We caught her at 8:30 at night trying to ride off on a bicycle with a camera, tape recorder, tapes, and a shopping bag with her clothes. Fortunately, she set off the alarm when she left the house, and we caught her, bag in hand, just as she was walking the bicycle out of the garage. Considering that Marisa was not able to ride the two-wheeler without trainer wheels and that her destination was a good twenty miles away, it was plain to see that Marisa was being unrealistic in what she thought she could do. Once again she lost all her home points for trying to do something that would clearly put her in great danger.

Although the pre-teen years meant there would be new problems arising out of the growing desire to be independent, Marisa was also maturing in ways that I hadn't realized would be beneficial till now. We had been using her goal chart for about six years at this point, and I started to notice Marisa's growing interest in it. She enjoyed checking her goals daily, adding in her points by herself, and she even initiated writing up her new chart at the beginning of each month.

In early November I decided to add a new goal to the chart and instructed Marisa to add it to the bottom of the goal list. The new goal was to take a chewable vitamin, and for this she would earn three extra points each day. Up to this point, Marisa had not been taking vitamins. She didn't like the taste of the liquid ones she had been taking as a baby, so I had stopped giving her that when she started drinking from a cup at age two. I had also tried the chewable vitamins, but Marisa would spit them out because she didn't like the taste. For a good eight years, she had no supplemental vitamins. I started to notice that her hair was thinning, and this prompted me to try the goal chart as a way to motivate her to take the chewable vitamins again. To my great relief, it worked.

I was so excited by this, not only because she was finally taking vitamins again, but because I knew that her eagerness to earn points would open up so many doors in terms of molding her behaviors. I realized that this was a real turning point! I thought that perhaps it would be helpful to consult with our pediatric neurologist about trying medication to help tone down impulsiveness and help Marisa focus better on her tasks. I decided to wait for a vacation from school to schedule an appointment, but was surprised to learn that there were no openings until February, so I scheduled an appointment for over the winter break.

In spite of the good that evolved with our home goal chart, a new problem developed at school. This set off a pattern I was going to have to take a real initiative to correct. At the end of November, Marisa started to mention a new boy that she seemed to have a crush on. She was so excited by a boy named Matt that she continually became distracted, looking for him throughout the day, when her class walked in the halls. She would dart off her line to run over and hug him when the opportunity arose. As a result, she lost her privilege of going to the school store. Her anger about this made her behave so badly that she had to spend time in the Thinking Room, where she had to do a planning sheet with an assistant. This was to be the beginning of a chronic pattern of trips to the Thinking Room, which would eventually lead to even more trips to the Isolation Room. According to the school's behavior plan, if the planning sheet done in the

Thinking Room did not work out, a student would spend time in the Isolation Room. Isolation, I was assured, did not mean time all alone in a room. It did, however, mean time away from the class, usually in a library or another available room doing class work with an assistant, when there were no other students using that room. Then if the Isolation Room didn't correct the problem, the student would visit with the school psychologist who would try to come up with a plan to correct the student's behavior.

Time and time again over the next few months Marisa would be taken to the Thinking Room to do planning sheets over incidents involving her hugging of Chris or Matt in the school halls. Then time after time, she would emerge from the Thinking Room only to do the exact same thing that got her sent there in the first place. Marisa would then end up in Isolation for thirty or forty minutes at a time and would continually repeat the unacceptable behavior, even after coming out of the Isolation Room for these extended periods.

I was disappointed in Marisa's teacher, who I thought would be willing to find a more creative and effective way of changing Marisa's behavior. However, the teacher was following the school behavior plan, which to me had some serious flaws.

I started to log all the incidents that the teacher wrote about in our communication book. I needed to come up with a plan to put an end to this ridiculously ineffective approach to handling Marisa's inappropriate behaviors. I knew that punishing the behavior by putting her in isolation was obviously not solving anything, since she would continually repeat the behavior.

If anything, this was the worst approach for an autistic child, who would probably have trouble with the concrete thinking involved in the planning sheets used in the Thinking Room. As for the Isolation Room, it seemed to me that it might seem like a reward for an autistic child, who tended to like being left alone. In effect, it was not a punishment at all, and most likely Marisa didn't even understand the reasons she was being removed from the class.

The other problem that I was concerned about was that the teacher was not doing an FBA (functional behavior assessment) for the repeated behavior. I knew it was very effective to do an FBA over a period of months in order to evaluate why a particular behavior was occurring and what the purpose the behavior served for the child. Once that was established, it would be more beneficial to replace the unacceptable behavior by one that would be equally rewarding for the child but that was also acceptable to those around her.

In the meantime, I decided to try adding penalties to our home chart as a way of deterring Marisa's impulsive desires to hug the boys she liked at school. I added to Marisa's home chart the new rule that she would lose five points every time she hugged someone against that person's wishes. Marisa clearly knew when someone didn't want to be hugged, but she seemed to do it anyway, not just because she wanted to hug, but because she found their negative response funny. I asked the teacher to keep me informed so that I could take appropriate action at home. I hoped that this would have some effect on her.

As I discussed the new rule with Marisa at home, she laughed at the thought of what she had been doing. I thought Marisa must also have been amused by all the times she sat in the Thinking Room with her aide, writing out plans for saying hello instead of hugging. All the times the aide escorted Marisa to the school psychologist, who told her repeatedly that she was engaging in inappropriate behavior by hugging boys she liked, Marisa would just sit and laugh about the startled reactions of the boys she approached to embrace. It was apparent to me that the startled responses of those around her were gratifying to her. She enjoyed the humor that she alone saw in the boys' reaction to her. I was determined to find a way to make an impact on her, and I hoped that the loss of points would do the trick.

Marisa's impulses continued to create problems so I decided to create a more specific point system for the teacher to use at school. On our home chart I added:

I will lose thirty points a day for every time I sneak out of the classroom.

This did seem to have an impact on Marisa, because she stopped laughing about the hugging incidents. At this point, Marisa started working hard each day to earn a total of three hundred fifty points that would go toward the purchase of a gift of her choosing. This was a very powerful motivator. In addition, I wrote to the teacher to inform him that if she ran from the classroom a second time in the same day, I would take Mutsy away for a day, and if the behavior repeated a third time, he should call me to pick her up. I knew that losing Mutsy for a day would be a devastating blow to Marisa, and for someone who loved school as much as Marisa did, being taken out of school would have to be the absolute worst punishment of all. I knew that Marisa would not laugh at these consequences.

I was hoping this new plan would prevent any further time spent away from the classroom. I became increasingly angry when I heard about yet another incident from Marisa's aide. Marisa had an outburst of laughter while thinking about Matt as she said, "I want to attack Matt!" Apparently the word "attack" had been used frequently at school while talking about the hugging incidents, and Marisa was laughing about this "attacking" behavior, which was actually meant to be a friendly hug. This time Marisa had been sent to the Thinking Room for laughing about her thoughts. There she was expected to understand that she was making Matt afraid by her overly friendly approach. What nobody seemed to realize was that making someone afraid of her friendly hugs was what Marisa found so funny in the first place. She was clearly enjoying the humor she saw in the situation, and the time spent trying to make her understand the fears of others was wasted. Children with autism frequently are unable to recognize the meanings of various facial expressions, and for Marisa this was clearly the case. For example, a frightened facial expression appeared comical from her perspective.

Because the planning sheets in the Thinking Room were not working, Marisa was graduated to the Isolation Room by the end of December. I was even more disturbed to read the teacher's note informing me that Marisa had spent the first hour of the day in Isolation for hugging Matt when leaving school to go on the bus the day before. According to the teacher, after that, Marisa's behavior remained unstable for the rest of that day. I was not happy about punishments being carried out at the start of a new day. I would have preferred to be given a phone call; I could have discussed the problem with Marisa and perhaps that would have been more meaningful to her.

I urgently tried reinforcing the rules on the home chart. I did not want Marisa to be spending so much time in either the Thinking Room or in Isolation. I knew that these techniques were having no impact and were probably even confusing to Marisa. She couldn't seem to understand why what she was doing was wrong; all she knew was that she wanted to hug someone. Her need for closeness and affection was not being met.

In a desperate attempt to prevent any further trips to the Thinking Room or Isolation Room, I continued to remind her about the points she would lose for hugging and leaving the classroom without permission. Daily, I went over the new rules on her chart. I would also try explaining the reasons why these rules were important. I knew she had trouble understanding the importance of the rules. However, I hoped that seeing the points she would lose for not following the rules would have an impact. Repeating the reasons for the rules, I thought, might eventually take on meaning for her as she matured and was able to understand more about other people's feelings.

I was happy that the teacher agreed to work with me in carrying out the new plan. He would inform me of all the incidents in which Marisa would leave the classroom without permission, leave the classroom line while walking in the hall, and hug boys against their wishes. I in turn, let the teacher know that Marisa was losing points on her home chart for those incidents. I hoped that this would bring about a change in Marisa's behavior, but unfortunately it was not soon enough.

Within a day or two, I received a note from Marisa's aide that was so typical of the frequent incidents that had been occurring at this time:

> *During music class Marisa was asked by the music teacher to leave the music room because of continual outbursts of laughter. An aide was sitting with her outside the music room, when she ran across to the OT room. Chris happened to be in the OT room, where Marisa went to give him a friendly hug. Due to this incident, Marisa had isolation for an hour. Isolation was being in the library with me and class work to do.*

It was unfortunate that Marisa had to sit right outside the music room in the hall, doing nothing but watching the things around her. Perhaps she could have been escorted back to the classroom to do some class work. Instead, the staff placed her in a vulnerable situation in which she would surely be distracted and provoked into doing something unacceptable. Then the resulting behavior only caused her to be further penalized with isolation time. How unfortunate and ridiculous this seemed to me.

Time and time again she would go from Time Out for thirty-minutes, into Isolation for an hour, for repeating the same hugging behaviors. It was obvious that the Time Out and Isolation were having no impact on the unwanted behavior. It was even clearer to me, that Marisa was frequently spending most of the time in her day alone and away from her classmates. This was not a healthy way of handling the problem, and I became angrier with each passing day.

Clearly, the school psychologist had no alternative to offer other than taking away points and removing Marisa from the class. This was not working, and I felt it was unacceptable, and once again I suggested that an FBA be done. I wrote the following note to the teacher:

> *I do understand the predicament you are in, but it is clear to me that isolation and loss of socialization time are not appropriate for a child who has severe communication and social deficits to begin with. I believe a functional behavior assessment and an autism consultant are imperative in this circumstance. Marisa probably finds isolation very soothing, and it may be more of a reward than a punishment at this point.*

I noticed, to my disgust, that Marisa had started talking to herself in two different voices while she was alone. It was obvious to me that she was becoming a very lonely girl. Though she craved interaction with her peers, she was not learning how to go about having meaningful peer relationships. I mentioned to the teacher that I would get in touch with the school psychologist to talk about how to resolve the problem. I scheduled a meeting with the psychologist for mid-January.

At the meeting, the psychologist started to fill out what he said was a functional behavior assessment form, which took all of about twenty minutes. He concluded that the unacceptable behaviors should be given consequences of Time Out or Isolation. I could not believe what I was hearing! Did he really think that I had scheduled this meeting so that he could come up with the same solutions that had not been working all year?

I informed the psychologist that as I had learned on my own, a proper FBA would take a few months of data collecting, during which time the behaviors in question could be categorized by motive, usually to fall into one of three categories: escape, attention, or tangible (seeking to get something). Seeking and testing out acceptable equivalent behaviors to replace the unacceptable behaviors should then follow this.

I recommended an excellent source for him to read, a book entitled *Communication Based Intervention for Problem Behavior (A User's Guide for Producing Positive Change)* by Edward G. Carr, Len Levin, and Christopher Smith. I pointed out that this book was enlightening and informed the psychologist that I was using the book's methods at home to resolve some of Marisa's problem behaviors. It made sense to try to understand the reason for any unacceptable behavior and then replace it with an appropriate and acceptable behavior. For example, if someone was continually fidgeting with her hands in public, which would be considered unacceptable, she could instead learn to put her hands in her pockets where no one would notice the fidgeting, which would be more acceptable. I tried to explain this to the psychologist, who didn't seem to understand that the goal should not be to come up with an appropriate punishment but to come up with an appropriate replacement behavior.

At our meeting it became clear to me that BOCES was unprepared to handle a properly done FBA, and the school's staff seemed totally unaware of the idea of changing behaviors through the replacement of acceptable behaviors. I was frustrated and angry to think that I had entrusted my child to a program that was unwilling to update its behavior plan to a more contemporary approach, especially since the approach being used up to that point had not worked. It was clear to me and should have been clear to the psychologist that if something wasn't working, a change of plan was needed.

As I attempted to explain the concept of the book to the psychologist, I sensed that he was not taking me seriously. I suggested that we needed to come up with an acceptable replacement behavior for Marisa's hugging. When I suggested that Marisa be taught to go hug Mutsy instead, for example, the psychologist thought I was joking. However, when the psychologist realized how serious I was, he agreed to try this replacement behavior. The teacher actually liked the idea and decided to add an extra incentive by rewarding Marisa with computer time for every time she used Mutsy as a replacement for hugging a boy in the halls.

I also sent in a copy of the home goal chart, adding a new incentive. I incorporated a new home goal to award points for good school behavior. The number of points earned for good school behavior could vary depending on how many school points Marisa earned each day. This flexibility in the goal chart created an incentive to do well rather than a constant reminder that she was a failure.

Marisa responded well to the idea of hugging Mutsy, which gave her something constructive to do when she had the impulse to run and hug. It seemed that hugging the stuffed dog actually made her feel the same warm feeling she wanted when she went to hug a person.

Though some of the hugging incidents were eliminated, at times Marisa would still lose control and run to hug someone. As was done previously, the teacher continued to send her to Isolation. I decided to ad another rule to the home goal chart and asked the teacher to keep me informed. That rule was that she would lose twenty points at home each time she was sent to Isolation. I hoped that this addition would have an impact.

In the meantime, I had kept a log of all the times Marisa had been in Isolation. I spoke to my district director of special services about the problem at school. This director was new in our school district and seemed much more receptive than the last director, who had only stayed with the district for a year. I sent her a list of all the dates and hour-long times Marisa had spent in either Time Out or Isolation. The director was surprised to see how many times Marisa had been separated from her class for hugging incidents. She said that if Isolation incidents continued, an emergency CSE (Committee on Special Education) meeting would have to be held. However, it seemed that the placement of the "lose twenty points for isolation" on the home goal chart had a big impact on Marisa, whose behavior started to improve dramatically from that point on.

The class had a trip scheduled for the end of January, and I hoped that things would go well. I was anxious to hear a good report on the trip and was disappointed to learn, when Marisa arrived home with her communication book, that things had not gone well at all. Marisa had apparently hugged another student twice during the day, made a fuss over where she was sitting at lunch, and also had some difficulties on the bus ride back to school. The teacher only informed me that, since it is Friday, there will be follow-up on the behaviors on Monday morning. I was infuriated to read that the follow-up would take place after the weekend and knew that most likely such follow-up would be time spent in Time Out away from the class.

I asked Marisa about the trip, hoping to get some verification of what had happened, and I asked if she had taken Mutsy along for hugging. When Marisa told me that Mutsy stayed back at school, I was just plain angry. After having planned out a functional behavior assessment that would allow the stuffed dog to be used for hugging as an appropriate alternative behavior, it was disturbing to find out that the dog had been left back at the school. A trip, when Marisa would need every conceivable support possible, would hardly be the time to leave behind something that could help. As a result of what happened, I had no choice but to subtract ten points on Marisa's home goal chart, but I was determined to use every means possible to prevent the unwanted behavior in the future.

I arranged for a phone conference with the teacher to go over the plan for handling out-of-classroom time. During the phone conference, I suggested to the teacher that if Marisa was out of the class without her stuffed dog, Mutsy, she should have a reminder card that stated the consequences of hugging someone in the halls. I encouraged the teacher to use a written reminder with a simple picture to go with it. The reminder should also clearly state that one hug of a student would result in a five-point loss on her home chart, and time spent in Isolation would result in a twenty-point loss on her home chart. Marisa clearly needed a visual reminder along with verbal reminders. I was willing to do anything possible to prevent Marisa from ending up in Isolation, even if it meant increasing the number of points lost on her home goal chart, which would be a big motivator for Marisa to behave well.

I knew this teacher was willing to work with me to find an acceptable way to bring about change. It was clear to him that Marisa was losing learning time and socialization time. He had disapproved of the way the teacher from the previous year had isolated Marisa at lunchtime, but now he was resorting to the same tactic. I knew he was as frustrated as I was, and so together we worked on the new plan. Marisa had been punished far too much with the deprivation of social interaction, the thing she wanted so much and needed practice in the most.

I had scheduled an appointment for Marisa with the pediatric neurologist during the winter break. Marisa and I had to wait for an hour in the waiting room and it was plain to see that Marisa was having difficulty. She was continually jumping up from her seat watching the other children and moving around the room checking everything out. When we finally were called in to meet with the doctor, Marisa was quite restless. As I spoke with the neurologist she observed Marisa who seemed to be constantly on the move. Every noise Marisa heard caused her to jump out of her seat to find the source. Then the doctor examined Marisa and suggested we try Adderall at a low dose at first to see how she reacted to it. If she did not become irritable on the medication, we would be able to gradually increase it according to the schedule she gave me.

When Marisa returned to school, she started taking a low dose of the medication but I didn't tell the teacher initially; I didn't want him to be biased knowing she was on medication. I wanted to see if he would notice a change.

Along with the new medication, I started to offer more rewards to Marisa to encourage her to control her urges. I told her that if things went well over the period of a week, I would reward her not only with her regular points on the goal chart but with the "Frosted Blue Minute Maid Treat" from Burger King on Friday afternoons. This was a special frozen treat that she had been asking for, and I decided to take advantage of her desire. The teacher and I started to see a big change. Marisa was also taking full responsibility for recording her points on a daily basis.

Now Marisa would stop and think before jumping up and running out of the room. It was a turning point that would prove to be well worth our efforts. When Marisa occasionally ended up in Isolation, I would deduct the twenty points from her chart. This had such an amazing impact that the number of such incidents greatly decreased over the next couple of months. I was happy things were improved but I couldn't be sure if it was the medication or the behavior plan or perhaps both.

I was grateful that the teacher was making a genuine effort to work with me and to listen to my advice and concerns. He was appreciative of my efforts, using picture reminders as I had suggested, and helping Marisa engage herself in more socially acceptable ways. Over the next few months, everyone began to relax a bit in dealing with Marisa's interest in boys.

Marisa's teacher even had a good sense of humor; he would stand with Marisa in the classroom doorway at the beginning of the day, engaging her in conversation about the boy she had a crush on. There they would talk and wait for the crush to pass by, so she could have an opportunity to say hello. At other times of the day, while walking in the halls, he reminded Marisa that it was OK to greet someone with a smile, a wave, and a friendly "Hello!"

The teacher wrote to me about a cute incident that occurred during reading time one day. Marisa seemed to be deep in thought, and when the teacher asked her if she was "going to read to me or what?" Marisa replied, "Or what!" and then laughed at her own joke. It seemed that she was becoming a happier, less frustrated child.

Over the spring vacation, Marisa enjoyed a couple of organized play dates with some of her old girlfriends. It was enough to keep her satisfied and happy for the week home.

Back at school in April, Marisa was doing exceptionally well. There were some incidents when she would start to run out of the room after a friend in the hall, but then the teacher would remind her of the consequences; these reminders seemed to be enough to stop the inappropriate behaviors before they occurred.

The class was to go on a spring trip, and though things were going well enough at school, I didn't want to take any chances of Marisa having a relapse. I reminded the teacher that if Marisa followed all the trip rules, she would earn an additional twenty points, a new addition to our home goal chart. I wrote out a rule card for Marisa to take on the trip. It wasn't good enough to just tell her she had to "behave" on the trip. Her behavior had to be very specific, so Marisa would know exactly what was expected of her. The rules were as follows:

1. No running off.

2. No grabbing.

3. Stay with the group.

4. Sit in assigned seat.

5. Follow instructions from the teacher and one-to-one aide.

The trip was a huge success for Marisa, and she was able to earn all twenty home points. I was pleased and relieved!

By the end of April, things were going exceptionally well at school. Unfortunately, Marisa had a major setback at home. Marisa had taken Shoshana's contacts and colored them blue, thinking she could use them to make her own eyes blue. This was such a dangerous and serious situation that I had to deduct all her hard-earned points. Although it seemed unfair to take away everything she had worked toward, there was no other way of impressing on her the seriousness of what she had done. I also knew that I had to find a way of satisfying her desire for blue eyes. In the meantime, I told Marisa that she was too young to wear contacts anyway, and coloring the contacts with markers was a dangerous thing to do and certainly not the way to change one's eye color.

I was happy to hear that Marisa was doing so well in chorus that she would be able to participate in the upcoming school performance during the evening. She was so proud to take part in the show.

She also had improved so much at school and started telling me that she didn't need an aide any more, insisting that she would be fine without the aide in the new school year. She had earned the privilege of walking in the halls without her aide right next to her and was being given the chance to show that she could do well walking in the halls while with the class.

We planned a craft party for Marisa's twelfth birthday. It turned out to be a beautiful day, and we held the party outdoors, where the kids played croquet, volleyball, and badminton and had pizza and decorated fabric caps with fabric markers. It was a fun day! Then Marisa painted her own beautiful photo album cover for her birthday album, where she proudly displayed her birthday pictures.

This year we celebrated Marisa's birthday a week early, because the whole family was invited to celebrate my cousin's sixtieth birthday. This day was actually very special, because my cousin shared the same birthday as Marisa. We were somewhat nervous about attending the party at the Marriott Hotel, but we were happy that Marisa was invited along with the rest of the family, so we were determined that she would behave in an appropriate way.

At the party, Marisa danced to the music and ate a special children's chicken nugget lunch. Though there was an enormous buffet to choose from, we knew that Marisa would not eat any of the adult-type foods offered, so we made arrangements in advance for her to have a children's meal. We were pleasantly surprised to see how well Marisa sat and listened during the speeches given in honor of the birthday hostess. Marisa earned five points on her goal chart in the category of a "visit well done." I was greatly relieved and happy that all had gone so well.

The school year was coming to an end with one last trip, to play miniature golf. Once again Marisa was to earn twenty trip points on her home goal chart if all went well. The trip was a huge success, and the teacher told me that Marisa had a very enjoyable day!

When the year ended, Marisa surprised her teacher and her one-to-one aide with photo albums. What made these albums special was that she hand painted the cover designs by herself. They were so beautiful that I had trouble parting with them. I was proud of Marisa's magnificent artwork, so I decided to photograph and frame enlarged versions for our home.

During the summer, Marisa had always attended the BOCES program, which was a full day. Up till now I felt the program was quite adequate, because half the day was spent on academics and the other half on outdoor activities, trips, and socialization. We were disappointed to find out that this summer, the BOCES program would be reduced to a half day of two and one-half hours. Because I hadn't known about this until late spring, I didn't have time to look into other summer programs.

I was disappointed about the shortened schedule, but when the summer program began, I was happy to find that Marisa was to retain her one-to-one aide from the school year. This was a surprise to us, since most of the staff usually took the summer off. The first day, the teacher sent a note stating that Marisa had commented about a girl in the class who was overweight. "It's the fat girl!" she said. The teacher said, "Marisa also mumbled something about how disgusting it was and bad breath."

The teacher explained to Marisa that this was inappropriate and rude, and she would not earn a check on her school chart for that period of the day. I was glad to be informed about the incident so I could talk it over with Marisa, explaining that the right thing to do was to apologize. This was an area that Marisa needed practice in. She did not know how to keep her inner thoughts to herself. This, too, was a trait very characteristic of autism. In effect, she was like an open book, not being able to discriminate between what was OK to share with others and what was better left unsaid.

I felt it was important to stress the kinds of things that were best left unsaid, explaining that Marisa should not say anything that would be hurtful to others. Since Marisa had difficulty knowing what things might be hurtful to others, I decided that I would look for opportunities in the community to point out things around her that were all right to comment on and things that were best kept quiet. Community outings were becoming more and more our living classroom.

In the meantime, Marisa's sister Deborah had graduated high school and had taken a summer position as a counselor at the GAP program in our town. GAP was the town program for kids and adults with special needs—the same program that I had attempted to have Marisa join some years earlier during the school year. They also held a wonderful, six-week camp program at one of the parks near our home. Deborah knew how unhappy Marisa and I were about the half-day program at BOCES. After two days at camp, Deborah informed me that, although Marisa had been disinterested in GAP previously, she was older now, and Deborah felt that the summer program would appeal to her.

I decided to call the GAP director to inquire about possibly having Marisa participate for half of the day. She was attending the BOCES program in the morning, and I thought perhaps the bus could drop her off at the park for the afternoon. As it turned out, the school district would be able to bus Marisa to school, bring her to the park for the afternoon, and then bus her home with the other campers at 3:00. It seemed like a wonderful idea! Marisa would get the best of both programs.

I arranged for Marisa to meet the camp director at the park for a screening and a trial day at camp; the director wanted to see how Marisa would behave. To my surprise and delight, Marisa was cooperative and happy to be a part of the camp program!

During the next few days, I needed to work out a plan for Marisa to be dropped off at the park and left in the care of the proper people at the GAP program. To make the transition from school to camp easier, I met the bus at the park for the first few days.

Marisa had a lot of things to remember to bring to school and camp. She was to wear her bathing suit in the morning and bring a towel, goggles, and extra underwear for after the pool at camp. As a special treat we went to the swim store, where Marisa selected a special pair of goggles. Unfortunately, the first day she brought her goggles she lost them; she apparently had a hole in the bottom of her bag, and the goggles had probably fallen out. Although we searched the park to find them, we were unsuccessful. Marisa was so upset after camp, she cried for a good part of the afternoon.

The loss of the goggles, however, had a surprisingly positive outcome. Marisa had been bringing Mutsy to school with her since she was three years old. I suggested to her that perhaps it would be a good idea to leave Mutsy home, where he could not get lost. With all the things Marisa needed to keep track of at school and camp, it seemed like one extra thing she could really do better without. To my surprise, Marisa agreed! I knew that any idea I presented to her had to make sense to her, and this one did. Marisa chose to leave Mutsy home from that day on.

The trauma of losing the goggles had initiated a milestone for Marisa. She was able to part with her favorite stuffed dog, which over time became less and less important to her even at home. Mutsy was downgraded from being carried around the house, to just going to bed with her at night, to a basket in the bedroom, and finally, some months later, Marisa tucked Mutsy away in a drawer. I felt that she was showing signs of maturing and felt this was a good thing.

During that summer Marisa attended the GAP camp program four days of the week. One day each week the GAP took an all-day trip, so Marisa would go straight home from BOCES on those days. The summer program at BOCES and the GAP program worked out well for Marisa, but because she was given a taste of camp experience, Marisa became discontent with the idea of ever again going back to a school program in the summer. She figured it would be better if she could go to camp for a full day, like everyone else, and she asked if she could attend only the GAP camp for the following summer.

I received a note from the teacher stating that Marisa told her speech teacher she was planning to take a bike and ride to JC Penny. She wanted a pair of fuzzy slippers she saw in the catalogue. By now I knew enough to take seriously anything Marisa had to say. I told Marisa that I would check out the store to see if they had the slippers, and then we would take a trip to select a pair for her. Although I rarely had taken Marisa out to a big department store before, it was an opportunity to practice some of her social skills. Going to a department store for something Marisa wanted would motivate her to be on her best behavior. We did take that trip to the store, and it turned out to be a rewarding experience for both Marisa and me as Marisa was given the chance to select her new slippers.

Though Marisa's summer was going well, she continued to find ways of surprising me by doing the unexpected. One weekend we spent a pleasant afternoon at her friend Peter's house. After returning home, she disappeared in her room, and she later reappeared with very short haircut that she had performed on herself. "What were you thinking?" I said to her. "I wanted to look like Peter!" she said. Marisa had cut a short cap haircut with bangs, which needed a bit of straightening out. She was not happy with the cut she gave herself. To this day, I still don't understand why looking like the boy she liked made sense to her, but it somehow did. Perhaps she thought that looking like him would somehow bring him closer to her.

As the end of the GAP camp program approached, Deborah informed me that she thought two of the GAP trips would appeal to Marisa. There was a trip to the aquarium in Riverhead and an end-of-summer trip to the amusement park Adventureland. I decided that Marisa would skip those two days at the BOCES program in order to go on the trips.

Marisa was very excited about the trip to the aquarium. Normally she didn't get up until 8:00 for school, but that day was special, and although she didn't have to be at the camp grounds till 10:00, she was up and ready at 7:30. Marisa went on the trip to the aquarium, and the head counselor told me it turned out to be a terrific day for her.

Marisa's one-to-one aide told me how proud she had been of Marisa over the summer. Good behavior at school had become pretty much the norm for Marisa now, and the trip to Adventureland was Marisa's reward. On the trip, Marisa was pleasantly surprised to see her friend Peter, who was participating in the Massapequa branch of the GAP camp program, which had also gone on the trip to Adventureland. Marisa was excited to be able to go on many rides at the amusement park with her friend Peter. It was a wonderful, fun-filled experience, and a rewarding way to end the summer camp program. Because Marisa had a taste of camp life, she eagerly anticipated spending her future summers at camp full-time.

Chapter   Twelve

CONTINUED SUCCESS

Since the GAP summer program had worked out so well for Marisa, she was eager to enroll in the weekend recreation program consisting of bowling events and day trips. I was happy to see that she was willing to participate in this program, because I felt it would give her an opportunity to take part in community activities and provide her with more social interaction.

Marisa started the new school year with the same teacher and one-to-one aide. I was greatly relieved, because I had established a good relationship with the teacher the previous year. The teacher was very receptive to using my home goal chart as an aid at school. Now we would have a chance to continue with the same technique.

The teacher felt that perhaps if Marisa had a network of friends at school to get together with for an activity of mutual interest, her focus on boys would decrease. As he had suggested last year, he established a "Girl's Club" in which a few girls from various classes would get together on Friday afternoons to give each other manicures and polish their nails. This was an activity that Marisa really enjoyed, and she also used her artistic talents to paint designs on her fingernails and those of her friends.

Though Marisa could occasionally be caught off track, when she might attempt to approach boys she liked in the halls, or run off the class line, in most situations she was able to stop herself. She would stop and think about the consequences, because she knew she would lose points on her goal chart, which was taped to her desk as a constant reminder. Though the director of special services from my district had written in Marisa's IEP that Isolation was not to be used as a punishment, I didn't want to take any chances. I felt that listing isolation in the "Lose Points" section of her home goal chart was extra insurance that she wouldn't end up there. I wanted to make Marisa feel more in control of her behavior by keeping the twenty-point loss for time in Isolation as an ever-present reminder for her. It seemed to work, because Marisa did not go back into Isolation ever again. This only confirmed my feelings that what I was doing was the right thing. It gave me a great sense of relief and accomplishment that Marisa was taking the initiative to maintain good behavior.

Marisa was such an inquisitive kid that she made it her business to know about anything special going on. During Marisa's five years at the Seaman Neck Middle School, she had learned about a trip available to students in February each year, to a camp at Frost Valley. Only fifteen to twenty students would be selected from the entire school, and Marisa was determined to be one of them. I inquired about the trip and found out it was a five-day environmental adventure for a select group of students whom the teachers felt would be cooperative.

Although Marisa was only in her third year at the middle school, I was determined to help fulfill her dream to be one of the privileged few to attend Frost Valley. The teacher promised to make the recommendation, and then all we could do was wait. To Marisa's great disappointment, she was not selected. She was saddened as she expressed to me that she might never get to see Frost Valley. I assured her that we would try again next year. After all, she still had a few years at the school, so her chances of being chosen were still good for the future. I reminded her that if she continued her good behavior and cooperated with the teachers, she would increase her chances of being selected for a future trip. With this optimistic approach, the prospect of being selected for the Frost Valley trip became a tremendous motivator for Marisa to control her impulsive behaviors and try harder to stay on task during school time.

During the year, I received a confidential social update form (a questionnaire to update progress in social and emotional development) to fill out for Marisa. Though I had every intention of filling out the form and sending it back to school as soon as possible, I could not seem to get to it soon enough for Marisa. One day, I found her in the kitchen filling out the form for me. As I then sat down to finish the form, Marisa stood over me, watching and reading my responses to the questions. She seemed very concerned with what my answers would be. She was satisfied when I finished filling it out, and I shared what I had written. She and I were both pleased to realize how much she had improved over the years. She almost sounded like the perfectly well behaved twelve-year-old. I realized then that she really had come a long way.

In early February, the class went on a trip to The Cradle of Aviation Museum. The teacher and I once again reminded Marisa to follow the rules of the trip as I had written them. We also reminded her that if all went well she would earn her twenty trip points. Later that day, I was happy to read that the trip had been a huge success!

Although Marisa's behavior had improved considerably, a new problem had developed at school and at home that needed to be addressed. Marisa had started to talk to herself frequently in many different voices, as if she were carrying on a conversation with other people. I thought that maybe she was practicing conversational skills, she was re-enacting something that had happened, or she was just plain lonely and was filling a gap for herself. Whatever the purpose was, I needed to find a way to reduce this behavior in public. I suggested to the teacher that we add "talking to myself" to the "loss of points" section of the goal chart, which might help deter some of the talking episodes. Then to replace the inappropriate behavior with one that would be more acceptable, I suggested that if Marisa needed to talk to herself, she use puppets or use her fingers as puppets, which would at least appear to be some kind of dramatic play activity.

To help Marisa understand why she needed to change this behavior, the reason had to be logical to her. I informed her that it would not look good to other people to see her talking to herself. If other people found the behavior weird, they might prefer not to be around her, which would mean she would be jeopardizing her friendships. I felt that since Marisa enjoyed being around friends, it might make her reconsider what she was doing in the presence of others. I told her that if she wanted to talk to herself, she needed to either go in her room and do it there or at least use puppets or her finger puppets. To avoid losing points, she did use her finger puppets. However, because she found it silly, she began to reduce the frequency of conversations with herself, but more importantly, she started to initiate conversations with her peers more frequently.

One of Marisa's favorite holidays was Valentine's Day, because it gave her a chance to reach out to others. Marisa prepared cards for all her friends both at her other schools and her current school. Marisa found a recipe for a "People Pleaser" cake in her American Girl magazine. She was so excited about it that she asked me to bake the cake for her to bring to school on Valentine's Day. It was a cake with chocolate cake on one half and vanilla on the other. Then by placing chocolate icing and vanilla icing in the opposite directions across the cake, it would create every possible combination of flavors. Marisa was so happy that this cake would give everyone a choice of their favorite combination of flavors. What a great idea this turned out to be! It was so nice to see Marisa showing a healthy concern for the wishes of others.

This year I made Marisa a red skirt to wear to the Valentines Day dance at school. The previous year Marisa, told her teacher that she was going to wear a red skirt for Valentine's Day. However, I had only learned of her desire to wear a red skirt the day before the dance and didn't have time to find a red skirt for the occasion. To help ease Marisa's disappointment at that time, I promised that I would make her a flared red skirt for the dance the next year. When Valentine's Day arrived, Marisa proudly wore her new red skirt and danced with one of her favorite boy friends. It was a wonderful day!

Although Marisa had a great desire for friendship, understanding the needs of others and expressing her needs to others was difficult for her, which is typical for most people on the autism spectrum. One day Marisa came home with an awful scratch across her right cheek. When I asked her about it, she said she had done it to herself. I was alarmed to hear that and asked her why. She managed to explain that it happened in music when the music teacher had invited her to stand on the stage for a song. When the song ended and the teacher asked her to sit down, she got very angry. Her anger was so intense that she dug her nails into her face, creating a two-inch bleeding scratch line. Marisa had never done this before, so I was somewhat concerned and eager to find out what the circumstances had been.

I verified the story with Marisa's teacher and then sat down to go over the incident with Marisa. I explained to her that she was asked to sit down because the teacher needed to give other students a chance to be on the stage and sing. Marisa didn't understand this and thought that she was being asked to sit down for doing something wrong. Not knowing what she had done wrong was frustrating, and because she was disappointed and frustrated, she scratched herself in a fit of anger. I needed to make it very clear to Marisa that if she continued to behave this way, the music teacher would not want to take a chance on having her up on the stage again. She had frightened the teacher with her unexpected outlash at his request for her to take her seat.

Though it was important for Marisa to understand what she had done wrong, it was equally important for the teacher to understand why things had gone badly. I explained the need for giving explicit instructions to Marisa so that she would understand each step of what was going to happen. She needed to know in advance what was expected of her. If she knew what to expect, she would not be disappointed, because there would not be any surprises. The teacher would also be more relaxed about giving Marisa more opportunities to participate, knowing what would work best for her. For example, if Marisa had known she was to be on stage for just one song and then take her seat in order to give someone else a chance, she would have been better prepared to handle the request to sit down at the end of the song.

To help Marisa improve and further her understanding of social skills, I enrolled her in a social skills class that was offered near my home. Marisa seemed to enjoy going to this class once a week, but I was disappointed that the class only consisted of three children: Marisa, another girl, and a boy the same age. I was hoping to see more students enrolled in the class, but it wasn't to happen. The good thing was that parents were allowed to watch what was going on in the class through a two-way mirror. By observing, I could see that Marisa seemed to be the most focused of the three, and that was very encouraging to me.

By the second half of the year the boy had dropped out of the class, because his mom did not feel it was benefiting him. He was a very talented child in one very special respect: he could draw beautiful horses and create horse sculptures out of colored tape, but at the exclusion of everything else. No matter what went on in the room, it seemed that his only interest was to draw the horses. This is an example of splinter skills that are often present in autism, but sometimes the skills are so extraordinary that they are called savant skills. It became frustrating for me to watch what was happening in the room with the three children, because I felt that there was a strong opportunity to apply the floor-time approach (following the child's interest) of Dr. Stanley I. Greenspan, which had been missed. Perhaps if the social worker had attempted to use the boy's strong interest in horses as a lesson for all three children, it would have been a bonding experience for the group. The second half of the year, when the boy dropped out of the class, there remained just the two girls. I was disappointed to find out that no other students enrolled.

When I inquired about other classes or other possible students joining the class, the social worker asked me to take brochures to Marisa's school in the hope of drawing more interest. This I was happy to do, if it would help expand the class size. Though parents who received the brochure eagerly called to inquire about the program, only one child was admitted to the group. I was angry to learn that many had been turned away because the social worker felt the group should not be larger than three. I sensed that the social worker did not feel she could adequately work with a larger group but felt that having me hand out brochures would draw enough candidates for her to interview and select one child that she felt would be a good fit for the group.

Marisa enjoyed this group immensely, but I had to wonder if it was because she was the shining star. As I continued to watch the activities, it appeared to me that Marisa was measuring herself against the other two in the group. I started to feel that although Marisa was enjoying the group, she needed more of a challenge. I felt that although she may have felt good about herself in this group, I would have liked to see her in a group where she would be able to emulate more mature behaviors of others. When I asked about switching Marisa to another group that was taking community outings, the social worker told me that Marisa was not high-functioning enough and was not ready for community outings. I did not agree, because Marisa had taken many successful trips with her GAP program. Although I was disappointed with the response, I decided to stay with the group through the remainder of the year, because Marisa seemed to enjoy the activities and extra attention.

Since Marisa was now participating nicely in the GAP recreation program during the school year, I decided to look into other social skills classes that she might enjoy and benefit from. After doing some research, I found that the special services department at the local JCC (Sid Jacobson Jewish Community Center) in East Hills had a social skills class that I thought might be a good alternative for Marisa for the next year. The JCC also had a less formal teen lounge program for Saturday evening that I thought was worth a try. Marisa was eager to participate, so I arranged to meet the director and discuss whether Marisa would be appropriate for the teen lounge. The director decided to give Marisa an opportunity to try out the group tentatively so that she could be observed in the group. The director usually was present at this group, but the day we were to try Marisa out, the director wasn't going to be there. Though I was a bit concerned, I decided to go ahead and let her attend.

Dan and I brought Marisa down to the Saturday night teen lounge after preparing her with the idea that she would earn five points for good behavior that evening. It was scary for us, because these people did not know Marisa, but I knew that we had to give it a try. After leaving our contact number with the group's supervisors, we reluctantly went off to dinner at a nearby restaurant.

When we returned after two hours, we could see right away that things had not gone well. Marisa's eyes were all red from crying, and the counselor in charge looked very frazzled, to say the least. "What happened?" I asked. "Why wasn't I called?" The counselor felt that they should ride out the difficulties because it was just for two hours.

According to the counselor, the evening had taken an immediate turn for the worse when Marisa wanted to spend the three dollars I gave her for snack. The snacks were a dollar each and children were allowed to buy up to three. In order to avoid any fussing over the snacks, I had given Marisa three dollars and told the counselors that I had done so. For some reason the counselor decided that it wasn't a good idea for Marisa to buy three snacks.

Then later that evening, Marisa had discovered that there was a live show going on in the auditorium, and she wanted to watch it. This show was a special performance being put on by the Y theatre group, and tickets had to be purchased. It was not something that the counselor could just take Marisa in to. Besides, even if the counselor did take Marisa in to see the show, there wouldn't have been enough supervision to watch the remainder of the group in the teen lounge. Marisa, however, did not understand this, and in frustration, she had a major outburst, screaming as she jumped up and down shooting her fists out in the air.

After hearing of the unfortunate events, the counselor informed me that Marisa would not be allowed to come back to the group. It was upsetting to me, but I realized that she just wasn't ready at that time. On one hand, it was an unfortunate failure, but on the other, it had a profoundly positive affect on Marisa. She pleaded to be given another chance, but I had to tell her that we could not try again till the following year. This idea took hold in her mind, and she became very determined to get it right when the time came to try the group again.

Meanwhile, back at school, where Marisa's behavior appeared well under control, I discovered that she had stolen a cell phone from someone in her class. While cleaning Marisa's bedroom, I found the phone in one of her drawers. When I asked her about it, she informed me that she took it from Monica, a girl in her class. She lost twenty points on her home goal chart, and I warned her that the next time she stole something she would lose fifty points. She returned the phone to Monica with an apology the next day.

In early March, I informed the teacher that we were trying out a new medication for Marisa. We had Marisa on Adderall, which appeared to help with the impulsive behaviors, but we noticed that Marisa developed slurred speech, which we thought might be caused by the drug. The doctor suggested that we switch to a new drug being used for ADHD that might also help with the focusing problems. This new drug was Strattera.

We started Marisa on a low dose of Strattera that was eventually increased to sixty milligrams. She seemed to be doing well on the new medication, and her behaviors continued to be well under control, but I really didn't believe that the drug alone was responsible for the improvements. I felt it was the combination of the drug and the home goal chart that produced the favorable outcome. I believed that there was an improvement with the Adderall and then the Strattera, but I also believed that perhaps the drugs made it easier for Marisa to focus on the goals she was working on at the time. We kept Marisa on the Strattera for a good two years. This seemed to provide a smooth sailing atmosphere for us, while she maintained good behaviors and achieved all her goals on her home goal chart.

Over time she had become very proficient at recording her points on her home goal chart and earning her chosen rewards. One of the rewards Marisa had selected for earning three hundred and fifty points was a Door Beads Kit. She loved stringing beads, and this kit was specifically to make a curtain of beads for a doorway. When Marisa received her new kit, she set to work stringing up the beads that would create a colorful curtain for her bedroom doorway. She was proud of her achievement and was happily engaged, as she kept herself busy arranging patterns for each seven-foot long string of beads to be hung.

Although Marisa was keeping busy with her new kit, she managed to get herself into trouble once again. One day I discovered in her bedroom drawer a Game boy Advance Harry Potter cartridge that I knew was not one I bought for her. Once again I was disappointed to learn that she had taken this from another student. When Marisa arrived home from school, I confronted her about the cartridge, and she admitted to taking it from a girl in her class, Monica. I asked Marisa to put herself in Monica's place and think how she would feel if someone took something of hers. As she had been warned before, she lost not twenty, but fifty points on her home goal chart for stealing. She returned the cartridge with another apology, and she seemed pleased to have done the right thing.

Over the course of the next few weeks, the teacher saw Marisa browsing through other classmates' backpacks. I felt this was only going to create a temptation to take something that wasn't hers. I decided that rather than wait for another stealing incident, it would be better to add a new goal to the chart, "looking in another student's backpack," which would result in losing two points. By anticipating the smaller problem, I was hoping to prevent Marisa from acting on the more serious urge to take things that weren't hers. My instincts were correct; this approach seemed to put an end to any further stealing.

In early April an opportunity arose that Marisa was eager to participate in. Shoshana, who had been working at a local cablevision news channel for Long Island, was looking for good news stories to suggest at the morning meetings at work. I had sent her some information on the reauthorization of IDEA (The Individuals with Disabilities Education Act). She became very interested in the topic and knew that there was a petition with signatures, from all over the country, on the Internet. The reauthorization of IDEA would impact the education of children with disabilities all across the United States, and some of the proposed changes were not favorable to the special needs students. She presented the story on the reauthorization of IDEA at work. It seemed to generate some real interest, but the executive producer told her that the story would not be aired unless a parent and child that would be affected by the changes could be interviewed. This would make the story more personal and bring it closer to home for the local viewers. I asked Marisa if she would like to do the interview with me, and though she was not happy about missing a morning of school, she seemed excited about the prospect of being on television.

Marisa and I were recruited and set up for a Friday morning interview at home. The morning of the interview was quite exciting! Marisa was very cooperative as she engaged herself in drawing and beading activities for the video, and she even answered the reporter's questions. Then when I was interviewed, Marisa sat quietly watching with Shoshana. I explained to the reporter that it was important for children with special needs to have annual reviews of their IEP because children's needs change and progress should be documented. The new proposal being set forth was to only review every three years. Another important point I stressed was that the IEP should continue to have short term goals along with annual goals so that learning could continue to be broken down in to the smaller goals necessary along the way to reaching the annual goals.

Later that morning I brought Marisa to school. She was excited to be a celebrity for the day, as she received lots of warm welcomes from the staff and her classmates. Later that evening we sat down to watch the five o'clock news, which was the first of many shows that the interview was to be aired on. When Marisa saw herself on the news for the first time, she jumped out of her seat a bit startled by the sight of herself on the television screen. Then she settled back to watch the interview with a smile. The next week I sent the interview in to school for Marisa to share with her class.

Although Marisa seemed happy and content most of the time, she would still occasionally feel sad that she did not see some of her old friends often enough. One day in May Marisa's aide sent me a note conveying that Marisa was sad because she wanted to talk to Peter. The aide promised Marisa that she would write to me asking if Marisa could call her old friend. I informed the assistant that Marisa had been calling Peter at least two times a week on a regular basis, and although he would never come to the phone or call back, it made her happy to make the phone calls and leave messages or speak to his mother.

One day Peter did call Marisa back, and oddly enough, when I excitedly rushed to tell her, she was busy playing one of her favorite Pokemon games and was not too happy about being interrupted. She took the phone for two seconds to say hello before shoving it back in my hand. Peter asked me why Marisa wouldn't talk to him, and I had to remind him that he is usually the one who is too busy playing video games to come to the phone and talk to her.

Later I reminded Marisa about Peter's call and pointed out to her that he was disappointed very much the same way she was when he was too busy to talk to her. How sad it is that these kids cannot even get to talk to each other when they want to because they are too absorbed in other activities to come to the phone. Unfortunately, all too often for people on the autism spectrum, the games they play or activities they engage in often seem to take priority over human interaction. This was something I wanted to help make Marisa more aware of, so she could work at putting her activity on hold long enough to respond appropriately to any friendly phone calls that might come her way.

Things had gone very well in music class since the music teacher had developed a better understanding of Marisa's needs. The spring concert was scheduled for the middle of May, and the teacher was giving Marisa an opportunity to sing a song with three other girls. This was a very exciting moment for Marisa, because she had earned the music teacher's trust, and she was excited and proud to prove that she could do a good job. We attended the concert, and we were proud and happy to watch as Marisa performed her song. There was pride and satisfaction all over her beaming face.

In spite of so many improvements in school, I was still concerned with Marisa's inability to express herself in writing. While attending a parents autism training group given by my school district, I expressed concern for Marisa's inability to master the skill of putting her thoughts on paper. The instructor suggested graphic organizers to plan out the various things that would go into a writing assignment. Graphic organizers would help break the writing assignment into sections by listing the subject, the people involved, and the time and place, for example, and then putting it all together. Other ideas were to use a camera and write about a picture the child took, or using a tape recorder to talk about what to write and then play it back and have the student write what he or she said. All these ideas sparked an idea of my own, and I decided to add a new goal to Marisa's goal chart. She would earn three points for writing the day's events, but I knew that Marisa wasn't ready to write by herself.

I purchased a notebook for Marisa to record day's events and explained to her that I would write down the things she said, and then she would read them back to me. For this daily activity, she would earn three additional points on her goal chart. As I sat down with her and asked her things about her day, I slowly managed to get bits of information from her. I would then rephrase and write what she said in sentence form. When she was finished, I would have her read what I had written. In this way, she got practice reading about her own thoughts and learning how those thoughts could be put into sentence form.

We continued this for the rest of the year and into the summer, until one day Marisa expressed an interest in putting her thoughts on paper by herself. To my great surprise, she had reached a new milestone and was able to complete the activity. Today, Marisa does her day's events by herself, asking for correct spellings when she needs to, and giving herself three points on her goal chart. This has also proven to be an excellent way for me to find out what went on at school each day. All I have to do is check her day's events book.

It was a very good year for Marisa. She went on numerous trips with her class and always earned her twenty points. She was also becoming more comfortable at handling herself in social situations. On some occasions, when she was given a choice between a movie and a game in a group, she would pass up the movie in favor of playing a game with some of the girls in her class. This was encouraging, because Marisa was learning to interact in socially appropriate ways with her peers.

Marisa's thirteenth birthday was approaching and Marisa eagerly gave out the invitations to her friends at school. Marisa's friendship list had increased to a large number of children. I was greatly surprised to learn that Marisa had a list of twenty-three children to invite.

The day of the party turned out to be a partly rainy and partly sunny day, so we decided to have the party indoors. Ten children attended the party, only three of whom were from Marisa's class. Although Marisa wanted to make decorated mirrors as the party project, I convinced her that the boys probably would prefer making tiled boxes. We gave the children both options, and everyone was happy. It was a fun day, and Marisa was happy, too, that her old friend Peter showed up at the party, although they hadn't spoken to each other almost the entire year.

A successful year was coming to an end, but I was saddened to find that Marisa had once again taken something that did not belong to her. She came home with a dog leash that she informed me she bought on a trip to Petco. It occurred to me that Marisa was making up the whole story. This was very serious, because not only had she taken something that was clearly not hers, but she was lying about it as well. Lying was not typical for Marisa. Usually, children with autism are prone to be truthful. This truly was a first for Marisa, and I attributed it to her improved ability toward creative thinking. Although lying in itself was not a good thing, the idea that she could be inventive was encouraging to me.

When I wrote to the teacher about it, I learned that the leash was actually for the class guinea pig. Marisa returned the leash and lost a hundred points for stealing and lying. I stressed my disappointment at the lie and the taking of the leash. Marisa said she was sorry and would not lie or steal again. I reminded Marisa that if she continued to take things that weren't hers, she would continue to lose more points.

At the end of the year, I received a surprise from the teacher and the one-to-one aide. They had put together a beautiful photo album of events and trips over the course of the two years Marisa had been in their class. I was so pleased to see all the beautiful pictures. Marisa and I sat and looked at the pictures together. I asked her about some of the pictures, and she eagerly explained them to me.

Marisa was excited that this summer she was going to attend the GAP camp program full time, which also meant that she would get to go on the group's weekly trips. My school district was able to arrange for a speech teacher to come to our home early each morning for a speech lesson before the bus arrived to pick Marisa up for camp. It was good to watch Marisa interact with her speech teacher. They worked on pragmatic speech and also some pronunciation problems. At the end of the summer, Marisa had the opportunity to perform a song with another camper during the camp show. Together they did a performance of "Sk8er Boi" by Avril Lavigne. What an amazing surprise this was! Shoshana and I were there to get the performance on video—every amazing moment of the song and dance routine! We were so proud! I knew that Marisa was very in to the latest pop music but hadn't actually seen her perform a song before.

Also during this summer, I decided to arrange for Marisa to take horse-back-riding lessons at a special-needs program once a week. I read that horseback riding had many benefits for children with special needs. Marisa already had excellent coordination and good muscle tone, but riding would help build self-esteem and develop compassion for animals. By learning to ride and to take care of the horse's needs, which was also a part of the program, I hoped that Marisa would also improve her sense of responsibility.

Marisa loved the idea of horseback riding and approached it with the seriousness of any eager student. Over the summer, we could see Marisa's interest in her pet cats and the horses change in a very positive way. She would approach our cats at home much more cautiously, so as not to disturb them, whereas in the past she didn't seem to realize that a quiet and gentle manner would be more welcome. Now she would come slowly and quietly toward them and gently reach out to pet them. It was nice to see that she was caring about the animals' feelings. She learned to approach the horses in much the same way.

When school resumed in September, Marisa was feeling very good about herself. She had fallen into a nice routine with her horseback riding. She had completed a summer at the GAP camp, in which her end-of-summer performance in the camp show had made her feel so special. The result was that she went back to school feeling accomplished and more self-assured than ever before. I was so pleased that Marisa's self-esteem had reached a healthy, all-time high!

Chapter Thirteen

BECOMING MORE
RESPONSIBLE

When school started, Marisa was happy to find that her new teacher was someone who had taught her during the summer program a few years earlier. She also was lucky enough to have the same one-to-one aide that she had for the past two years, which made the transition to the new class easier. However, as I had always done at the beginning of each year, I sent a note to the teacher to give her some tips on what worked best with Marisa.

In the meantime, the teacher sent me notes to let me know about the class schedule and expectations for homework. This teacher had something she called D.E.A.R. time, which stood for "drop everything and read." She sent home a chart that I was to sign every night when Marisa spent at least fifteen minutes reading. Marisa could read by herself, or I could read to her. This was an excellent idea, but I knew that Marisa would not want to do it. Comprehension was an area of weakness for Marisa, and although she was able to decode words phonetically, she had a great amount of difficulty understanding what she was reading. Because of this, reading was not very pleasurable for her. I decided to add "reading at least fifteen minutes daily" in the bonus section of her home goal chart. Marisa would earn three points each day for reading with me. This had an immediate impact on Marisa, who eagerly reminded me to read with her each night from that day on.

In the middle of September, the instructor of the horseback-riding program asked me if I would let Marisa participate in the annual horseback riding show. I was not prepared for this and was surprised to be asked; I didn't know about the show and I didn't think Marisa was ready to be included in such an event. However, Marisa was so excited about the idea so I signed her up to participate!

That weekend, on a miserably rainy day, we went to the horseback riding show, where Marisa competed in a beginners group. She came in second place in her group and was very excited when she received her medal. The judge asked Marisa how long she had been horseback riding, and she said, "Since July." He was very surprised and congratulated her on a job well done! Though we walked away soaking wet and covered in mud from the torrential rains that day, I was happy we had participated; it was an exceptionally rewarding experience for Marisa.

Later that month, I was stunned to learn that Marisa was going to run for treasurer on the student council. Marisa was good with numbers but I had no idea that this was a job that she could handle. The teacher told me that Marisa really wanted to run for an office and because of her ability with numbers, she was encouraged by the staff to obtain signatures of her classmates. Marisa was so determined that she managed to obtain the required number of signatures to be able to run for treasurer. Once she had aquired the necessary signatures she had to start planning her campaign. She needed to make posters to display in the school halls and prepare a speech to present to her classmates. I helped Marisa prepare the posters which gave her the chance to think about the qualities she had to offer that would make her a good treasurer. With the help of her speech teacher, she prepared and practiced reading her speech. Although she did not win the election, it was a valuable experience for her.

In late September I received a call from the center where Marisa was enrolled in a social skills class. The previous year, while Marisa was in the social skills group at the center, I had brought in the news interview Marisa and I had done on the reauthorization of IDEA. The social worker remembered how relaxed Marisa had looked during the interview, and she asked if we would be willing to do an interview on *The God Squad*, a cable TV show covering human interest stories and hosted by a priest and a rabbi. The show was to cover the topic of autism in order to raise public awareness. It was to be aired the week before the Long Island NAAR (National Alliance for Autism Research) walk at Jones Beach, an annual walk that raised money for research in finding a cure for autism. They were looking for a child with autism who would not be afraid to be interviewed. Marisa seemed perfect for the spot!

I asked Marisa if she would mind missing a morning of school to be interviewed on the TV show. She was very excited about the idea, so we agreed to do it. It turned out to be a terrific experience for Marisa. She got to see what the television set was like and even got her face made up for the interview. Once again, she felt like a star! I was so proud of how well she sat for the interview. Here was this thirteen-year-old child with autism sitting attentively on a television set interview. She was even answering questions! After the interview, we rushed off to school, where once again Marisa was treated as a celebrity. She loved every minute of it!

At around this time I was deciding whether to continue Marisa in the social skills group that she was in from the year before. The other girl had dropped out of the group, but the social worker assured me that there would still be at least three students, one of which was a new boy. Once again, I asked about placing Marisa in a group that did more community outings, but my request was denied. I decided to give the group one last chance, since Marisa seemed eager to participate. Over the past year, I had come to the conclusion that Marisa was capable of much more than was being expected of her. After all, she was doing well in the GAP trip recreation program. Although I enrolled her in the group that fall semester, I had decided it was time to move on to alternative programs.

Marisa knew how I felt about the social skills group that she was participating in. She took advantage of my disappointment in the group to bring up the idea of trying the Sid Jacobson JCC Saturday night teen lounge once again. It was a new year, and Marisa had not forgotten my promise to let her try it out again. We talked about what had happened the year before and how she had lost the chance to stay in the group because she could not comply with the counselor's instructions. Marisa pleaded to be given another chance. She promised to be careful and follow the instructions of the counselors. I wanted so badly for this to work for her, and I could see how eager and determined she had become. I knew that if it didn't work this time, it would be a devastating blow to her.

Nevertheless, I had no alternative. If Marisa was going to succeed, she needed to be given the chance; this was a chance we had to take. I called the JCC to arrange for Marisa to come back. Once again I was told she would be given a trial opportunity. The evening arrived to bring Marisa to the teen lounge, and again Dan and I left her and went out for a dinner close by. It was the most nerve-wracking two-hour dinner we had ever had. When we returned, we were relieved to find that things had gone very well.

The greatest joy was seeing our daughter's smiling, happy face; she knew that she had finally managed to be accepted into this group. The rewards would be having the opportunity to mix with other kids, to talk with, play games with, and listen to music and dance with. Here was a group of about twenty teens with varied disabilities who could come together in a relaxed and safe environment to practice their social skills with the guidance of the teachers, social workers, and counselors running the group. I was so happy that Marisa was finally able to participate. We continued to bring her to the teen lounge throughout the first half of the year, and once I saw how well she did in the group, I considered the idea of enrolling her in a social skills class there during the week.

Although Marisa's behaviors had improved immensely, she still did strange things at times, but for everything that we considered odd, there always seemed to be a perfectly logical explanation from Marisa's point of view. One evening, after taking her bath, Marisa emerged from the bathroom looking quite odd. I couldn't quite place my finger on what was wrong, but she just didn't look right. Something about her looked oddly off, but what? Oh my God! It came to me! She had shaved off her eyebrows.

"*Why? Why?!*" I yelled.

Marisa said, "Danny has no eyebrows. I want to look like him."

I asked her, "Who is Danny?"

When she said he was a boy at school, I asked, "Why do you want to look like him?"

"Because he has blond hair, and I want to have blond hair too!" she said.

I asked Marisa to get one of her yearbooks to show me his picture. There was Danny, a boy with very blond hair and very blond eyebrows—but the eyebrows were very much there. I showed Marisa how Danny's eyebrows were very light. Marisa started to cry, because she realized she had made a big mistake. She would now have to walk around with no eyebrows until they grew in. I knew that punishing her was not going to serve any useful purpose. I assured her that I would go buy an eyebrow pencil.

In spite of occasional upsets like this, it was an exciting time for my family. My sister and I had been planning a sixtieth wedding anniversary for my parents, to be held at my house. Marisa was very much aware of all the preparations for the party, which had been going on for months. Deborah had designed and printed up the invitations. Shoshana had prepared and edited a special movie presentation of my parent's lives from their old family movies. She planned to put the movies to favorite songs from their early years, and she received help with the project from a news editor at her job.

The day before the party, we removed all the furniture in our large atrium center hall to set up tables for the guests. We had purchased and wrapped party favors and put together the last-minute flower arrangements for the seven tables the evening before the big event. Marisa was very excited, too, that Deborah and her boyfriend were flying home from Montreal, where Deborah was in her second year in school at McGill University.

The party on Sunday afternoon, October 12, was a huge success. It was so nice to see Marisa participating at this party. She sat with her sisters and cousins, ate with the guests, listened to speeches, and watched the forty-minute-long movie that Shoshana had prepared over many months. She did not once leave to go off in her room by herself to play with a video game in private. We were so proud and happy to see how well she interacted with the guests.

The school year was going well. Marisa was enjoying her new class, and during this year I rarely heard a word about disruptive behaviors. Occasionally, I would receive a note stating that Marisa left the class line for one reason or another. In such instances, I would deduct five points off her home goal chart. These deductions served as reminders, and the result was that, over time, they occurred less and less often. Marisa was coming home with perfect behavior scores on her school chart.

The teacher was planning an environmental overnight trip with the class. This was an opportunity for Marisa to show that she could be a good candidate for the five-day Frost Valley trip she still longed to go on. There were some concerns about Marisa's dietary habits on the overnight trip. I assured the teacher that if there was any problem with the foods they should call me. I was willing to bring food for Marisa, if necessary, since the Brookville Environmental Center was close to my home. However, I told the teacher that Marisa had been expressing an interest in going to sleep-away camp the next summer, and if she wanted to do this, she had to start eating more varied foods. This actually was a great motivator for Marisa. To the teacher's surprise and mine as well, when she went on the overnight trip with her class, she ate all the foods offered.

Thanksgiving was coming! Marisa always enjoyed preparations for special family holidays. This year I decided to let her make napkin holders out of beads. Marisa carefully prepared fourteen napkin holders and helped color turkey place settings. It was a happy and settled time, so with great caution and uncertainty, we were considering taking a big step in a new direction.

Because of Marisa's strong interest in going to sleep-away camp, we had started our search for the right placement. Although Marisa was eager to go away, we were somewhat skeptical; I was having difficulty finding the right camp. We had visited a camp that was recommended to us during the summer, but I was not happy with the abrupt manner of the camp director. The result was that I needed to continue my search.

One day in early November, I came across an article in the local autism newsletter that commended the work of a special camp director, Gordie Felt. He was the director of a seven week special needs sleep away camp called Camp Northwood, located in Remsen, New York, near Utica. I was very impressed with the two parent letters commending him on the wonderful care he had given their children at his camp. As I read their personal stories, I felt I had possibly found a good match for Marisa.

I decided to check out the Web site, after which I contacted the camp. Within a few days, I received an information packet in the mail and immediately called the director. He set up an interview for us to bring Marisa to a meeting place in Manhattan so that he could evaluate Marisa and decide if she would be a good fit for the camp. We would also have an opportunity to learn more about the program and see a video of the facility. Our interview was scheduled for November 23, a Sunday morning.

When I met the director I could understand why those parents had spoken so highly of him. After a two-hour interview, we walked away feeling assured that this was the right camp for Marisa. The director was a gentle, compassionate person who was able to make a connection with Marisa. He seemed to have a sense of who she was. In essence, I liked his approach and gentle nature. Although we were still not fully certain Marisa would be able to handle a sleep-away program for seven weeks, we felt it was worth a try. It was worth it if it would help her improve her social skills and mature into a happier, more independent, and confident individual.

The camp seemed to have so much to offer, and the ratio of camper to counselor care was two to one. Three counselors would be with the six campers around the clock; I didn't think it could get much better than that! We decided to take the plunge and sent in our deposit. Marisa was ecstatic!

At school, things were going well, and Marisa was hoping to be selected for the school Frost Valley trip. Again I wrote to the teacher and asked if she would recommend Marisa for the trip, and once again, Marisa was not selected. I assured her that if she continued to behave well at school and follow the rules, she would still have a chance to go the next year. Though Marisa took the disappointment well and continued to keep up the good work, I knew that there was just one more year that she could have this opportunity. I hoped that her good behavior, which had been improved by the prospect of attending Frost Valley, would pay off in her final year. Little did Marisa know how worried I was that, after all her efforts, she might be disappointed that one last time, dealing her a hard life lesson.

In the meantime, the first semester in the social-skills class had come to an end, and I decided not to enroll Marisa again. Instead, I placed her in a social-skills group at the Sid Jacobson JCC in East Hills, Long Island. There she would have an opportunity to participate in a larger group, doing varied, in-house activities and also going on community outings to a movie, bowling, and dinner in a restaurant. I felt this would be a good change for Marisa and good preparation to going to sleep-away camp. The good thing was that she had gotten to know some of the participants, because many of these kids were also attending the Saturday night teen lounge program. I felt that since things were going well at the teen lounge, then the social skills class would likely work out as well.

We continued horseback riding throughout the remainder of the year. Although the activity was enjoyable and rewarding, we decided to discontinue it. It was very costly, and although Marisa had developed compassion for animals and improved her self-esteem, we felt she should pursue other more sociable activities.

The year went well, and Marisa did get to go on one more environmental trip with her class, and this time it was for two nights. Once again the trip was a huge success! At the end of June, Marisa celebrated her fourteenth birthday with lots of friends around her. Marisa chose decorating nylon wallets with fabric paint as a craft for this year's party activity.

In preparation for camp, I had requested that Marisa's teacher put together an academic work packet for Marisa. The camp had a one-hour academic period as the first activity each weekday morning. The academic packet from the teacher would help the camp set up a program that would focus on the skills Marisa was working on.

We prepared for the upcoming summer with reservation and concern. We were excited by the prospect of Marisa being able to go away but were worried that she would be unable to handle it. With all the preparations and information I provided to help the camp understand Marisa, I still had to wait and wonder if this would actually work out all right. At the camp director's direction, I sent a letter mentioning all the things I felt would be helpful for the counselors to know about Marisa. Then there was not much else to do but wait till the day when we would drive her to the bus pick-up point in New York City on the first day of camp. From that time on we had to anxiously wait and see how things went.

The first day of camp arrived. Marisa had packed up all the last-minute essentials that would go with her. She had her CD player and some twenty or thirty CDs, her Game Boy Advance and twelve cartridges, her toothbrush, her hair drier, her *Harry Potter* book three, her *Pokemon Player's Guide*, and a lunch for the ride up on the bus. We headed off to the city at seven in the morning. The buses were to leave from the designated location in Manhattan an hour later, so we needed to allow enough time to get there.

When we arrived at the drop-off point, we were told to find Marisa's counselor, Victoria, and wait with her. Victoria was a young college student from England studying to be a teacher, and she greeted Marisa warmly after recognizing her from a picture we had sent the camp. After about thirty minutes of waiting for all the campers to arrive, we were told that the kids could start boarding the bus. Marisa was anxious for us to leave as she eagerly went up the steps and into the bus. We waved and with hesitation walked down the street to a nearby Starbucks, where we sat drinking coffee.

It was a strange kind of day for us. We didn't know what to expect. We seemed to think that within a day, if not sooner, we would be getting calls for help. We worried about tantrums. We worried about Marisa not being able to express her needs clearly. I consoled myself with the one thing I had put in place that I hoped would help Marisa get through the summer successfully. I had sent her along with a goal chart specifically made for camp. She had six goals all related to following very specific rules. I had written to the head counselor to explain that Marisa could earn two points for each goal each day, and only if she deserved the points. I also informed the counselor that I had promised Marisa something very special at the end of the summer if all went well. This special reward was to have her ears pierced.

The first day came and went without a phone call, as did the second, third, and fourth. A week went by, and the only call we got was the scheduled weekly call from the head counselor. Victoria called to let us know how things were going, and we were relieved and delighted to hear that all was going smoothly. Though Marisa had had a few difficult moments, they were handled well and resolved without having to consult me.

I didn't know it at the time, but one of the counselors in Marisa's group was actually a college student who herself had high-functioning autism, and had a clear understanding of her campers. She herself had been a camper at Camp Northwood. Over the phone the head counselor explained to us that on the first day of camp, Marisa was upset because she didn't have her vitamins and medicine in her cabin with her. The staff decided to take her to the nurse to show her rather than just tell her where the vitamins and medication was. Because Marisa is such a visual learner, that approach had worked well, easing her concern over the whereabouts of her medication. I later suspected that it might very well have been the insight of this counselor on the autism spectrum that helped resolve that situation.

One of the best things that kept Dan and I assured at home was having access to the camp Web site. Every day the director would write a newsletter to inform the parents of what was going on, and he would post thirty to forty pictures of the campers each day. We would anticipate these newsletters and pictures, which made us feel very connected to the camp. We were overjoyed when, on the first day, the director posted a picture of Marisa. She was sitting with her bunk group on the lawn with a broad, happy smile on her face. We were relieved to see that she was happy.

The camp had a special e-mail lab that the campers could use a few times a week. During that first summer, Marisa learned to e-mail her sisters and us. We started to realize that writing about the day's events at home was good practice for the e-mails and letters she wrote to us and other family and friends.

Because I had incorporated "writing a letter each day" into Marisa's camp goal chart, she sent us letters daily. She was writing not just to us at home but to other people as well. Over that first summer, I received some forty-four letters from Marisa, and that was in addition to the letters she was sending to her sisters, friends, aunts, uncles, cousins, and grandparents. Her letters were always so beautifully written, and when she ran out of stationery, she would create a beautiful card of her own, usually with a flower on the front page. Over the weeks, the letters improved. Marisa became more descriptive in her writing. Early in July 2004 she wrote this letter:

> *Dear Mom and Dad,*
> *I wrote a letter to Michelle, and I want to get my gel pen set, and my pyjama set from L.T.D., and I went banna boating, and it was a fun day, and I want to send my sutf from L.T.D. in my mail.*
> *Love, Marisa*

I loved receiving these innocent, self-centered notes from Marisa and would write back, trying to help her to make her letters sound a bit more caring about the person she was writing to. I encouraged Marisa to show the letters to a counselor who could perhaps help her make spelling or grammatical corrections. By August there was much improvement in the letter writing. On August 12 she wrote this note which only contained one spelling error:

Dear Mom, and Dad,
How are you?
I am doing good.
Yesterday, I had a chesseburger, corn, and fries for dinner, and I went to the green
dance, and I danced to "Get the party started," "Hey ya," and "Baby one more
time."
Today, I had a donut for breakfast, and I went to the bears, and I went to haba,
and I didn't go sailing, and I had grilled cheese for lunch. My favorite activity has
been arts and crafts.
Love,
Marisa

We were excited to see Marisa on visiting day, and though it was a miserable and rainy day, we were overjoyed to be with Marisa. As Marisa led us around the camp to various activities, it was quite apparent that she was maturing. There was a calm peacefulness about her. She seemed content and happy to show us around. I immediately saw a change in her manner while we were standing on a long line leading into the dining room for a buffet lunch. Marisa was holding her plate and utensils, along with her raincoat. She didn't dump her raincoat on me, as she might have done in the past.

As we walked along the buffet lunch line, it became apparent to me that Marisa had developed a taste for many foods. There was so much to choose from, and she was making many selections I had never seen her try before. Though she hadn't selected any vegetables, she was clearly adding to her very limited diet.

We were so pleased with what we saw. We knew then that we had clearly made the right decision to send her to this sleep-away camp. We stayed at camp for the day and attended the camp show of *The King and I*, in which Marisa was happy to participate as a royal dancer along with the other girls in her bunk. Marisa had no problem saying good-bye to us at the end of the day, as she had planned to return to her bunk for some quiet games, letter writing, and daily-events writing.

Over the next few weeks, I anticipated Marisa's return and was worried that she would feel a let-down upon arriving home. To ease the transition, I wrote letters to her, telling her about some of the things I had planned for when she came home. We would plan some get-togethers with friends and go shopping for new school clothes at the mall.

Marisa arrived home in mid-August, and as she stepped off the bus smiling, tears of joy rolled down my cheeks. It was a happy reunion, and she did well getting back into a routine at home. I kept Marisa busy over the next few weeks, and she also kept in touch with her camp friends through letter writing and e-mail, skills she had mastered at camp. Marisa had achieved a great deal more independence in taking care of her personal needs, and she felt good about herself because she had friends that she had common interests with, that she could contact through her letters and e-mails. The letter writing and e-mails also gave her the opportunity to practice her writing and reading skills.

One evening while helping Marisa dry her hair straight with the hair drier, I discovered that a good section of hair at the back of her neck had been burnt off from using the hair dryer at camp. Apparently, Marisa had been putting too much heat on her hair as she dried it.

I decided to use this unfortunate happening as an opportunity to introduce Marisa to vegetables. I used the ruse of making her think that vegetables would make her hair grow back faster. The last time Marisa had eaten any cooked vegetables was when she was a baby on pureed foods. I told her that her hair would grow back faster if she would eat all kinds of vegetables. I could not believe how easily this worked! From that day on, Marisa started to eat not only her vegetables, but also everything that we ate for dinner. I no longer had to prepare separate meals for Marisa. The finicky eater that she had been for the past thirteen years was gone.

Chapter Fourteen

REWARDED AT LAST

The new school year began, and Marisa was lucky enough to have the same teacher. However, the principal decided that Marisa would be better off with a different one-to-one aide. Marisa was beginning to be resentful of the aide, and though she did give Marisa her space, the principal felt that Marisa would appreciate the change. Marisa felt she was able to function well on her own, especially after being away at camp for a full summer. The new aide turned out to be a good choice for Marisa. She was an experienced Boy Scout counselor and encouraged Marisa to work independently, not hovering around her.

Because Marisa was doing so well, Dan felt it was a good time to try taking Marisa off medication; he felt it was time to see if she was showing real gains or just improving with age. As a neurologist, he knew from the latest literature that there was no evidence that Strattera benefited children with autism. It was however, beneficial for children with attention deficit disorder. Also, he knew that there were always risks in taking medication; he felt that it should not be taken unless there was evidence of a significant benefit. Although I was worried, I knew it was the only way to find out if her good behavior could be maintained without medication. To my relief and surprise, Marisa's behavior remained much the same once we discontinued the Strattera. She remained the same happy, bright-eyed Marisa I had become accustomed to seeing. Perhaps it had served its purpose well, helping Marisa focus on the behaviors she needed to learn, so she could now manage on her own.

It was Marisa's last year at the middle school, and it would also be her last chance to go on the Frost Valley trip. Marisa was going to try her best to convince her teacher that they should recommend her for the trip. I also spoke to the teacher again, explaining how important this was to Marisa. Throughout the first half of that year, Marisa would frequently approach the teacher in charge of the trip to remind him that she was an eager, responsible candidate.

In the meantime I had enrolled Marisa once again in the Saturday-night teen lounge at the Sid Jacobson JCC. I also enrolled her in the social skills class there. Marisa did well in these groups, as she had become very comfortable in her ability to get along with the other class participants. At school, the class went on visits to the Brookville Environmental Center, and Marisa also did well on these trips.

Then in January we received a letter from the teacher in charge of the Frost Valley trip. Marisa had been selected! It was such an exciting moment for her. After all the years she had been pleading to be accepted for this trip, she was finally getting to go along with ten other children in the school. How proud she was to be a part of this select few!

The five-day trip was scheduled for February. The children got to sleigh ride and tour the surrounding wooded area with an environmentalist. Back in the camp classroom, the group studied real reptiles and snakes. Marisa did so well on the trip that the teacher in charge of the trip rewarded her on the way home with a free Burger King lunch for having the cleanest and most organized bunk in the camp cabin. After the Frost Valley trip Marisa's aide sent me a warm and beautiful note:

March 10, 2005
Dear Mrs. Rubin,
Please find enclosed some photographs I took during the Frost Valley trip. I am not the world's best photographer, as you can see, but the photos show Marisa during a few of the activities we all participated in. There are notes on the backs of the pictures.

To repeat from my rushed notes on Marisa's target sheet for the week of the trip, Marisa was terrific! She participated in all the activities fully and with confidence, she was respectful of both staff and her peers, and engaged with others socially. It was a pleasure to see a young lady eat heartily of such a variety of foods, and with excellent table manners.

I'm thankful for the opportunity to have shared this experience with Marisa, and to have gotten to know her better. Marisa is a really great person. Thank you for the kind note and the box of chocolates; I enjoyed every calorie!

It was so nice to receive this note to confirm that the trip was a successful one, and I was grateful that Marisa had the opportunity to prove to all who attended that she could keep her word and be on her best behavior.

Another exciting event during that last year at the middle school BOCES was a special ceremony for the Helping Hands Committee of students. Marisa was always eager to participate in community work and had become a member of the Helping Hands Committee this year. These students were a select few that had been able to go out in the community to participate in various community service events. They would visit nursing homes to entertain the residents, distribute gifts to needy children at Christmas time, and help gather non-perishable foods, used clothing, and books for the poor. A special assembly was being held in their honor and the students were to receive certificates from Congressman Peter King.

Marisa's fifteenth birthday surrounded her with many friends. She was making contacts at school and her social skills class as well as maintaining friendships from her earlier years. Once again she enjoyed bringing her friends together for pizza, yard games, and a rainbow-and-glitter scratch art project.

The year came to a close with a graduation ceremony. Marisa received an award in art, with an honorable mention in physical education. The students had been asked what they cared about, and next to Marisa's name in the graduation program she was quoted: "I care about my friends." This was so typical of Marisa, who always enjoyed being around other kids and finding new friends. Marisa was also happy to receive beautiful pearl earrings as a graduation gift from her one-to-one aide.

It was a good five years at the middle school BOCES. Marisa graduated feeling good about herself. She was ready for a second year away at Camp Northwood and was eagerly anticipating starting school at the BOCES high school program in the fall.

When we arrived at the Camp Northwood drop-off location in New York City on July 3, 2004, Marisa walked down the street feeling confident and happy. She passed familiar faces; she smiled and waved as she called out a friendly "Hi," usually followed by the person's name. She approached the director, and to his and our surprise, she greeted him with a "Hi, Gordie!" and a big hug.

Then it was much as it had been in the previous year. Marisa went to meet her new head counselor and wait with two other campers who were to be in her bunk. When it was time to board the bus, Marisa eagerly said good-bye and climbed the steps. Once again Dan and I went down the street to the local Starbucks and reminisced how things had been the year before. We were somewhat more at ease this year as we drove home and thought about the previous summer.

Over the course of the next few weeks, Marisa sent us many letters and e-mails. She was once again adjusting well to the camp schedule. The nice thing, we learned, was that the bunk roster had remained much the same, with the exception of one new girl. The group of girls had developed a camaraderie that was visually noticeable in the online pictures that the director posted each day. The counselors had changed, though the one counselor who herself had high-functioning autism had remained with the group, and even she looked so much more relaxed and happy in the pictures.

Marisa wrote to us about a new boyfriend she had gotten close to, and she was anxious for us to meet him when we arrived for visiting day. Alex was a boy from Park Slope that Marisa seemed to like a lot, and it appeared that the feeling was mutual. The two seemed to enjoy hanging out together during visiting day. Marisa and Alex were over at the soccer field when the bell was sounded to call all cast members to the theatre to prepare for the show. We saw them running across the field hand in hand.

Another noticeable change this summer was that Marisa had clearly gotten over her finicky food habits. We saw her eat a big salad followed by a plate filled with a variety of foods, including the vegetables she had become accustomed to eating at home.

During the camp visit, Marisa made the rounds to her friends and literally dragged us to meet their moms. She wanted to be sure that I developed some kind of a relationship with the people who were becoming important to her. We met Alex's parents, who actually did not live unreasonably far from us. We also met the parents of a few other friends with whom Marisa was hoping to get together once camp was over.

Just before the performance of *Beauty and the Beast* was to begin, Marisa quickly rushed over to me. "Marisa, what are you doing? You should be back stage getting ready!" I said. Marisa was holding the hand of someone else's mom, who she knew happened to live right near us. She literally dropped the mom's hand in front of me, saying, "This is Sam's mom!" as she then hurried back behind the scenes, leaving the mother and me to get to know each other.

The most interesting thing that happened that summer was that Marisa's goal chart had become a hot item in her bunk. The head counselor informed me that because the counselors could see how effective the chart was for Marisa, they decided to create similar goal charts for the other girls in the bunk. Marisa's chart had initiated a behavior plan for her bunkmates.

When the summer came to an end, Marisa returned home with a renewed spirit. She typed up a list of her friends from camp and immediately set out to correspond through e-mail and paper mail. She made phone calls to arrange get-togethers. With all the letter writing, e-mails, and dates, followed by recording her daily activities in her journal, she kept very busy till school was to begin.

Marisa's reward for maintaining an excellent goal chart at camp was to have highlights put in her hair. This I cautiously did myself. While working on Marisa's hair, Marisa once again expressed a desire to change her eye color. This had been one request I had not been able to come up with a solution for. As I was brushing the highlights into her hair, an idea came to me. I told Marisa that we would take a trip to the drug store to purchase blue eye shadow, which would highlight her eyes in the color of her choice. I felt the blue eye shadow would satisfy her desire for the color blue around rather than in her eyes. Marisa's highlights turned out quite pleasing, as did the blue eye shadow. She was happy with her new look as she prepared to start the year in her new school.

Marisa went back to school with tremendous enthusiasm. This year Marisa was going to attend school without a one-to-one aide. She had earned the right to work independently on her own. She was eager to start the new program where many of her older friends already were in attendance. The high school BOCES program is located in the Rosemary Kennedy Center in Wantagh, Long Island. There are many programs in the Rosemary Kennedy Center, and Marisa was to attend the CCA (Center for Community Adjustment) program, which is a combined academic and skills program.

The participants in this program spend a good deal of time in the community, learning activities of daily living. The students learn to comparison shop, work at various job sites, learn how to prepare for an interview, and learn to take public transportation. Learning to live independently is the goal. At the same time, the students continue their academic education. It is a program that teaches life skills to students that are not necessarily college bound but are preparing to find jobs in the community that are both appropriate and of interest to them. The students develop a sense of responsibility as they train in various positions. By trying out different jobs, they develop a sense of what kind of work they might enjoy and do well when they graduate.

While Marisa was starting at the new school, I was also going to try to make my way back into the working world. I worked as an early childhood teacher some twenty-eight years earlier and had spent the interim time home with my four daughters. Now was a good time for me to make a gradual change in my own life. I was preparing to go back to work as a substitute teacher, so I would have a chance to learn what changes had occurred in teaching during the time I had spent at home.

I had started to prepare Marisa for this over the course of a two-year period. It was important to teach her how to open the door with her key and turn off the house alarm. We had spent a good year practicing with the key before I felt Marisa was ready to open the door without me by her side. This was a slow process, but it was well worth it. This became very apparent one day when, unfortunately, I couldn't make it home in time for Marisa's arrival, because I was tied up in a traffic jam. The bus driver knew that if he didn't see my car in the driveway, I wasn't home. I didn't know if the bus driver would leave Marisa off or come back after dropping off the other children. As it turned out, he let Marisa off the bus. When I arrived home I found her safely indoors. She had locked the door and reactivated the alarm! Although the bus driver should not have released her without seeing my car in the driveway, he probably felt it was all right since he knew she had a key. I congratulated Marisa on a job well done and assured her that she had shown how capable she really was.

Another skill that I started working on with Marisa around this time was her ability to take written phone messages. Although Marisa had been earning points for answering the phone and asking who is on the line and whom the person wants to speak to, I felt she was now ready for the next step. She was to start earning points for taking written messages. Marisa currently is able to record the date, name, and time the person calls and earns an additional two points on her goal chart for these written messages.

In spite of all the skills Marisa has achieved, there's always something else to explore and learn from. Such was the case when in early September we received information from the local Autism Society that a special event was to take place at the West Hills Day Camp. This was to be a "Common Connections" day sponsored by the Asperger Foundation International (for Aspergers and high-functioning autistic children.) We also learned that Marisa's counselor from Camp Northwood, also on the spectrum, was going to be there speaking about her own personal experiences before college and her goals to become a teacher. There were to be many helpful groups and agencies at the Common Connections event to give information and offer support to parents of children with autism.

When we arrived at the camp, Marisa immediately headed for the beautiful pool and water slide. She spent at least a half-hour there before she decided to try another activity. As she was drying herself off and getting ready to move on, a boy about her age came into the pool area with his mom. While he was putting his things on a nearby bench, I could see Marisa watching him.

As he was about to head for the water slide, Marisa approached him to ask his name, his age, and where he lived. He answered the questions and then, to my surprise, asked her the same. Next, Marisa put her things down and decided to follow him back to the water slide. The two hit it off at the slide, and I went to sit next to his mom.

As we talked and watched, it became apparent that these two had found that "common connection" that the event was hoping to nurture between children with common interests. They walked arm in arm up the steps to the water slide, waiting their turn, talking, holding hands, and just looking very happy to be together. They went down the slide together, but when the lifeguard informed them that they were to only go down one at a time, they started taking turns. The one waiting at the bottom of the slide would greet the other with a high five! It was so sweet and exciting to watch the two of them that we hadn't noticed others observing them as well.

Before we knew it, *Newsday*, a local Long Island newspaper, had come to interview the other mother and myself and then asked our permission to speak to Marisa and her new friend Kyle. As it turned out, the story was featured that Sunday with a photo of Marisa and Kyle going down the water slide. These two on the spectrum had made that common connection that the event was set up to achieve, and to this day Marisa and Kyle e-mail, talk on the phone, and plan get-togethers during holidays.

More recently Marisa has taken up Scrabble, and for this I credit my brother-in-law, Eddie. If it weren't for Eddie, who is a Scrabble lover and true pro, Marisa might not have taken an interest in this vocabulary-building game. Whenever we see my sister and brother-in-law, there is always a Scrabble game, and since Dan likes to play the game as well, it has turned out to be a regular activity in our house. Now Marisa asks to play Scrabble, and she will sit and concentrate on the game for more than an hour at a time. Her dad teaches her to use strategy to earn the most points, and Marisa seems to learn quickly, even remembering the little Scrabble words that she looks up in the Scrabble dictionary.

Marisa is now fifteen years old, and though she still has many more years to grow and mature, it is obvious to anyone who has known her from her earlier years that she has come a very long way. At age two, I could not take her anywhere, because I never knew what to expect. Today I know I can count on her to at least try her best to do the right thing. I am fully confident that she will be able to attend any event that might come her way, whether it be dining out, a show, a wedding, a museum, or even her sister's graduation. I know that Marisa will be able to handle anything. We have tried to give her the tools to help her find her way. With our faith in her ability, we believe she cannot go wrong. Over the years of working with Marisa, I have developed an understanding and made an amazing connection that enables me to trust her. In essence, I have finally found Marisa.

In concluding this story, I have to say that if I could wish one thing for Marisa and all my daughters, it would be to find happiness. That, I feel, should be the goal for all people. All the education in the world does not make a person happy, unless the knowledge and skills acquired are what that person wants. Therefore, focusing on individual strengths such as art, music, computer and organizational skills when seeking employment and learning to navigate her way socially are the things I strongly believe will lead to a happy and favorable outcome for Marisa.

Marisa is not a neurotypical person, but she must find her way in this world just like anyone else. Right now I can safely say that she is happy doing just that, and she approaches new experiences with an eagerness that is refreshing to see. She seems confident as she faces her future. She is meticulously well organized, artistic, musical, computer literate, and extremely outgoing; she is always seeking out new friends. To me, those are qualities that could lead to a successful future.

I am grateful that I have had the time to spend helping all my children through their growing years, and I can only hope that they are all happy with the choices they have made along the way. As I look forward to Marisa's future years, I will continue to help her reach the goals that will lead her to a happy, successful life—not by my standards, but by her own.

Chapter   Fifteen

HELPFUL TIPS

1. As a parent, always stay true to your feelings and instincts. If it doesn't feel right to you, then don't do it just because someone says you should.

2. If you have the chance to visit or observe your child's early intervention classroom, take advantage of that. Visiting the classroom may spark ideas of your own or at the very least give you ideas that you can implement at home.

3. Always follow your child's lead. Children are individuals, and they have interests that are clearly their own. These should be encouraged and nurtured. It is so much easier to teach when the interest is already there.

4. Try joining your child in her self-initiated play activities. This is a wonderful way to connect with your child and share in her interest.

5. Respect the learning style of the child. We all learn in our own unique ways.

6. Think of each day as a new learning experience. You never know how a new experience may enlighten you to new ideas.

7. When selecting goals to work on, choose those related to safety first. These goals can never be stressed enough.

8. Don't try to work on too many goals at once. Every little goal accomplished is a tiny but significant step in the right direction.

9. Don't ever assume that your child doesn't understand your words. Speak to him the way you would any child. You never know how much he's grasping,

so don't deny him the chance to hear your words. Some day, you may be surprised by a reply.

10. Don't ever underestimate the knowledge you have about your own child. What you know can and should be a treasure chest of information for your child's teacher.

11. Evaluate what kind of learner your child is, and try to utilize methods that stress her area of strength. For example: a visual learner does well with picture clues, written scripts, social stories, and charting.

12. The strengths children possess while young will most likely remain strengths into adulthood. That is why you should encourage and nurture these strengths.

13. Don't assume your child is unaware. He may just be seeing the world around him from his own unique perspective. Give him the benefit of the doubt.

14. Use written scripts, such as small sentences with picture clues, to help your child communicate needs.

15. Never underestimate the power of a reward, but be consistent in what is required to earn the reward.

16. Praise and a positive approach will more than likely result in a positive outcome.

17. When things aren't going smoothly, try to take a step back and evaluate where the difficulty is. Sometimes a problem can be solved simply by making a small change in one's approach. For example: while waiting in a long line, a child may become restless. Providing some small distraction to keep her busy may be very helpful.

18. A laid-back attitude is more likely to reward you with results. Pushing children to do something before they are ready will cause more harm than good. When they are ready, it will be that much more rewarding.

19. Create incentives to complete a task. You will not only be encouraging your child but rewarding yourself with results.

20. Use visual aides to help structure your child's day. A written plan will often be helpful, giving your child a sense of what comes next in the schedule throughout the day.

21. Remember to revise the goals and rewards to go along with the age of your child. As your child matures, expectations and capabilities change. The rewards should also change. Review and update goals. Replace stickers with a more sophisticated point system as your child gets older.

22. Read as much as you can about your child's disability, so that you will empower yourself with the knowledge that will enable you to understand and better handle the obstacles that may come your way.

23. Help your young child sort out her thoughts by writing what she has to say, so that you can read it back to her. Drawing pictures to go with the written words may also be helpful in sorting thoughts and feelings.

24. Use videos, DVDs, audiocassettes, or CDs to model skills and appropriate behaviors like table manners and phone manners. The power of music is amazing, too! So many skills can be learned through songs.

25. Never underestimate the advantage of siblings as role models during play. Siblings are also usually eager participants in safely helping your special needs child practice his social skills.

26. Use family gatherings as an opportunity to practice social skills.

27. Take advantage of many of the educational computer games on the market. So many autistic children, being visual learners, are able to acquire many skills through the use of these programs.

28. Encourage friendships with children who have similar interests. It will be easier to share when there are similar interests, and topics of conversation will flow naturally.

29. Make sure the rewards you offer as incentives are chosen by your child, not by yourself.

30. Knowing your child makes you your child's best advocate when looking at school placements. Every child is different, and therefore the uniqueness of

each individual should be taken into consideration when looking for an appropriate school placement. Inclusion is not for everyone.

31. Obtain medical documentation to back up your request for services at your CSE meetings. School districts are held accountable when requesting funds, and professional evaluations will make it easier and quicker to obtain the needed services.

32. Respect your child's feelings and take them into consideration when creating the behavior plan.

33. Take cues from your child. Try to take your child's requests into consideration when planning activities.

34. Be assertive when advocating for your child, but don't have a confrontational attitude with your child's teacher. Be respectful and listen, and try to work with the teacher while planning what is best for your child. With the right approach, you may learn something helpful, and the teacher will be more open to learning something from what you have to offer too.

35. Have an open mind, but follow your instincts.

36. Where possible, use community outings to teach appropriate behavior. There is no better way of learning than through practice. Make the real world your everyday classroom.

37. Most of all, try to have faith in your child's ability. Trust your child to carry out what you request. In time, you will reap the rewards of your efforts.

Afterword

Marisa is now in her second year at CCA. She continues to be happy at school as she participates in all activities. Marisa has expressed an interest in community service, because she likes being around people and being involved in all aspects of helping people. This year she has joined the Key Club at her school. Key Club is the single largest high school service organization in the world and Marisa enjoys participating in all fundraising activities planned by Key Club at her school.

At home, Marisa continues to take part in many recreational activities with the town program for children with special needs. She attends a drama club on Wednesday evenings, goes bowling every Thursday afternoon, and attends a weekly Friday evening program for bowling, ice-skating, and gym activities. On weekends she takes part in day trips to museums and shows, while being in the company of other children.

She continues her participation in the Saturday night teen lounge at the JCC and also attends their vocational and recreational after-school program three days a week for children with autism.

This year Marisa is hoping to attend her school prom, and is busy like any other teen, surfing the Internet for the best dresses and accessories to purchase for her special day. Looking forward to the prom is her incentive to maintain her best behavior at school and at home, as she continues to record her goal points on her self-evaluating goal chart.

I have watched Marisa developing her own preferences in novels, clothing, recreational activities, music and friends just like any other teenager. The only difference is that Marisa has autism which makes her a bit more unique than the typical teen.

I see Marisa as the unique and very special person that she is, and feel that all parents with a special needs child should embrace their child in this positive way. Parents should see themselves as the special people they are too. You are special because nobody knows your child the way you do.

When feeling down, don't be discouraged because children do mature on their own to a certain degree and what seems like the impossible when your child is two years old will be a much different picture when he or she is 14 or 15 years old.

I hope that this story provides insight and encouragement to those families struggling to understand their child with autism.

Bibliography of Helpful Resources

Included in this list are not all but some of the books I have found most helpful through the years.

1. Adams, Janice I. *Autism-P.D.D. More Creative Ideas from Age Eight to Early Adulthood.* Ontario, Canada: Adams Publications, 1997.

2. Barron, Judy and Sean. *There's A Boy In Here.* Arlington, Texas: Future Horizons, Inc., 2002.

3. Carr, Edward G.; Levin, Len; McConnachie, Gene; Carlson, Jane I.; Kemp, Duane C.; Smith, Christopher E. *Communication Based Intervention for Problem Behavior ... A User's Guide for Producing Positive Change.* Baltimore, Maryland: Paul H. Brookes Publishing Co., 1994.

4. Fouse, Beth and Wheeler, Maria, M. *A Treasure Chest of Behavioral Strategies for Individuals with Autism.* Arlington, Texas: Future Horizons, Inc., 1997.

5. Gray, Carol(editor) and students in Mrs. Johnson's Psychology and Sociology classes at Jenison High School in Jenison, Michigan. *The Social Story Book 1994.* Arlington, Texas: Future Education, 1994.

6. Grandin, Temple. *Thinking In Pictures.* New York, New York: Doubleday, 1995.

7. Greenspan, Stanley I. and Wieder, Serena. *The Child with Special Needs*. Reading, Massachusetts: A Merloyd Lawrence Book, 1998.

8. Hodgdon, Linda A. *Visual Strategies for Improving Communication Volume I: Practical Supports for School and Home*. Troy, Michigan: Quirk Roberts Publishing, 1998.

9. Lovass, Ivar O. *Teaching Developmentally Disabled Children, The Me Book*. Austin, Texas: Pro-Ed, Inc., 1981.

10. McAfee, Jeanette. *Navigating the Social World*. Arlington, Texas: Future Horizons, Inc., 2002.